D1472473

Elementary-school children in Pezuela de las Torres stage a back-yard bullfight.

OTHER BOOKS BY TAD SZULC

TWILIGHT OF THE TYRANTS
CUBAN INVASION (with Karl E. Mayer)
WINDS OF REVOLUTION
THE DOMINICAN DIARY
LATIN AMERICA
BOMBS OF PALOMARES
CZECHOSLOVAKIA SINCE WORLD WAR II
THE UNITED STATES AND THE CARIBBEAN (Editor)

Portrait of SPAIN

by Tad Szulc

Photographs by
JACK MANNING

Special Interest Guide by
MARI DE OLIVA and JILL JARRELL

A New York Times Book

American Heritage Press
A Division of McGraw-Hill Book Company
New York   St. Louis   San Francisco   Düsseldorf
London   Mexico   Sydney   Toronto

Book design by Elaine Gongora.

Copyright © 1972 by The New York Times Company.
Published by American Heritage Press, a division of McGraw-Hill Book Company.
Published in Canada by McGraw-Hill Ryerson Ltd.

Library of Congress Catalog Card Number: 76-95732
07-062654-5

THIS BOOK IS FOR JANINA

Contents

The Castilian town of Pezuela de las Torres

Preface

Spain is a many-splendored, multifaceted, infinitely colorful, immensely attractive, enormously gifted, yet contradictory, frustrating, and frequently unnerving nation. As the Spaniards themselves like to say, with both pride and self-depreciation, "Spain is different."

Perhaps more than most countries, Spain must be taken for what it is—at its best and at its worst. Otherwise, I can only advise leaving Spain alone. It is fruitless to approach the country with the attitude that it would be a superb place if, for example, Spaniards did not have a penchant for civil wars, if they had not accepted living for more than thirty years under the Franco dictatorship, if they all did not drive as if they were alone on the highways, and if Castile were not such a bleak and parched plateau. People with any one of these reservations had perhaps better spend a morning at Madrid's Prado Museum admiring the Goyas, El Grecos, and Velázquezs and an afternoon at the Ventas bull ring watching the "moment of truth" but not quite perceiving the crowd's differing reactions to the great old Antonio Ordoñez (who retired in mid-1971) and the young El Cordobés. This kind of visit to Spain could end with an evening at a flamenco *tablado* listening to music born during the Moorish occupation but not really knowing why an aging

One of the older quarters of Madrid

cantaor sounds better than a young one or why a plump *gitana* dances more convincingly than a slim beauty.

On the other hand, the traveler who accepts Spain as it is can be richly rewarded, because this is a country in which moods are often more important than facts, where gestures and courtesies carry more meaning than words, and where emotions can overrule reason.

This uniquely Spanish blend is what Washington Irving discovered in the palaces of Granada and while riding through Andalusia on horseback. This is what Goya and Ernest Hemingway saw, each in his own way, in the disasters of the Spanish wars. This is what the great old historians meant when they pointed out the relationship between the nation's tortuous geography and its people— a people who discovered and colonized half the world but kept forgetting their own country.

Written in part at an old mill near a tiny Castilian pueblo, where sheep and goats still graze among the ageless houses of stone, this, finally, is what this book is all about.

T. S.

San Benito Mill, Pezuela de las Torres, Province of Madrid, Castile, Spain
Washington, D.C.

BOOK ONE

This Is Spain

The Sierra Nevada

GONGORA

1 The Castle of Spain

I came to Spain for *The New York Times* on July 18, 1965, the twenty-ninth anniversary of the outbreak of the Spanish Civil War. Madrid was quietly enjoying the holiday and basking in the hot summer sun. Foreign diplomats, in the white tie and tails that stiff Spanish protocol requires, were at the palace of La Granja, an hour's drive from the capital, presenting their compliments to Generalissimo Francisco Franco Bahamonde at an annual ceremony. Spaniards by the millions had fled homes, offices, and factories for vacations at the seaside or in cool sierras. Spain in 1965 appeared to be relaxed, well-ordered, even prosperous.

A quarter of a century earlier, almost to the week, I had paid my first visit to Madrid. I had been fourteen, and my mother and I had been escaping from France ahead of the advancing Nazi armies. We had crossed the French–Spanish border high in the Pyrenees and taken a rickety bus down winding mountain roads to a village near Lérida. There we spent the night at the home of a pretty young woman who was always dressed in black. Her husband had been killed in the Civil War, which had ended a little over a year before, but I never knew on which side he had fought. We knew no Spanish at the time, but the widow and her family showed their compassion and friendship through gestures and smiles. They gave us a huge meal even though the war-ravaged country was on the verge of famine and it was evidently a sacrifice to feed strangers. Curiously, I also remember the village band in the small central plaza playing on their tubas the long-forgotten English tune called, I believe, "How Do You Do, Mr. Brown?"

From Lérida we traveled by train to Saragossa and thence to Madrid through a landscape ravaged by three years of civil war. Standing by ruined houses were emaciated children who watched silently as the train went by. On hillsides the winners had painted enormous signs proclaiming *"Arriba España"* or *"Viva Franco!"* Madrid was still scarred by the prolonged siege it had undergone. The tall telephone-exchange building off Gran Vía, the crowded main street, was pock-marked by artillery shells. The suburbs, where Loyalists and Nationalists had fought hand to hand for years, were in ruins. The Prado's magnificent and priceless paintings were still packed away to protect them from destruction.

The Axis powers were at the apex of their glory: France had

Off to the spring fair, in and on the scooter

been overrun and the Germans were preparing to invade England. Nationalist Spain, which had won the Civil War largely because of German and Italian aid, was considered to be an ally of the Axis. Nazi flags with swastikas hung from buildings on the Puerta del Sol, the center of Madrid, where my mother and I spent a week at a modest little hotel before continuing our flight to Portugal and the New World. But three months later, Franco met Hitler at the French border and stubbornly refused to bring Spain into the war on Germany's side. This was the beginning of Franco's extraordinary political trajectory that over the next three decades was to turn him from a virtual enemy into a military ally of the United States.

Twenty-five years later, I returned to a changed Spain. Despite the survival of profound economic and social distortions, her industries were humming, her people did not, by and large, go hungry, and they were decently dressed. This was my first impression of Madrid on that July day in 1965 as I toured the city seeking to recapture old memories. But there was little to bring them back. The small hotel on the Puerta del Sol was gone. The once-battered suburbs had become attractive residential areas built around exclusive clubs. The Ciudad Universitaria, the battlefield of the Madrid siege, had been rebuilt into a splendid new campus. But Spain's political transition from the Civil War days lagged behind the physical transformation. Student and labor unrest and the emergence of militant progressive factions in the Roman Catholic Church demanding a rapid change in national life—these problems were to be my prime concern as a newspaper correspondent during the three years I was assigned to Madrid.

Having learned Spanish during many years spent as a correspondent in Latin America, I found it relatively easy to establish something of a rapport with the Spaniards of every class and profession whom I met. I have accepted the admonition that *no* foreigner can ever truly understand Spain, but within those limits I have found the Spaniards to be an impressive, perplexing, strikingly individualistic, stubborn, prideful, creative, and occasionally aggravating people.

The area of Spain is 190,100 square miles, slightly less than France and somewhat more than California. Stretching 640 miles from the Atlantic to the Mediterranean and 530 miles from the Pyrenees to the Strait of Gibraltar, it has all the contradictory characteristics of its thirty-three million inhabitants. It is essentially a land of mountains ringed by the sea, and early in Spanish history, the mountain valleys and passes became invasion routes—into and out of Spain—and the seas a link to the world for this nation of restless discoverers, conquerors, and adventure seekers.

Madrid, the capital, sits high on the majestic Castilian plateau in the exact center of the Iberian Peninsula. It is protected from the north and west by the Sierra de Guadarrama and the Sierra de Gredos. To reach Madrid from the north, the traveler or invader must cross mountain passes at an altitude of five thousand feet. The Montes de Toledo bar the way in the south, and ramparts of mountains rise to the east in the direction of Valencia and the Mediterranean coast. The Andalusian range watches over the southern coast of Spain. The Pyrenees guard the northern approaches to Barcelona, the great Mediterranean seaport. The north coast—the

Basque country and Asturias and Galicia—is outlined by the Cantabrian range. The Sierra de Gata guards the approaches to Portugal.

Mountain ranges defend the outer perimeter of Spain and form smaller fortresses within the country. Just as Madrid hides behind its mountain walls, so do Barcelona, Valencia, Málaga, Bilbao, San Sebastián, and La Coruña. Rivers further divide the Spanish regions. The Ebro, flowing through Aragon, separates Castile from Catalonia in the northeast. The Tagus divides Old Castile from New Castile. The Duero cuts off central Spain from the northwest and Portugal. The Guadalquivir slashes Andalusia as it flows from the Sierra Nevada past Córdoba and Seville into the Atlantic above Cádiz. The Guadiana divides Estremadura in the west at Mérida and Badajoz. Even the Balearic Islands of Majorca, Minorca, and Ibiza in the Mediterranean are rimmed by protective mountain chains. Foreign invaders—from Carthaginian and Roman generals to Moslem caliphs and Napoleonic marshals—have learned the hard way about Spain's defensive geography.

Each visitor to Spain must find for himself a central point of reference from which his understanding of this strange country and its astounding people may flow. It may be the museums and archives of Madrid. It may be Barcelona, with its special Catalonian point of view. It may be Seville, Granada, or Córdoba, linked to the multisplendored Spanish past and the Andalusian echoes of Moorish music. It may be the mysticism of the Basque country. It may be the crowded tourist playgrounds along the southern Costa del Sol or the eastern Costa Brava. My chosen point of reference was an eighteenth-century mill, once the home of Benedictine monks, at the foot of the ancient Castilian village of Pezuela de las Torres. I spent much of my free time at that mill during my Spanish years, for it made me believe that I was close to the roots of Spain. Although barely an hour's drive from Madrid, Pezuela de las Torres is decades if not centuries from the capital in terms of history and levels of civilization.

Pezuela de las Torres is a hilltop town mercilessly baked by the sun in summer and bitterly lashed by a winter wind that rises in the eastern ranges of the Sierra de Guadarrama. So raw and bone-chilling is this wind that Castilians have been saying forever, in their somber and fatalistic way, that it "may not douse a candle, but it will take a man's life."

The wind, the heat, and the drought, haunting but never quite obliterating tableland pueblos like Pezuela de las Torres, have forged the strength of the Castilians. That is why for nearly a half a millennium the region of Castile has proudly ruled the rest of Spain, subordinating if not subjugating the sophisticated and supple Catalonian tradesmen of the eastern Mediterranean coast, the brave knights of the Valencian kingdoms, the romantic and lackadaisical Andalusians of the dry south, and through an extraordinary medieval marriage, even the tough Aragonese living along the Ebro River between the foothills of the Pyrenees and the fertile northeast. Then, in the Age of Discovery, Castilian resilience and wanderlust and greed went on to build a fabulous overseas empire.

If there is a valid central theory about Spain's history—and the Spanish temperament being what it is, there are as many theories as there are Spaniards—it concerns the intimate relationship between the harsh land and the character of the people. This relationship has been recognized by such leading Spanish historians as Rafael Altamira y Crevea, who published a formidable four-volume *Historia de España y de la civilización española* in the first decade of this century, and by Salvador de Madariaga, the octogenarian resident of Oxford and author of *Spain, A Modern History,* which is still the best and most readable work on the market. Rafael Altamira begins with an essay on "The Influence of Geography on the History of Spain." Madariaga opens with these words: "The main fact about the land is its inaccessibility . . . Spain is a castle."

The top of this Spanish castle is Castile—geographically, historically, politically, and even linguistically, for in Spanish *castillo* is the word for castle. The province has dominated Spain since the marriage of Isabella of Castile to Ferdinand of Aragon in 1469 and their formal recognition ten years later as equal sovereigns of their respective domains. The Catholic Kings, as Ferdinand and Isabella are called, united the individual kingdoms of the Peninsula under their twin crowns, ended nearly eight centuries of Arab and Moorish occupation by taking Granada in 1492, and sent Columbus off on his voyages to the New World, thus launching Spain's scintillating four-hundred-year career as a global empire.

Ever since Madrid became the capital of Spain in the sixteenth century, men from all over the country have sought to dispute its supremacy, for individualism and a sense of independence have always been dominant Iberian personality traits. The contenders

Washday near a Galician village

have fought the central power, besieged the capital, and sometimes even conquered it. But when they finally did so, they ruled Spain from Madrid in their turn.

Francisco Franco Bahamonde—"by the Grace of God, the Caudillo of Spain," the Generalissimo of the Armies of the Land, Sea, and Air, and for more than three decades the dictator of Spain— came from green Galicia in the northwest to rule Spain from Madrid at the end of the Civil War in 1939. And no one since the days of the Catholic Kings has been as convinced of the need for a centralized government for Spain from the Castilian plateau. Others —kings, ministers, poets, painters, and scholars—have likewise been attracted or forced toward Castile in the past five hundred years. They have dotted the province with great universities at Salamanca, Valladolid, and Alcalá de Henares and with castles and palaces in Toledo, Ávila, Segovia, and Aranjuez.

To know and understand Spain, therefore, it is logical to start with Castile. And to understand Castile, one may as well begin with Pezuela de las Torres.

E ntering the village from either direction, the traveler is greeted by a weather-beaten wooden sign in the shape of a yoke and arrows. It stands a few feet from the rectangular road sign proclaiming that this is Pezuela. The yoke-and-arrows emblem marks the entrance to every village, town, and city in Spain, and is the symbol of Generalissimo Franco's National Movement, the only political organization that has been allowed to exist in the country since the Civil War. Like Pezuela, the emblem spans Spanish history. It first appeared on the coat of arms of the Catholic Kings, and was borrowed as the symbol of the Falange by that political party's young founder, José Antonio Primo de Rivera, in the early 1930's, to remind Spaniards of their nation's past greatness. José Antonio was executed by the Loyalists in 1936, but the Falange and its yoke and arrows have survived. Generalissimo Franco, who is not an ideological Falangist, has neatly fitted this Fascist party into his National Movement along with the other rival groups that supported him during the Civil War.

The complex geometry of tile and stone in Pezuela de las Torres

2 Journey Through Time

Water is precious in Spain.

P ezuela de las Torres is only thirty-five miles east of Madrid. Through the narrow valley below the town flows the Tajuña River, a rare gift of water in this parched land. It irrigates the valley even in the hottest days of summer, when hundreds of Spanish rivers, brooks, and rivulets go bone-dry, and it makes life in the pueblo on the hill economically plausible if not necessarily comfortable.

Water is probably the most important single fact of life not only in Castile but in much of the rest of Spain. Where rivers have dried out because of soil erosion at their headwaters or prolonged droughts, villages have died. The inhabitants have emigrated (fled is a better word) to more promising areas of Spain or to jobs in western Europe. When the stone-hard soil has ceased to produce, the villagers have sold their ancient homes for a pittance—a centimo on the peseta—or simply abandoned them. In Castile, and in

Andalusia and Estremadura as well, one passes ghost villages, or villages in which only a single family or just a few old women and a handful of children have stayed behind to stare balefully at passing cars. The churches are closed because the priest has gone, too. The village bar, where men once gathered for a glass of red wine and a game of cards or dominoes, is boarded up. The old sign for San Miguel beer or Coca-Cola flaps in the wind, half-broken. The flowerpots in the windows of the houses, those eternal spots of color in a Spanish village, are empty. The cemetery, usually a small square or rectangle surrounded by a high wall, seems the only reminder that people once lived in the pueblo. Everything is for sale: houses, the church, the bar, even the cemetery, but there are no takers. In the Province of Toledo a whole village—lock, stock, and barrel—was advertised for sale not long ago. When I made inquiries, out of curiosity, a provincial official discouraged me. "You would be buying pure grief," he said. No one made a bid.

Arable land is always at a premium in this mountainous country, and a drought year brings on an economic crisis, or a period of stunted growth, as was the case after the 1964–65 droughts. As much as Spain may earn from tourism and from such exports as citrus fruits (which are seldom touched by drought or frost in their Mediterranean groves), it loses as much or more by having to increase food imports. In a typical recent year those imports exceeded one billion dollars in value, or one-twentieth of the total national income.

Even accepting the fact that the climate and topography of Spain —the most mountainous country of Europe after Switzerland—will never allow it to become agriculturally self-sufficient, some Spanish government someday must grant the water problem, and, therefore, the farm problem, the priorities that nowadays are so generously given to the prestige-creating and fashionable industries. No government can create water where it does not exist, but it can distribute it better. There have been large-scale irrigation schemes in Spain, but nowhere on the scale that is both possible with modern technology and urgently required. The World Bank has been telling this to the Franco regime for well over ten years. The people of Spain have been saying it even longer. The walls of villages throughout the south are covered with large hand-painted signs imploring "FRANCO—AGUA—FRANCO—AGUA!" In parched Almería Province in the south a sign says: "Franco: You Gave Us Victory in War—Now Give us Water in Peace. . . ."

Thanks to its river, Pezuela is relatively well off by Castilian standards. It also has electric lights, a telephone operator (which is a part of the great saga of Spanish communications), and half a dozen small stores and bars. Flowerpots decorate the fronts of the ancient whitewashed houses, and television antennas sprout from many of the roofs—when civilization comes to Spanish villages, it comes in a rush.

Nearly one thousand people reside in Pezuela, but no one is really sure of the number because there has been no national census since 1960 and because more and more young people go to work in Alcalá de Henares or in Madrid. Once employed, they usually stay in the cities, sending money but only occasionally returning for visits.

Many of those who have remained in Pezuela go down to the Tajuña Valley daily to work the fertile land sown in corn (for the animals), wheat, and vegetables. There are cattle and pigs on one or two big farms, belonging to Madrid people, on both slopes of the narrow valley. The trip from the pueblo to the fields is just under three miles down a winding mountain road. The more prosperous farmers and farm hands travel by motorcycle. The others walk or ride their tough little burros. Old men and women, sometimes children, carry huge earthenware jugs down to the river and back up to the village. That is how Pezuela obtains water for drinking and washing. Burros bring up loads of hay or grass for the animals that are kept in the pueblo. At sunset, which is beautiful and multicolored in summer and winter, the shepherds bring in the sheep and the goats that graze among the boulders along the road. There is something Biblical in the sight of the solemn, sun-scorched men and women riding donkeys that are also burdened with water and fodder. But, then, there is something Biblical about all of Spain that has known the Roman invasion and Moorish rule.

In winter Pezuela, like all Castilian pueblos, is shut tight against the cold and the wind from the Guadarramas. In summer the shutters are closed against the burning sun as they are in Jaén, Almería, Granada, and Seville. When you walk into Don Justo Castillo's general store in Pezuela, pushing aside the rough sackcloth curtain, it is so dark that you have to blink before your eyes are emptied of the bright sun and you can see again.

Men of this toughness and resilience have made Spain what it is today.

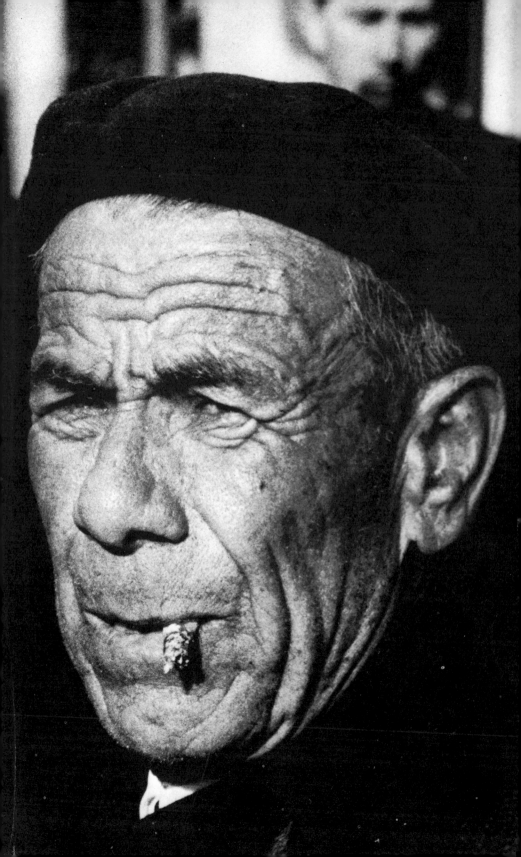

The people of Pezuela are as hard as the huge boulders in their fields and as resilient as the plants that fight for survival on the terraced hills. But all the villagers of Castile are a hardy race—the quiet old men in their black berets, puffing on black-tobacco cigarettes, and the black-dressed women unbent by the weight of the water jugs—and this is why Castile has become the brightest jewel in the crown of Spain. It was cut from their dignity, their sweat, their toughness, their resistance, and their fatalistic optimism that life will go on despite all hardships.

Driving from Pezuela to Madrid, the first town of consequence one passes is Alcalá de Henares, fifteen miles to the west. It is the threshold of modern Castile and the Spain of the twentieth century. The blacktop road that runs through Alcalá to Madrid is the main highway for heavy truck and car traffic from as far off as Barcelona and Gerona in wealthy Catalonia, some six hundred winding miles to the northeast. It also brings tourists who have crossed from France at La Junquera and followed the tortuous and narrow but very picturesque route skirting the Costa Brava resorts on the Mediterranean. All year round the intensity of movement on these eastern approaches to Madrid is reminiscent of that on the great western European and American highways.

But because this is Spain, Alcalá de Henares is also a city with an inescapable past. It was once surrounded by a wall, and its gates, built by Philip III in the early 1600's, still stand. It was here that one of Spain's first and most famous universities was founded in 1508. Among its earliest scholars was Ignatius of Loyola, the fighting Basque, possibly Spain's most important mystic and the founder of the Society of Jesus, who was canonized in 1622 by the Roman Catholic Church. During his Alcalá days Loyola was arrested by the Inquisition, another extreme form of Spanish mysticism, for wearing sackcloth and preaching in the streets.

The university buildings, which still stand in the old town, are a curious blend of Italian Renaissance, Andalusian, and Moorish architectural influences. The resulting hybrid opulence was known as the Cisneros Style during the sixteenth century, in an apparent tribute to Cardinal Francisco Jiménez de Cisneros. This formidable cardinal, the founder of Alcalá University, was a man to whom Spain still owes much of what is right and what is wrong about it. He was the Archbishop of Toledo (a post nowadays equivalent to

The main street of Alcalá de Henares

Primate of Spain), the private confessor of Queen Isabella, the Inquisitor General, and, briefly, regent after the death of the Catholic Kings.

The cardinal advocated architectural experiments of which both the towering Toledo Cathedral and Alcalá University are unrelated examples. His era also brought to Castile the heavy, ornate work of the *plateros,* the silversmiths of Moorish Seville and Granada. After a while, every Castilian nobleman from San Ildefonso to Ávila felt that he had to have sculptured silver doors or similarly ostentatious *platero* adornments on his castle or mansion.

Paralleling these innovations of extravagant form in what previously had been a fairly forbidding Castilian environment, a wave of sensual romanticism swept the tableland. Early in the sixteenth century the countless anonymous bards of Castile—the *infinitos poetas*—turned out romances, or ballads, that were touching, romantic, amusing, and sometimes downright sexy. They sang of love and war and conquest, and of errant knights, lovesick princesses, and midnight intrigues. In so doing, Castilian became increasingly established as the language of writers and poets.

As expressive as any of these anonymous love ballads is the *Romance de Rosaflorida.* Rosaflorida, a Castilian princess, refuses to be betrothed to seven Lombard counts and three Lombard princes while awaiting her dreamed-of Montesinos, a wandering knight whom she has never met. When he comes, she says, "he will be the lord of seven sweet Castilian castles, and the lord of silver gates, and the lord of my water sources, and the lord of roses at dawn." And when he wishes to take more, she says, "I shall give him even more. . . . He shall be the lord of my eyes and the prince of my lips, the cardinal of my breasts, and of my white thighs the count he shall be. . . . Sovereign and princely, over my body he shall rule, and no sweeter body is there nor in France nor in Castile. . . ."

Does this sound extravagantly sensual and risqué for the dour mystics of sixteenth-century Spain? Rosaflorida was remarkably well behaved compared to, say, Melisenda, "the daughter of the Kings of Castile" and the heroine of the *Romance de la Linda Melisenda.* The "lovely" Melisenda, to believe the bard, awoke one midnight from libidinous dreams about a Prince Airuelo, slipped out of the paternal castle clad only in a white mantle, and proceeded across town to her beloved's palace. Challenged by the prince's

The way of the cross, enacted during Holy Week in Seville

night watchman, Hernandillo, Melisenda borrowed his "sharp dagger," professing to fear the black of the night and the stray dogs, and "seven times plunged it in his back and thrice in the heart." As Hernandillo "fell dead, touching the earth with his cold lips," the barefoot Melisenda threw open the heavy sculptured silver doors and rushed to the prince's chambers. "Shout not, milord," she whispered to him, "do not awake your sleeping dogs, nor have fear of the virgin. . . . No daggers shine in the darkness, 'tis my body that glistens in the night." Indeed, Melisenda could put Shakespeare and the Elizabethans to shame.

It is important to remember, however, that these extravagances coexisted with the asceticism of Loyola and others like him. After Spain locked her doors to the Protestant Reformation of the 1500's, it was Castile that provided the mystics who helped to defend the Catholic faith. Among them were Cisneros in Toledo and Tomás de Torquemada in Ávila, both Grand Inquisitors, and Saint Theresa and Saint John of the Cross, also of the very Castilian walled town of Ávila.

Superficially at least, Spain has lost the penchant for ascetism, and its present thrust is toward the materially enjoyable gifts of life. But on Good Friday thousands and thousands of hooded penitents, heavy chains clanging at their bare feet, painfully retrace the route of Calvary along the streets of Seville, Madrid, and scores of other Spanish towns and villages. At Easter, 1968, for example, I learned that more than three hundred tons of iron were sold in Madrid alone for the use of the penitents. Then there is the politically powerful lay order known as Opus Dei, which is not altogether different in some ways from the sixteenth-century Jesuits. The order was founded in 1924 by Monsignor Josemaria Escrivá de Balaguer y Albas, a pragmatic Aragonese priest who now lives in Rome. Since late 1959 Opus Dei members, with Franco's blessings, have assumed most of Spain's key government posts.

The vast bleak palace and basilica that Philip II built at El Escorial from 1563 to 1584, and where Generalissimo Franco presides every February during severe rites for Spain's dead monarchs, is another Castilian monument to undying Spanish mysticism. So is the Basilica of the Valley of the Fallen, between El Escorial and Madrid, which Franco had hewn out of the rock by prisoners he took in the Civil War. He built it to perpetuate the memory of his soldiers who had died in the war. For that matter, was not the terrible and stubborn Civil War itself a supreme display of Spanish mysticism—that war in which each side fought to the death convinced of the cosmic justice of its cause?

Finally, there must be an element of mysticism in the drama of the bullfight—the *fiesta nacional,* the national feast, as the Spaniards have always called it. Why else would a man deliberately defy death in the crowd-ringed solitude of the arena?

Alcalá de Henares offers a touch of contemporary mysticism in the form of a theological seminary, where many Spanish priests of the new generation are trained. Unlike their conservative predecessors, these young priests often emerge as the revolutionaries of the new era, preaching social justice and political freedom in a society that has not quite yet shaken off its feudal past and post-Civil War dictatorial shackles. Their mysticism is nowadays inspired by the socially conscious proclamations of the Vatican Council, but the drama is eternal and very Spanish.

Twenty-five miles of road separate Alcalá from Madrid, and the drive tells a great deal about the economics and politics of modern Spain. Factories rise beside the busy highway on once-empty fields. They form the perimeter of Madrid's fast-growing industrial belt. Sheep and goats still graze around the factories, but the shepherds listen to music and soccer games on their transistor radios. A new Labor University, a contribution of the Franco government, stands on the outskirts of Alcalá. A paratrooper brigade is based in Alcalá, emphasizing the rapid modernization of Spain's armed forces in the last fifteen years or so.

Halfway along the road to Madrid sprawls the joint American-Spanish air force base of Torrejón de Ardoz, a formidable reminder of Spain's involvement in the West's nuclear-age defense system and of the support given by the United States to the Franco regime when it hovered on the brink of bankruptcy.

The $120-million Torrejón base, along with air bases at Saragossa in the north and San Pablo and Morón de la Frontera, both outside Seville, in the south, were built as part of a military agreement reached by the United States and Spain in 1953. The bases formed the backbone of the Strategic Air Command's Cold War defense in

Sheep move across the foundation of a Madrid housing development.

southwestern Europe. From these bases SAC bombers initially flew
nuclear airborne-alert missions along Soviet borders. Later, when
aerial technology improved and the B-52's began flying round-trip
missions directly from the United States, the Spanish bases served
as the home of the aerial tankers that refueled the bombers in transit.

Thirty-two naval-communications and radar installations and a
485-mile Seville-Saragossa pipeline for aviation fuel were also part
of the American military establishment in Spain. Between 1953 and

1963, when the agreement was renegotiated, United States aid to Spain totaled more than $2 billion, including $600 million worth of modern weapons. Credits, loans, and investments arising from the construction and maintenance of the bases eventually aided the country's recovery and what is currently but inaccurately called its "economic miracle." In 1963 a five-year renewal of the bases agreement provided for the construction of $250 million worth of special facilities for United States nuclear submarines at the Rota naval base near Cádiz. In 1969 Spain sought an astronomical price for another renewal of the agreement. After a year of negotiations the arrangement was extended for another five years on much more modest terms than Franco would have liked. But the Generalissimo had the satisfaction of a visit from President Nixon repeating the Eisenhower embrace that had sealed the original agreement in Madrid in 1959.

The Eisenhower Administration acted for purely military reasons, but to Spain—and to Generalissimo Franco—the bases agreement and General Eisenhower's visit also had extraordinary political, psychological, and economic value. Most significantly perhaps, they marked the end of Spain's international isolation that dated to the Allies' victory over the Axis in World War II and to the 1946 vote in the United Nations to withdraw ambassadors from Madrid and keep Spain out of the new world organization.

The leaders of western Europe, particularly the socialists, have apparently found it easier to bury the memory of World War II and to accept West Germany in NATO, to say nothing of Portugal under Salazar, the late dean of world dictators, than to forgive Franco for having won the Spanish Civil War. The real reason, conscious or unconscious, may lie in those leaders' guilt feelings for having allowed the Republican side to lose that war. The view that there is still a need to isolate Franco more than two decades after NATO's creation possibly does more harm than good to the prospects of restoring Spanish democracy. It has also caused the proud Spanish to resist making concessions to Western thinking as a price for acceptance. Franco has always demonstrated that he and Spain could wait. Only in 1970 did Spain manage to negotiate a preferential commercial agreement with the Common Market, her largest trading partner. But the agreement gives Spain no hope of membership in the foreseeable future.

29

American and Spanish personnel working together at the Torrejón de Ardoz air base

The United States returned an ambassador to Madrid long before the UN ban was lifted, and Spain was admitted to full membership in 1955. The bases agreement virtually made Spain a military ally of the world's greatest power. (No formal alliance exists thus far, and none is contemplated.) It also made Spain a participant in the Western defense system, even in the absence of actual ties to NATO. Above all, it vindicated Generalissimo Franco's stubborn refusal to step down, mend his ways, restore representative democracy, or do any of the things that were being demanded of him to end Spain's international ostracism.

The air base at Torrejón is another steppingstone to the reality of modern Spain, but because this is Spain, it offers the most startling contrast to the village of Torrejón that lies less than a mile away.

The base is the usual piece of America that our military men carry with them overseas as inevitably as a snail carries its home on its back wherever it goes. There is standard base housing, a well-designed network of internal roads complete with bilingual signs ordering drivers and passengers to "Fasten Your Seat Belts," first-rate schools, officers' and noncoms' clubs, swimming pools, hospitals, and post exchanges filled with American food and goods. It is a superbly administered township that could have been dropped in France, Britain, Italy, Turkey, or Saudi Arabia and would still look and feel pretty much the same.

The village of Torrejón de Ardoz is another world. It has as little in common with the base as it does with Madrid, which can be seen in the distance from its rutted main street. Torrejón de Ardoz, in fact, may well vie for the title of Spain's least attractive place. Its houses are dilapidated. Its bars and cafés, numerous because of the American trade, are primitive and uninviting. The people one sees in the streets lack both the hardiness and dignity of Castilian hill-dwellers and the verve of the Madrileños. This link between the American military presence next door and the explosive animation of Madrid down the asphalt straightaway can only be described as nondescript, and that can be said of extremely few Spanish towns and villages. Torrejón has considerably less character than tiny Pezuela de las Torres, to say nothing of Alcalá or Guadalajara. The only comparison that comes to mind is La Línea de la Concepción, the town on the doorstep of Gibraltar. In both cases, the traveler's overwhelming desire is to get out, in either direction. Perhaps foreign establishments simply drain the personality from contiguous Spanish towns.

The village of Torrejón, however, does offer an introduction to the unique national telephone service. Direct dialing exists nowadays between most of Spain's big cities, but in the countryside service among the small towns and villages and between them and the cities belongs to the dawn of the telephone age. The relays are all manual, which means that to talk to Madrid from, say, Pezuela, the operator must go through the regional exchange at Torrejón and several other open switchboards where calls are blended into a cacophonous sound that makes individual voices almost inaudible. The delays are so great that often it takes less time to drive to one's destination than to get a call through.

On the other hand, the rural telephone operator in Spain is far more of a social, cultural, and emergency-aid institution than her counterpart in the United States or Britain. With the village telephone station usually installed in the front parlor of her home, the operator knows everybody for miles and miles around. If a call came for me from Madrid, the Pezuela operator would send a message with the bus driver or with someone about to go down to the valley on a motorcycle. The typical Spanish operator also considers scores of other telephone operators in the region her friends, although most of them have never laid eyes on one another. This, in turn, leads to waves of gossip that Anglo-Saxons would not tolerate over such distances but that the garrulous Spaniards could not do without.

The following is typical of the conversations that would take place between María Teresa, the Pezuela operator, and Chelo, her counterpart in Torrejón, while I waited for my call to go through to Madrid:

"How are you behaving?" asks María Teresa, who sews as she operates her telephone.

"Like a Yé-Yé mule," Chelo answers. Both girls giggle over the private joke.

"What about this fellow Carmen has been going out with?" María Teresa inquires.

"Oh, he's sort of fortyish," Chelo says.

"You mean just like that Nicolás?" María Teresa remarks, cranking up her phone again.

I hasten to add that María Teresa and Chelo are efficient and courteous operators who must work with unspeakably deficient equipment. It simply means that rushing modernization has not yet done away with the human charm of Spain—even in Torrejón de Ardoz, a village between the air force base and the capital.

A turnoff from the six-lane highway leading from a point past Torrejón to Madrid takes one to Barajas Airport, the chief gateway for a large proportion of the twenty-four million people who visit Spain every year. There are also airports at Barcelona, Gerona, Málaga, Seville, Almería, and Alicante on the southern coast, and in Bilbao, Oviedo, and La Coruña in the north. Other international flights, often tourist charters, go directly to Majorca in the Mediterranean and to the Canary Islands off the African coast.

Life in the villages of Spain is on an intensely human scale.

Spain's former isolation has been further eroded by unending streams of automobiles that cross into Spain from France during most of the year. In summer one sees more foreign license plates—West German, French, British, or Scandinavian—than Spanish ones on the highways of Spain.

Foreigners—Phoenicians, Greeks, Carthaginians, Romans, Moors, the French armies of Napoleon, and now the invading tourists—have always crossed Spain more or less at will. Hannibal led his elephants from Africa past the orange groves of Spain's eastern Mediterranean coast and into France along the same roads that tourists travel today in Volkswagens and Peugeots. The Romans and Moors lived for centuries in Spain, and there is hardly a square mile on which they have not left a monument to their presence—a castle, an aqueduct, a watchtower, a palace, a garden, or a mosque hidden today inside the shell of a church or cathedral. For sheer abundance and historical variety of ruins no country in Europe is a match for Spain.

The paradox is that Spain has long been less accessible to her own people than to foreigners. Indeed, only in this generation have inexpensive, mass-produced automobiles permitted the Spaniards to see their own country. The Seat, a domestic version of the Italian Fiat, has caused something of a social revolution. Retailing at the equivalent of $1,200, it has given the eternally restless Spaniard perhaps his first opportunity in history to free himself from the shackles of his geography.

The Seat has also saddled Spain with the fearful menace of the "first-generation driver." Impatient and lordly, a combination of Don Quixote and a death-defying matador, the Spaniard drives with his hand on the horn, thinks nothing of high-speed turns from the wrong lane, and without a twinge of conscience will occupy the whole width of the highway. He righteously criticizes other Spanish drivers for doing the same things, by calling them *sinvergüenzas,* "shameless ones."

The full flavor of this social revolution on wheels can best be appreciated on a Spanish country road, where the overlapping stages of civilization are clearly visible. A man on a burro passes a woman on foot balancing a water jug on her head; a bicyclist passes the burro rider; a motorcycle passes the bicycle; and the unleashed Seat passes them all. The Seat may carry valises and even a folded baby carriage on the roof rack. Counterpoint is provided by a mule-drawn gypsy cart, the whole family bundled inside and the dog trotting behind on a rope.

Spanish highways are slowly but steadily improving, and there is a spreading network of glass-and-chrome service stations with neon signs and sometimes even girl attendants dressed in black leather. The economic implications of this transition are typified by the un-expected sight of a buglike Seat parked in the majestic solitude of a wheat field or an olive grove while its driver and passengers work the land around it.

The six-lane *autopista* that leads from Barajas into Madrid picks up streams of cars from the new suburbs and industrial plants in

New housing is continually going up in Madrid.

35

the area. The huge residential blocks of Ciudad Pegaso, where the employees of the government-owned Pegaso automotive works are housed, and the middle-class districts of Ciudad Lineal and Parque Avenida form veritable satellite cities just outside the congestion of midtown Madrid. Ciudad de los Angeles, a series of low-cost housing projects, provides the city's new outer shell to the south, and is gradually displacing the suburban slums and the caves in which some Spaniards still live.

Cave No. 5 near Granada is home to these two boys.

Like Madrid, Barcelona, Bilbao, Seville, Valencia, and the other cities have been affected by massive migrations from the chronically impoverished countryside, and they too are applying the same defensive urban-development tactic of spreading out to deal with the modern age that is so impatiently imposing itself on Spain.

The hour-long car trip from Pezuela de las Torres to Madrid is like a flight in a time machine from the closing years of the fifteenth century into the present.

Madrid's flea market is called the Rastro.

3 What Things!

Y qué cosas!"—"And what things!"—exclaimed Ramón Gómez de la Serna as he set out to describe, catalogue, admire, deplore, deride, and love the truly incredible riches of Madrid's vast open-air market called the Rastro. Gómez de la Serna, a turn-of-the-century Madrileño literary gentleman, labored from 1900 to 1914 to collect material for his celebrated "Guía del Rastro," but essentially nothing has changed there in the ensuing half-century. The Rastro is still right off the Puerta de Toledo, the ancient southern gateway to the city. If anything, it has become bigger and more varied as the population of Madrid has grown from considerably less than a million when the century began to more than three million today. Gómez de la Serna's admiring *"Y qué cosas!"* can now be applied to the exploding capital as a whole, not just to the Rastro.

Visually, the "things" of the capital range from Castilian austerity oddly blended with the baroque in old Madrid to the clean, modern buildings that line the new avenues. Art runs the gamut from the priceless Prado Museum collection, which is among the world's greatest, to new galleries exhibiting the works of contemporary artists like Tápies, Saura, Canogar, Sempere, Rueda, Tornos, and Genovese. These are men in their forties who have won international recognition (and commensurate prices) within the last decade. As happens periodically, Spanish art was "rediscovered" during the 1960's. Bridging the gap between the Prado and the galleries are the Picassos and Mirós to be found in smaller museums and private collections around the city. Picasso, incidentally, has refused to have any of his works hung in the Prado so long as Generalissimo Franco remains dictator of Spain. But in March, 1970, he donated hundreds of his early works to the Berenguer de Aguilar Palace museum in Barcelona, in Catalonia. Picasso is a native of Málaga, but he apparently regards the fiercely independent capital of Catalonia as his spiritual home.

The same spirit of defiance has kept Pablo Casals, the world's greatest cellist, from returning to Spain during Franco's lifetime. He will come from his home in Puerto Rico only as far as Prades on the French side of the Pyrenees. Yet, in one of those typical Spanish paradoxes, the government's radio network frequently and proudly broadcasts recorded performances by the Prades Festival

Orchestra conducted by Casals. And the regime has never stopped thousands of Spaniards from traveling to Prades to see and hear the self-exiled nonagenarian maestro who played at the White House for Theodore Roosevelt in 1904 and for John Kennedy in 1961. I saw Casals in Jerusalem in the summer of 1969, conducting his Biblical oratorio *The Manger* and chatting in Spanish and Catalonian with Israeli musicians of Sephardic descent.

Even without Casals the musical life of Madrid is active. The recently rebuilt Teatro Real has nearly the best acoustics in the world, according to the pianist Artur Rubinstein, who now comes to play there annually. On the less exalted end of the scale, there are performances of Spanish operettas known as *zarzuelas* and Spanish ballets by famous dancers like Antonio. And, inevitably, there is the flamenco, which attracts sophisticated Spaniards just as it does the package-tour visitors who are uncomprehendingly shepherded by their guides from the Corral de la Morería to the Zambra, the two temples of the Madrid schools of flamenco dance and song. (Seville flamenco is faster and merrier and more romantically Andalusian than the Madrileño variety, and serious scholars eternally debate in print and in person the relative merits of each.)

Few bullfights can compare with the Madrid performances during the week of the Feria de San Isidro, the feast of the city's patron

The matador moves in for the kill.

saint, late in May. I was there during the feria one year and watched the greatest bullfighters of our times—Antonio Ordoñez, Diego Puerta, Paco Camino, Paco Linares, and El Cordobés—give their best. They did not always try quite so hard during the rest of the March-to-October season.

There is a theory, not susceptible of scientific proof, that Spaniards eat massively and steadily to make up for the lack of sleep caused by their habit of dining close to midnight. True or not, one can eat well virtually around the clock in Madrid.

Six restaurants catering to foreigners and to Spain's rich and powerful deserve international notice: the Jockey Club, Nuevo Valentín, and Escuadrón are deluxe establishments on the French model with superior service; Botín, Casa Paco, and the "old" Valentín in downtown Madrid are classic, old-fashioned restaurants known to generations of Madrileños and visitors. There is no rating system in Spain like the stars awarded by Michelin in France. The practice followed by the Ministry of Information and Tourism of grading restaurants with one to five "forks" is less a guide to good eating than an ascending guide to the price of a meal. The conscientious diner who knows his circuit will often eat better at a one-fork than a five-fork restaurant.

Besides the great restaurants, there are scores of satisfying but lesser-known establishments. One that is relatively short on official forks but long on good food, service, quality, and atmosphere is Figón de Santiago, a seven-table restaurant in old Madrid known to virtually no foreigners and to only a Mafia-like group of Spaniards. Figón operates behind an unmarked black door that is usually locked. When a prospective customer knocks, the owner or a waiter peeks out through a small barred opening to determine whether the face on the other side belongs to a desirable client. The criteria have never been spelled out. Figón belongs to a florid and courteous Andalusian named Manuel who saved the money to start the restaurant during his years as a street photographer on the Gran Vía. The cooking is done by Carmen, his wife, a corpulent lady who on some evenings presides over flamenco sessions in the restaurant's stone cellar. There is no menu, and Manuel requires that his regulars phone him a day ahead to discuss their meal. In the case of diners who have not called ahead, Manuel recites what is available, referring to the soup or appetizers as "Act One," to the main course

One of the many *tascas* in Madrid

as "Act Two," and so on. In the final act, it is no effort to pay sixty or seventy dollars for a meal for four that has included excellent Spanish wines.

A dozen fine, old-fashioned restaurants in the general area of the old town serve seafood flown in from the Bay of Biscay, the Mediterranean, and in the case of some lobsters, the Canaries; excellent salmon from Asturian rivers; and Castilian specialties—principally roast piglet and roast lamb. The best of these roast meats are actually to be found in Castilian towns like Segovia or Escorial (where Philip II built his immense and somber monastery-palace).

Madrileño dishes call for a strong stomach. They range from tripe (*callos*) and garlic soup with egg to the formidable *cocido* (boiled meat served with vegetables). All these dishes are served at lunch and dinner. Between meals, Madrileños frequent the hundreds of *tascas*, where one may drink red wine, beer, or cognac and eat dark *serrano* ham, *manchego* cheese, shrimps, crayfish, lobster claws, olives, and a variety of sausages. The accepted system as one eats and drinks standing up at the crowded *tasca* bars is to drop the debris on the floor. Every hour or so a young boy sweeps up after the customers. European-type bars include the Chicote, with its encyclopedic collection of bottles; the Balmoral Bar, which attracts the foreign-ministry crowd, generals, aristocrats, and politicians; and the bars at the big hotels.

Fortunately, Madrid's rapid modernization has not yet overtaken its superb small craftsmen. Seseña's, for example, has been making capes for more than two hundred years. It is possible for a Spaniard to walk in and ask for "the same kind of cape you made for my great-grandfather around 1815. . . ." The clerk will ask the ancestor's name and check it in the venerable order book. Two or three weeks later, the handmade cape will be ready. The cost will be around $100. My most spectacular acquisition in Spain was a black

Hand-binding books in leather, shown here in a Madrid atelier, is a once widespread Spanish craft that is now dying out.

Seseña cape with scarlet facings, a Christmas gift from my wife. I have worn it proudly in Paris and Bucharest, Prague and Washington.

A few Madrid craftsmen still make huge wineskins in the shape of cows. These were originally used to transport wine without bruising it from the wholesalers' wooden barrels to bars, restaurants, and even private houses. But according to the wine people, there are only four or five men left in Madrid who know how to carry the wineskins on their backs and compensate for the shifting tide of wine without toppling over onto the pavement. Aging wine in the skins is another vanishing art because it is no longer economical. It is, however, said to survive in the mountain village of Polop in the Mediterranean Province of Alicante, where a whole ham is placed inside a wineskin full of young red wine. The wine, the story goes, is allowed to "eat" the ham during the two or three years' fermentation and aging process, thus acquiring a special raw taste prized by the villagers.

Bootmakers, castanet makers, and guitar makers are among the traditional Madrid craftsmen. The bootmakers and the castanet carvers are in diminishing demand, but the guitar makers are enjoying a boom as the wave of guitar playing among the world's youth keeps them working overtime. The most famous Spanish guitar maker is Ramirez of Madrid.

Directly or indirectly, the government bureaucracy of Spain accounts for quite a slice of Madrid's wealth, and probably involves more than half a million of its inhabitants.

Bureaucracy is one of the most cherished Spanish traditions. It has grown fantastically since the Catholic Kings first centralized the administration of Spain in Castile. In a sense, the Spanish bureaucracy has become an end in itself. Since Generalissimo Franco came to power more than thirty years ago, the normal Spanish bureaucratic apparatus (by *normal* I mean something roughly comparable to the bureaucratic nightmare of the Austro-Hungarian Empire, which was reputed to have been the worst ever seen in Europe) has been expanded to accommodate and include the powerful bureaucracy of the National Movement, which is the regime's political and patronage organization. Aside from running the official trade unions (Spain has no independent labor movement), which have an enforced membership of more than twelve million, the National Movement has created parallel "delegations" in all the government's administrative areas. The Movement operates on the national, provincial, and municipal levels, supervising local governments as well as such peripheral activities as sports and organized youth. It has its own ministry in Madrid—one of the eighteen that make up the Spanish government—in order to administer itself and the labor unions.

For a Spaniard, bureaucracy means the endless completion of documents, in triplicate at least, to prove that he exists, that he is paid monthly by his employer, that he belongs to his labor union, that he pays his dues, social security assessments, taxes, and so on. Employer and employee must go through this operation every month of the year. To obtain a passport to go abroad, a Spaniard must be cleared by the *Dirección General de Seguridad,* the political police, so that the authorities may be sure that he is not an enemy of the Franco regime attempting to flee the country. Buying and registering a car requires visiting an infinite number of offices, and collecting an infinite number of stamped documents. The purchase of a house or land requires bureaucratic pilgrimages and title searches that may go on for months or years. Every citizen must have an identity card, a union card, and a variety of other documents proving his employment, his right of residence, and so on.

This is the financial and administrative price Spain pays for the existence of the Franco regime. The regime is based on the corporative system that was initiated by Mussolini in Italy in the 1920's and later imitated by Salazar in Portugal. It is officially described as reposing legally on Family, Municipality, and Syndicate (labor union).

As a foreigner with quasi-official standing, I was reasonably well protected from Spanish red tape. Still, my involvement in a minor disturbance at a provincial bullfight caused the police to confiscate my press card and require me to report to the local police station three days later to reclaim it. And in many instances, I found it much easier to be received by a cabinet minister than by the mayor of a provincial town. In the latter case, my request was often sent to Madrid for clearance.

A refreshing aspect of Spanish bureaucracy is that some of its

The main post office in Madrid

innumerable branches are housed in beautiful buildings of historical interest. The Foreign Ministry, for example, is in a lovely seventeenth-century house, a stone's throw from the Plaza Mayor, the principal and classically elegant square of old Madrid. On display are fine tapestries, including Gobelins, and a respectable collection of paintings. A section of the ministry once served as a prison for noblemen, hence the original name for the building: Carcel de Cortes. The Presidency of the Government—the regime's political and policy-making ministry—is housed in an early nineteenth-century mansion on the tree-shaded Paseo de la Castellana. It has some good paintings, mainly portraits of solemn ministers and nobles, and some fairly interesting Spanish and French furniture. The prime minister will have his offices here if and when General Franco decides to fulfill his own 1966 constitution (the Organic

One of Spain's resplendent civil servants

Law of the State) and names a premier for this monarchy without a monarch.

The Commerce Ministry has likewise been assigned a classical building on the Paseo de la Castellana, but most of the original furnishings and decorations are gone. The War Ministry, overlooking the Plaza de la Cibeles, one of Madrid's principal intersections, dates from the eighteenth century. Its vast gardens separate it effectively from the roar of the traffic in the Plaza de la Cibeles, the Paseo de la Castellana, and the street of the bankers, Calle de Alcalá.

Visiting government offices, a stranger may develop the idea that the real burden of Spanish bureaucracy is borne not by the cabinet ministers but by the immensely haughty and decorative porters. In the conservative ministries they are dressed in black uniforms with broad silver or gold stripes on their sleeves, while the less traditional ministries now decree light-gray uniforms with less braid or none at all. These porters jealously guard the inner doors, sift the callers, and escort them to waiting rooms with the dry courtesy of ducal major-domos. Most of them are older men who have seen ministers come and go, and *they* are what make Spanish bureaucracy truly impressive in this age of intercoms and businesslike girl receptionists.

Spain being a country of ironies, the visible seats of government in Madrid are not necessarily the actual seats of power. For example, since Franco reorganized the Cortes, or parliament, in 1942, it has been little more than a rubber stamp for legislation proposed or previously approved by the government. The Caudillo, wearing an army uniform, usually appears before the Cortes once a year to deliver a monotonous "state of the union" speech. It is vigorously applauded by *procuradores*, hand-picked deputies who appear in white tie and tails or in National Movement or Falangist uniforms, depending on their function and background. These sessions, incidentally, are the most graphic illustration of the astounding ruling coalition that Franco has hammered together from capitalists and Fascists, aristocrats and generals, monarchists, right-wing political mystics and conservative Roman Catholic churchmen.

Another illusory seat of power is the great two-thousand-room Royal Palace in Madrid. Now a museum, it has been uninhabited since King Alfonso XIII was ousted by the Second Republic in 1931. General Franco has always refused to live there, but as a man of tradition he receives foreign envoys there, allowing them to present their credentials in ceremonies richer in pomp and circumstance than anything in Rome or London.

The permanent center of power in Spain remains El Pardo, Franco's cool suburban palace eight miles from the Puerta del Sol, the Madrid square from which all distances in Spain and all street numbers in the city are measured. At El Pardo, Franco and his family are guarded, in successive layers, by the police, the green-uniformed Guardia Civil, which is Spain's armed *gendarmerie,* and the Guardia de Franco, an elite corps of bodyguards armed with submachine guns. El Pardo, remote as the Generalissimo himself, is closed to visitors.

It is not infrequent, however, for Madrileños to see their Caudillo, at least from a safe distance. Several times a month, his motorcade crosses the city to take him to an inauguration or ceremony or to Barajas Airport for an out-of-town trip. An hour or more before Franco is to drive through Madrid, policemen in white gloves are posted fifty yards apart along his route. At the approach of the motorcade, traffic policemen clear the streets and avenues of all vehicles. Finally the Caudillo's black Rolls sweeps past at fifty miles an hour surrounded by twenty-two motorcycle policemen wearing white gloves. The motorcade is preceded and followed by black Cadillac convertibles, their tops down, carrying the members of the Guardia de Franco with their submachine guns.

The Royal Palace in Madrid, photographed through its ornate gate

The popular reaction to these rapid street appearances is virtually nil, and this suits Franco just fine. He has never been a man to court popular applause in the manner of a Mussolini. He simply takes it for granted that he is accepted as Spain's leader, almost by divine right, as the Castilian kings were. And in a sense, this is nearly true. He has become such an institution that even his worst enemies seem prepared to live with him as long as God lets him live. This is both Spanish realism and Spanish fatalism.

At this writing, Franco has never been the target of an assassination attempt, hot-blooded and trigger-happy as his fellow citizens are and numerous as the opportunities have been. Professional

political opposition and rising resentment against him among Spain's younger people have never led to actual conspiracies to oust him. But this does not mean that he is popular with Spaniards. The masses have simply become accustomed to his existence. In fact, more than half of Spain's population today has not known life without Franco. This is why there are bland stares in the streets of Madrid when he whizzes past at the center of his motorcade, though drivers often honk impatiently when traffic jams are created by his passage.

During ceremonial appearances, when he is driven slowly in an open Rolls Royce on state visits to cities like Barcelona, Seville, or San Sebastián, or when he inaugurates a plant or museum, he is much applauded. Still, one always wonders how sincere the applause really is. When Franco delivered one of his short, set-piece speeches during a visit to Seville in June, 1968, the official news agency included in the text it distributed to the newspapers this parenthetical aside: (A voice: *"Olé, Viva tu Madre!*—"Long Live your Mother!" Great applause). The Caudillo's mother, of course, has been dead for a long time, but this is a very Spanish, emotional remark that the official propagandists evidently wanted to pass on to newspaper readers. It was another vignette in the enforced pageantry surrounding the aging chief of state.

Thoughtful Spaniards often argue that too many resources are wasted on the bureaucracy and on the vast security forces, and that only widespread corruption keeps the Franco system from falling apart. However, despite the cumbersome and expensive bureaucracy, the cities of Spain, if not the countryside, are catching up rapidly with the rest of Europe. Most historians believe that three centuries of decline in the country's fortunes finally began to be arrested during the 1960's. And Madrid, bursting at the seams, is the center of this twentieth-century reconquest of Spain by the Spaniards.

B y mid-1967 it had become evident to Madrid's mayor, Carlos Arías Navarro, that something had to be done about the city's suffocating traffic congestion. Close to five hundred thousand cars, trucks, and buses were registered in Madrid (one for every six inhabitants), and tens of thousands came into town every

At 5 P.M. traffic at Madrid's busy Puerta del Sol is bumper to bumper.

day from the provinces and abroad. At rush hour it sometimes took almost an hour to drive from the Foreign Ministry to the Avenida del Generalísimo in the uptown residential section, a distance of roughly one mile across the heart of Madrid. Traffic lights were installed and more policemen were deployed. Many avenues were made one-way. But having acquired their little Seat's or Spanish-assembled Dodge Darts (at more than six thousand dollars each), Madrileños were not about to do without them on the way to and from work. This raised the impossible question of where to park, for few people could afford chauffeurs who would drop them off at the office and pick them up again in the evening. The introduction of heavy fines and municipal tow trucks made little difference. In one instance, the indignant owner of a car being towed away by the police insisted on riding in it to the municipal parking lot. His pregnant wife was with him, and he argued angrily that he *had* the right to park illegally on a narrow street while visiting the family doctor.

In the end, the city had no choice but to construct underground parking lots. The decision was made by Mayor Arías, an efficient and energetic man whom Generalissimo Franco named to run

Madrid (no public officials are elected in Spain) after a long tenure as national director of security.

The most spectacular of the subterranean garages was built beneath the Plaza Mayor, a grand open space created in 1617–19 to imitate the Place des Vosges in Paris. Juan Gómez de Mora, the first Spanish architect to try his hand at the baroque style, gave the delightful symmetrical square colonnaded passages on all four sides. The two entrances to the plaza are through archways that pass under buildings. In the old days the cobbled square was used for afternoon promenades in carriages and on foot. In modern times the Plaza Mayor has featured outdoor restaurants and hundreds of parked cars. By tradition, one corner of the plaza is an informal outdoor exchange for traders in postage stamps. With the approach of Christmas, the Plaza Mayor is covered with wooden stands selling crèches, Christmas ornaments, tree bark, and green boughs and branches. When Christmas trees first gained acceptance among Spaniards after the Second World War, the gypsies, who monopolize certain activities in Spain, began to turn the Plaza Mayor into a forest of pine trees, firs, and spruces from the foothills of the Pyrenees. Presiding over all these activities from the center of the plaza was the majestic equestrian statue of Philip III, a rather undistinguished but very Madrileño monarch.

When Mayor Arías resolved to put an underground garage under the Plaza Mayor, his first step was to send Philip III away to the temporary oblivion of the municipal warehouse. The city promised that Philip would be replaced in the Plaza Mayor after the garage was completed and the square cleared of cars. The garage has opened and the cobbles have been turned over to pedestrians, but Philip is still in storage, along with a number of other sculptured heroes and quasi-heroes that have been displaced as streets and plazas have been broadened to accommodate more traffic. Only the statues of Franco's Civil War heroes have not been disturbed.

To the regret of traditionalists, the beautiful oak and plane trees along several of the most elegant avenues have been sacrificed to the demands of traffic. This fate has befallen the section of the Calle de Serrano where fashionable stores give way to private mansions, and the tree-shaded median on the Calle de Velázquez, which had been a cool summer oasis for strollers, children at play, and coffee and beer drinkers in the little improvised cafés.

Outdoor cafés are one of the charms of Madrid.

The institution of the outdoor café still survives in Madrid. But nobody knows for how long. With mild spring weather bars and restaurants spill out onto the sidewalks. Avenues that still have shady miniparks dividing the traffic are turned into extensions of the cafés with tables and chairs placed on the greenery. One of the interesting sights of Madrid is to watch waiters rushing through traffic, dexterously balancing their loaded trays. In Spanish cafés, indoor and outdoor, by the way, the customer is never rushed, and the time he may stay at his table is not related to what he spends. The writers and artists who used to meet at the Café Gijón on the Castellana are increasingly giving way to miniskirted young ladies and hippie-like characters. But one may still safely spend the whole afternoon at a choice window table for the price of a cup of coffee. The aging waiters do not hurry themselves or the customers.

In the old European tradition, the Gijón and several similar cafés also provide newspapers secured to a round stick, which is one way of saying that their clients are welcome to stay as long as they like.

Smog, however, is making life in the outdoor cafés, and other outdoor activities, less and less pleasant. It is at its most irritating between November and March (when a mild autumn or spring often allows the sidewalk cafés to stay open). Madrid now has the same concentration of smog as Milan, an industrial city, and the reasons are both modern and old-fashioned.

The modern reasons are, of course, the more than half a million vehicles in the streets and the industrial plants that are forming a tightening belt around the city. The old-fashioned reason is the continued use of coal and wood-burning furnaces in Madrid. By mid-autumn the coal trucks, and even surviving mule-drawn carts, appear in Madrid's streets to make their deliveries. The coal is either dumped down chutes into building cellars or carried inside in huge leather baskets by coal-blackened men. The coal dust then begins to rise in the streets.

To complicate matters, Madrid suffers from the phenomenon of atmospheric inversion. Because the city lies in a bowl atop the Castilian plateau, clouds tend to hang over it and trap the smog above the roofs. Not even the breezes from the nearby Guadarramas succeed in blowing it away. The progressive elimination of green-leaved trees from Madrid as part of Mayor Arías's solution to the traffic problem tends to aggravate the smog problem, for the greenery had helped to absorb the smog. Fortunately, Madrid still has two great green areas that are unlikely to be paved over—the Retiro, behind the Prado, and the Parque del Oeste, stretching from the approaches to the Plaza de España downtown to Ciudad Universitaria uptown.

After smog, noise is the worst by-product of Madrid's modernization. To be sure, Spaniards have always preferred to talk loudly rather than softly, and they do not mind producing a steady cacophony of sounds ranging from banging doors and clattering kitchen pots to the spontaneous singing of flamenco songs in the hallways of apartment buildings. Thus, when a Spaniard drives a car, his hand automatically seeks the horn at the slightest provocation. In Madrid this medley of steady honking has as its counterpoint the machine-gun bursts of starting and backfiring by tens of thousands of motorcycles and scooters. For some reason, the scooter and the motorcycle riders seem particularly to enjoy the sound effects they create in what passes for the stillness of the night.

Actually, the stillness of night never really comes to Madrid. The city simply goes through various thresholds of noise. Motor traffic abates after midnight but never ceases as it does in the financial district of Manhattan or in sections of Paris and even Rome. Just as silence is on the verge of descending on the uptown residential areas, the Spanish army's politically crucial División Brunete decides to move its Sherman tanks from barracks northwest of the city to barracks in the southeast, or vice versa. These exercises usually take place between three and four o'clock in the morning, with the tanks rumbling up or down the Avenida del Generalísimo at least once a month. At five o'clock in the morning, six days a week, it is the turn of the garbagemen and the *traperos*, the ragpickers. Madrid has a modern sanitation department, but for obscure reasons of local politics it has not been able to rid itself of the men and women who pick up trash at dawn in carts drawn by mules or donkeys. The carts seldom have rubber tires—hence a great rattle and clatter on the pavements in the small hours.

Most of the *traperos* are gypsies, for private garbage collection is another of their special monopolies. The *traperos* have their own association headed by a former army colonel. They do so well in their business that they continually try to persuade the municipal garbagemen, who work for low fixed wages, to join them and stop competing with them in the city's modern garbage trucks. The Rastro's merchants, processing factories of various kinds (mainly glass and paper), and other establishments are the clients of the *traperos*. Food scraps are fed to the pigs that the *traperos* keep around their shacks on Madrid's outskirts. The fattened pigs then feed the *trapero* families or are sold to slaughterhouses. In the end, many a *trapero* is better off financially than a white-collar worker who drives his Seat to the office and has to worry about his fixed budget.

As Madrid expands in every direction, the city's old elegance inevitably vanishes. Along the *Paseo de la Castellana* modern office buildings are gradually replacing the large and graceful houses that made Madrid's reputation for elegance. The luckier mansions are not actually torn down but merely transformed into banks or cor-

poration offices. The official argument is that the economics of a growing modern city demands these sacrifices. But it may be a spurious argument. Rome and Athens, for example, have succeeded in saving their best buildings by an official policy of preserving historical monuments and municipal elegance. In Madrid when an impoverished aristocrat has to sell his mansion, nobody comes forth to try to save it, and the pile drivers start working immediately on the foundations of a new building.

Ironically, one thing Madrid does not need in its current expansion is expensive housing. Along and around the Avenida del Generalísimo brand-new buildings with unfurnished luxury apartments in the $500-a-month class are half-empty. There is, however, a tragic dearth of moderately priced housing for small families. The young professional, to say nothing of the new arrival from the provinces, can seldom find or afford decent quarters with up-to-date comforts. Obsolete housing laws are presumably maintained for political reasons, since the regime portrays itself as a defender of the working class, and the frozen rents make it impossible to maintain or modernize old midtown and downtown buildings. Some Madrid apartments still rent for $15 a month, but the hallways are dark and smelly, the elevators (when they exist) may be used only to go up so as to preserve the equipment, and the plumbing is slowly deteriorating. I know a Spanish diplomat who owns a lovely old building near the Royal Palace. His worry is not to make money but to keep the early nineteenth-century building from collapsing, for he is not allowed to raise the rent of his apartments above the frozen level of $10 a month.

Yet Spanish coupon clippers, bankers, and real-estate operators see the expensive apartment buildings in the Generalísimo area as a hedge against inflation and a better investment than industry, which has been in a general state of crisis since 1967. Amid the uptown construction, flocks of sheep and herds of goats still make their way through traffic while going from their grazing meadows to their pens and back. So fast is Madrid growing that sometimes one cannot tell where the city ends and the countryside begins.

Madrid is still a worthwhile old city in the midst of all this rush to change. To sense it, one has only to go to such havens as the Prado and, improbably, the Rastro. In an odd way, these two seemingly unrelated institutions are linked. When the Prado acquired a long-lost Antonello da Messina painting from a private owner in 1966, a museum official marched off to the Rastro on a Sunday morning to look for a suitable frame. He was not particularly surprised to find within the space of an hour a fifteenth-century Venetian frame for the fifteenth-century picture by a master who had, in fact, died in Venice. Knowledgeable about the Rastro, the official not only went straight to where he thought a frame of this kind could be found but was able to buy it for the bargain price of less than ten dollars.

The Prado houses the fantastic art collection begun by Charles V and continued by Philip II, Philip III, and Philip IV. These kings were such avid collectors and art patrons that by the time Philip V ascended to the throne in 1700 the Spanish crown owned 5,539 pictures by such artists as Titian, Rubens, Velázquez, El Greco, Botticelli, and Hieronymous Bosch, to name only a few. Different as these kings were in personality, they all had fine and daring taste. Charles V and Philip II commissioned paintings from Titian (the 1548 equestrian portrait of Charles V at the battle of Mühlberg is now at the Prado). Philip II brought back Veroneses, Tintorettos, and Bassanos from his travels in Italy. Philip III, the weakest of these royal connoisseurs, had Rubens painting at his court for eight months in 1603. Philip IV brought Rubens back to Madrid twenty-five years later. For forty years this art-loving king was a personal friend of Diego Velázquez.

The Castilian monarchs filled their palaces with their acquisitions: the Buen Retiro palace that stood where the Prado is today, the suburban El Pardo palace, and the Escorial Monastery. The overflow went to private palaces and churches in and around Madrid. Ferdinand VII, one of Spain's most disastrous kings, ordered the Prado built as a national picture gallery. Thanks to his art-loving predecessors, it opened in 1819 with one of the world's most dazzling collections. The works of Francisco Goya, who was painting at the time the Prado was inaugurated, quickly found their way into the new museum, as did the works of his contemporaries. Among the most notable Goyas at the Prado are the drawings, some sarcastic, some amusing and fanciful, and some heart-rending.

In the mid-nineteenth century Queen Isabella II had many paint-

The Prado—one of the great museums of the world

ings from the Escorial moved to the Prado. She also had the National Museum of Painting and Sculpture incorporated into the Prado. It had housed art from monasteries that had been closed by the anticlericalism of the time.

The Prado's collection is literally priceless today. A sample of its hypothetical value was provided in 1968 when the museum insured for $10 million a shipment of nine of its paintings, including several El Grecos, on loan to the HemisFair exhibit in San Antonio, Texas. It is a safe guess that the Prado is a greater treasure than Spain's gold and foreign-currency reserves, which were over the $1 billion level in 1971.

On the other hand, display techniques lag lamentably in Spain, suggesting a certain national indifference to art riches. Visitors to the Prado often find the lighting unsatisfactory and occasionally must strain their eyes to make out a picture half lost in shadow or hung well above their heads. In Toledo the situation is even worse. The works by Rubens and Velázquez in the sacristy of the Toledo Cathedral are cracking because of the lack of temperature control, and the lighting is so bad that it is quite impossible to see some of

61

the pictures hung in the side rooms. In El Greco's house several of his works sit on easels, making irresistible targets for the thousands of tourists who pass through the tiny rooms each year. Only the ghost of El Greco knows how many sweaty fingerprints these pictures have suffered.

Art is not Madrid's only treasure. The National Library contains 100,000 manuscripts, and although cataloguing began in the middle of the nineteenth century, it has not yet been completed. Indeed, as recently as 1967 it suddenly developed that the collection contained two hitherto unknown volumes of Leonardo da Vinci's sketches and drawings, annotated in his mirror writing. They had been accidentally discovered there two years earlier by an American researcher who was looking for medieval ballads. It is presumed that they were brought to Spain by Pompeo Leoni, an Italian sculptor in the service of Philip II. Leoni appears to have acted for Philip as both a court sculptor and an art procurer, a forerunner of England's Lord Duveen. Most probably, the notebooks were stored at the Escorial and transferred 250 years later to the National Library when it was inaugurated by Isabella II. As an internationally famous art scholar remarked recently, Spain is so rich in artistic treasures that "she does not even begin to know what she has."

Even Madrid's Rastro still remains a source of surprises, as it was in the days of Gómez de la Serna. Along the crowded and hilly Ribera de Curtidores, the street of the tanners, which is the market's central thoroughfare, and along the Plaza del Rastro and the Plaza de Vara del Rey and the ten other streets constituting the Rastro, almost anything can be found in the stores and on the outdoor stands. The chief change from Gómez de la Serna's era is that now the market also offers old automobile engines, complete or in pieces, tires, transistor radios (smuggled, stolen, or purchased), and other modern odds and ends. But basically, it still is a vast repository of furniture, bad and occasionally great paintings, medals from forgotten wars, crosses and Christs, mirrors that have seen one knows not what faces, musical instruments, bidets, tubs, clocks that may not work, "glasses for mysterious strabismus," weapons that "may once have killed or not," rugs, Moorish braziers, candelabra, hats and cloaks, books describing "ancient deflorations," canary birds, and almost any item that may or may not be needed by someone.

In human terms, as in Gómez de la Serna's day, the Rastro remains the province of "supreme beggars," of the "hostile, cruel faces of the women" who buy and sell, and of peddlers who are darker and "more Moorish-looking" than the average Madrileño. It is an immutable Madrid institution that links the modern capital with its past.

But, then, Spain can never really break with her past.

In the old quarter of Madrid

The town of Cuenca, in the province of Old Castile

4 The Kingdoms of Spain

Despite Spaniards' new mobility, Spain remains in many ways a conglomeration of former kingdoms that have retained regional identities far more pronounced than, say, those distinguishing the North and the South in the United States or Calabria and Tuscany in Italy. It is a tribute to the indestructible influence of Spanish geography and the unconquerable individuality of Iberian man that the thirty-three million Spaniards speak four main languages—Castilian, Catalan, Basque, and Gallegan (Galician). Each has a literature of its own, while Catalan and Basque have important subdivisions.

Administratively, Spain consists of fifty provinces, but to speak of these provinces individually does not convey the regional nature of the country. It is more to the point to divide the country into nine distinctive regions—Castile, Aragon, Catalonia, Valencia, Andalusia, La Mancha, the Basque country, Galicia, and Estremadura. These regions include the Balearic Islands in the Mediterranean but exclude the Canary Islands in the Atlantic, the Spanish Sahara, Equatorial Guinea (which became independent in 1968), and the Moroccan enclaves of Ceuta, and Melilla. Ifni, another Spanish enclave, was returned to Morocco. Administratively, however, Spanish holdings in Africa are also considered a part of mainland Spain.

The tableland of Castile is politically the most important region of Spain. It is made up of Old Castile and New Castile, which lie respectively north and south of Madrid. The two Castiles are separated by the Guadarramas than run northeast to southwest and by their continuation to the west, the Sierra de Gredos. Travel between the two Castiles is principally over the high Navacerrada Pass in the Guadarramas along the road linking Madrid and Segovia or through the new tunnel under the mountains along the Madrid-Ávila highway.

Old Castile is more forbidding, ascetic, and traditional than New Castile. It is, in fact, the cradle of the harshness of character, courage, and determination that underlie the Castilian rule of Spain. The kings of Castile held court at Valladolid until Philip II established the capital of the newly unified nation at Madrid. The first important university on the Iberian Peninsula

The landscape of Old Castile is well worn by time and weather.

was established at Salamanca about 1220 by Alfonso IX of the Kingdom of León. Ávila became the spiritual and mystical center, just as Valladolid and Madrid were the political centers and Salamanca, León, and Burgos the intellectual and cultural centers of a region that was shifting in the mid-fifteenth century from feudal to urban rule. The Castilian tongue, now known as classical Spanish, and its Leonese variant were developed before the end of the eleventh century and a hundred years later became the written and literary languages. Leonese has subsequently vanished, thus sparing modern Spain yet another dialect. Galician, which emerged in the eleventh century as a Castilian variant, blended later with Portuguese influences to become one of the present living languages.

The Duero River basin north of Madrid, deep in Old Castile, has more castles than any other part of Spain. They served first as bases from which to repel the Moorish invaders who reached deep into Castile and the Basque country on their way to France. Later, the Castilian and Leonese kings and princes fought one another interminably from these castles before the advent of the Catholic Kings. Today, most of the castles are abandoned and roofless shells, a favorite hunting ground for the members of Spain's Society of Friends of Castles (Sociedad de Amigos de Castillos), an organization of castle buffs.

Old Castile has never allowed itself to remain a frozen monument to its own past. When Renaissance influences began to show

New Castile, south of Madrid, is a gentler region than Old Castile.

themselves in Catalonia and Aragon, Old Castile was quick to respond. In the early fifteenth century decorative Italian and plateresque designs influenced such famous structures as the façade of the University of Salamanca, Salamanca Cathedral, and Valladolid's Colégio de Santa Cruz.

Alexandre Cirici-Pellicer, the Barcelona art historian, has called New Castile "the heir to Old Castile." It is the softer, more pleasure-seeking part of the tableland, irrigated and beautified by the Tagus River. In it are situated Madrid and the sumptuous

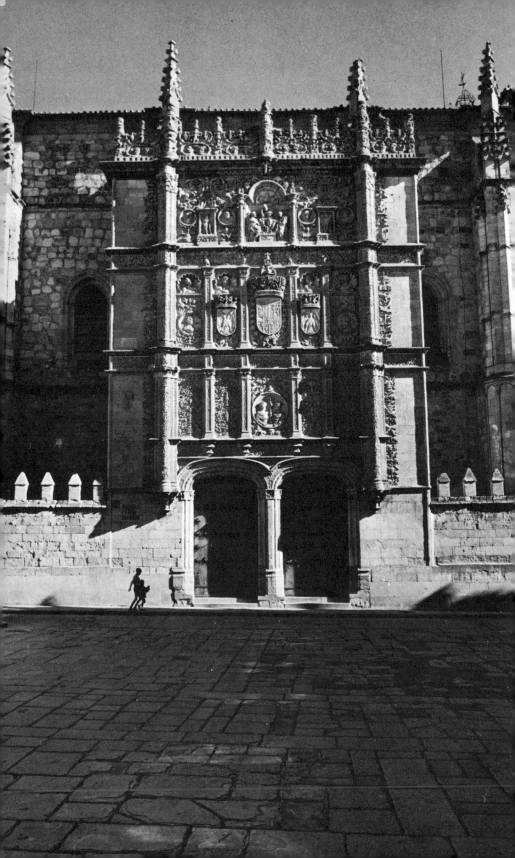

eighteenth-century summer palace at Aranjuez built in the style of Versailles for Philip V and Charles III by Etienne Marchand. Philip V's love of France made itself felt across the Guadarramas in Old Castile, too, when he almost simultaneously commissioned Theodore Ardemans to design La Granja palace near Segovia, another Versailles-type summer retreat. However, the superficial gaiety of Madrid and the relaxed elegance of Aranjuez do not compensate for the bleakness of Philip II's Escorial Monastery, nor for the nearby overwhelming memorial to the dead of the Spanish Civil War known as the Valley of the Fallen.

As heir to Old Castile, New Castile took what the older region had to offer and usually improved on it. By the end of the sixteenth century the university at Alcalá de Henares rivaled the older University of Salamanca as a center of learning, for Cardinal Jiménez de Cisneros had assembled in Alcalá the greatest humanists of the day. Architecturally, New Castile took up Renaissance and plateresque design with enthusiasm. The outstanding examples are Alcalá and Toledo.

The walled city of Toledo has imposed itself over the centuries as one of Spain's greatest historic and artistic monuments. It is a city that has known three faiths: Roman Catholic, Moslem, and Jewish. Its great Gothic cathedral stands on the site of a sixth-century Christian church. When the Moors took Toledo in the eighth century, a mosque was erected in its place. After the Christians reconquered the city, the construction on the present cathedral began in 1227. But the memory of the Moors and their easy coexistence with the Catholics is preserved by the custom of saying daily mass in the exotic Mozarabic rite of the Moslems who once embraced Christianity. The cathedral itself is an immense vaulted sanctuary rich in liturgical and artistic treasures. A side chapel contains the tall monstrance made of the first gold brought to the Catholic Kings by the fifteenth-century conquerors of the Americas. On the feast of Corpus Christi in the spring the monstrance is carried through Toledo's narrow streets, which are shaded for the occasion by canopies stretched from rooftop to rooftop. The sacristy of the cathedral contains El Greco's twelve apostles and his *Expolio* painting of Christ carrying the cross.

The Jewish faith is represented by the synagogues of Santa María la Blanca and El Tránsito, both of them now museums. El

The early-sixteenth-century façade of the Salamanca University library is in the plateresque style.

Toledo's magnificent cathedral was begun in the thirteenth century.

Tránsito synagogue stands near El Greco's house, which, it is said, was built by the Jewish banker Samuel Levi, who served the crown of Castile before the Spanish Diaspora. El Greco lived in Toledo for thirty years, and it was there that he discovered the extraordinary tones of the Spanish sky: the metallic blues, the dreamy greens, the soft pinks, and above all, the incredibly translucent and harsh quality of the light. I became aware of that sky and light one late afternoon at the Toledo bull ring when dark storm clouds suddenly rolled toward the setting sun and everything was bathed for an instant in a symphony of colors. Total silence enveloped the crowd, and the moment of truth in the arena below was abruptly forgotten.

The thirteenth-century Puente de Alcántara now takes only pedestrians across the Tagus and into Toledo.

Today's Castilian is the product of centuries of intermixing. If he can be distinguished from other Spaniards, it is mainly by his pronunciation, notably the lisped letter *c*. In Madrid first-generation migrants from the south and west tend to remain together for social, cultural, and economic reasons, and the working-class suburbs have their neighborhood communities of Andalusians, Murcians, and Estremeños. The children of the migrants, however, are quickly absorbed into the new environment, as is usually the case everywhere. The parents, if they can afford it, still try to visit the pueblo they came from at least once a year. Their grown children will rarely bother. Less and less can one make the anthropological distinction between the longheaded Castilians of Iberian stock and the roundheaded Spaniards of Celtic and North African descent.

In the back country of Castile, away from the mainstream of migrations, the race is probably purer. So are both the quiet pride and the grave courtesy, which often come more spontaneously from the villagers than from the grandees of Spain. There are isolated villages on both sides of the Guadarramas in which the human stock probably has not changed greatly since the days of the Catholic Kings. Today's shepherd is most likely to be the linear descendant of the shepherd of four centuries ago. As a general rule, the Castilian hinterland sends out people and does not receive much new blood.

Aragon, the second of the nine regions into which we have divided Spain, is Castile's natural bridge to the Mediterranean and to wealthy and crucial Catalonia.

When Ferdinand of Aragon married Isabella of Castile in 1469, he contributed a whole Mediterranean empire in addition to the small Kingdom of Aragon along the Ebro River valley. Since 1164 the larger and richer Catalonia had been incorporated into the House of Aragon. Successive rulers had added the Balearic Islands (Majorca and Ibiza), Sicily and Sardinia, and the duchies of Naples and Milan, thus giving Aragon more than half of the Italian mainland, as well as the Rousillon region of France. The Aragonese absorbed the proud Catalans not through conquest but by political attraction. The seafaring Catalonian members of the Aragonese confederacy in effect made a gift of the Mediterranean

Ferdinand and Isabella are joined forever in the round central medallion that adorns the façade of the Salamanca University library.

to the House of Aragon. A sound historical theory is that the Ebro Valley Aragonese exercised the same attraction on the coastal Catalonians that the haughty Castilians later exercised on the Aragonese. Inasmuch as Castile had similarly attracted the northwestern Kingdom of León to its fold, the historical corollary favored in Madrid is that Castile was an almost mystical pole of attraction for all the people of Spain. As for Aragon's empire building and its pull on the Catalonians, Salvador de Madariaga attempts to shed light on it through his comments on the Aragonese man: "Spontaneous, frank, he is apt to form extreme opinions; he is uncompromising, stubborn, richer in intuition than in conscious intellect, independent, proud and individualistic. Goya was an Aragonese, and his genius conveys the genius of Aragon better than any work of literature." But Spanish regionalisms apart, this description could, of course, fit almost any Spaniard in the past half-millennium.

The story of how Catalonia joined Aragon, and how they both united with Castile, serves among other things to emphasize the complexities of Spanish history. For example, the archives of the Crown of Aragon are housed today not in an Aragonese city but in Barcelona. The title of the Bourbon dynasty's pretender to the Spanish throne is the Count of Barcelona. This is the title used by Don Juan de Borbón y Battenberg, who lives in exile in Estoril, Portugal.

In 1969 Generalissimo Franco selected his son Prince Juan Carlos to become the king of Spain after the Caudillo retires or dies. As heir apparent to the throne Prince Juan Carlos carries the traditional title of Prince of Asturias.

The visitor will discover that there have been Alfonsos of Aragon, of Catalonia, of Castile and León, of León and Castile, and of Spain. The last two were the Bourbons Alfonso XII and Alfonso XIII. Alfonso XIII, Spain's last king, was Don Juan's father. There have been Ferdinands of Aragon, of Castile, of León, of Castile and León, and of Spain. There have been Henrys of Castile and Henrys of Castile and León, including Henry the Impotent. There have been Pedros of Aragon and Pedros of Castile and León, among them Pedro the Cruel. There have been Charleses of Spain and Pretender Charleses, who began the still bitter Carlist schisms. James I of Aragon, the Conqueror, was also the king of Valencia, but that is another story.

In any event, Aragon is today a prosperous if relatively small inverted triangle of land, its point touching Valencia, its base along the Pyrenees, and its flanks bounded on the east by Catalonia and on the west by Castile. In the days when the Kingdom of Aragon included Catalonia, the Aragonese spoke both Castilian Spanish and Catalan. Today they confine themselves to Castilian alone.

It is the Ebro, the Blue Ebro of uncounted Spanish songs and poems, that is the central fact of life in Aragon. Born in the Basque mountains, it broadens when it enters the northeastern plain, and its waters irrigate the whole region. It accounts for Aragon's agricultural, and therefore economic, importance in a nation chronically short of food. The Ebro empties into the Mediterranean at the Catalonian town of Tortosa. One of the bloodiest battles of the Civil War was fought at the river near Tortosa—so bloody that the waters are said to have actually run crimson. This stretch of the river is known as the Red Ebro. A heroic monument to the Nationalist victors stands today at Tortosa.

Saragossa is a pleasant Aragonese city with medieval monuments and a renowned sixteenth-century cathedral known as La Seo. It was as commandant of Spain's military academy in Saragossa that General Franco made his name in the highest echelons of the Spanish army shortly before the Civil War. In 1953 the United States built a major air force base on the outskirts of Saragossa.

Catalonia, the third of the great Spanish regions in this *tour d'horizon,* is both a gift from God and a perpetual problem for Spain. There was a "Catalonian Question" in the eleventh and twelfth centuries and throughout the Middle Ages, in the Renaissance, and before and during the Civil War (when Franco's Moorish troops erupted into Barcelona and ordered the inhabi-

A well-stocked kiosk along the Ramblas in Barcelona

The upholstery for a Seat car is sewn in a Barcelona plant.

tants to "speak Christian now" instead of Catalan); and there is a Catalonian Question today, thirty-odd years after Franco reunited Spain with his "crusade."

In its simplest terms today's Catalonian Question is the desire of some six million Spaniards inhabiting the vast northeastern section of the country to preserve their cultural identity as Catalans and to win as much home rule as they can. Catalonia enjoyed an autonomous government from 1931 until the Civil War, and there are Catalonian sentimentalists who still dream of a "free" Catalonia stretching from the Pyrenees to the Balearic Islands and including the French Catalonian lands of the Rousillon. But the majority are too pragmatic to take this seriously. As Spain's principal industrial region, Catalonia probably could not survive the loss of its natural markets if customs barriers were suddenly erected between it and the rest of Spain. Catalonia's powerful textile industry has survived because of the protection afforded it by the Spanish tariff system, and it could not in the foreseeable future compete with European exports. Most of the hundreds of thousands of the Seats that have put Spain on wheels are built around Barcelona. So are motorcycles, typewriters, appliances, and hundreds of other manufactures for the hungry Spanish market. Catalonian industrialists may pay lip service to the idea of a separate Catalonia, as some do, but the chances are that they fear it even more than the possibility of Spain becoming a full-fledged member of the European Common Market (to which Spain loses about a billion dollars annually in trade).

The Catalonian Question today boils down to attitudes. Catalans are contemptuous of Castilians and, for that matter, of everybody else in Spain. A Catalan talking about Catalonia sounds like a Texan talking about Texas, except more so. His self-justification is one thousand years of Catalonian history, and Catalonia's current wealth, which, in his judgment, pays the freight for the rest of the country.

Objectively, there is a lot to be said for Catalonia's pride. The Province of Barcelona, one of the five Catalonian provinces, leads the nation in value of total production. The five provinces together represent only 17 per cent of Spain's population but account for nearly 25 per cent of Spain's production. Barcelona's bankers and industrialists argue that the central government takes considerably more out of Catalonia in taxes and invisibles than it invests in the region. The most extreme Catalans claim that this is a form of vengeance because Catalonia was on the Republican side in the Civil War. However, Catalonia is vastly important to the Spanish economy, and Franco, who has appointed a Catalan head of the national Economic Development Plan, knows it. The province's contribution to the national exchequer includes hundreds of millions of dollars from tourists who year-round invade the Balearics and in the summer swarm over the Costa Brava.

The second attitude—perhaps more difficult to argue these days —is that Catalonia, and especially Barcelona, are more European-oriented and more cultured than "arrogant" Castile, isolated atop its central plateau. This may have been true in circa 235 B.C., when Hamilcar Barca, a great Carthaginian general, is said to have founded Barcelona. Castile was nonexistent in terms of civilization at that point in history. But in the intervening centuries, and par-

Some of the Roman remains in Barcelona

ticularly in the past fifty years or so, it has become a matter of personal taste whether Barcelona or Madrid is more civilized, cultured, or European. Barcelona does have the Teatro del Liceo, one of the three or four most outstanding opera houses in Europe, but the opera season is increasingly becoming a social rather than a purely artistic event. Barcelona women dress better for openings than Madrid women do when attending the Teatro Real (Balenciaga, Pertegáz, and Rovira are, after all, Catalans), but it might be dangerous to draw too profound a conclusion from this fact. The Catalans may also have a point when they insist that the Castilians in Madrid are essentially lazy because they still observe the siesta, but one must not confuse the Madrileños with the hard-working backland Castilians. That Madrid is unquestionably more frivolous than Barcelona is illustrated by the dinner hours: in Madrid few people eat before ten or eleven o'clock in the evening; in Barcelona restaurant kitchens tend to close after eleven. But in the end, this whole rather artificial argument bogs down in contradictions. Is it more European, civilized, and cultured to be serious and hard-working or to be frivolous? As the age of leisure spreads over western Europe, the Catalans may find themselves on the losing side of this debate.

Culture is the third and most important attitude that makes up the modern Catalonian Question. The Catalans feel that their language and culture, being almost a thousand years old, have the right not only to survive but to flourish. While the province was autonomous in the early 1930's, Catalan was made the official language. But Franco, in his eagerness to do away with regionalisms after the Civil War, forbade the teaching of Catalan in the schools and the teaching of school in Catalan. This was rightly regarded by the Catalans as a slur on their culture, and inevitably, it contributed to a renaissance of that culture. Over the years, the Franco regime has greatly relaxed its opposition to the Catalan language. There are no obstacles to the public use of the language; about 750 books are published annually in Catalan; mass is said in Catalan; there is Catalan theatre; and the first movie in Catalan was recently produced. However, the regime's continued prohibition against the use of Catalan in schools has become a fighting issue.

Some recordings in Catalan are sold freely, but there is a ban on songs by Raimón, a young Barcelona protest singer (actually born in Valencia) who specializes in inspirational ballads about the greatness of Catalonia. When Raimón sings at recitals at Barcelona University or in Catalonian villages, the audiences give him standing ovations. Almost always he appears because a special police permit has been obtained by sponsoring Catalan Roman Catholic priests, who are the most Catalonian of all Catalans.

Spanish is the official language of the offices of the Civil Government of Barcelona Province, which represents the Franco regime, but Catalan is spoken freely at the Barcelona city hall. Whereas a generation ago Catalan was chiefly the language of the working classes, especially in the countryside (where even today whole villages cannot understand Castilian Spanish), now it is fashionable for the rich and influential to speak Catalan, too. Its use, in fact, has become the middle-class form of protest against the Franco regime. Since the late fifties, when the university students, then the progressive clergy, and finally the workers began to clash with the regime over broad issues of civil liberties, their sense of being Catalan has developed into a common denominator and a stimulus for further struggle.

This elegant Gothic court is on the second floor of the Diputación, a fifteenth-century building still used by the Barcelona city government.

The diversity of Catalonia mirrors that of Spain itself. Catalans live from the high Pyrenees (the Andorrans are mountain Catalans) to the shores of the Mediterranean and in the Balearic Islands. Their language includes a number of dialects: the Ampurdán, from the Ampurdán area north of Barcelona (where the Greeks established themselves in the seventh century B.C.), which is said to be the purest; the Majorcan dialect, related to the Ampurdán; and the most common dialect, incorporating Castilianisms, which is heard in the streets of Barcelona and in its satellite towns of Sabadell, Hospitalet, and Tarrasa. There are subdialects in the Pyrenees and elsewhere in the countryside. Catalan, a neo-Latin language,

belongs to the Hispanic group, though it has been markedly influenced by the dialects of Provence and Roussillon in France and by the Portuguese.

Ramón Lull, a thirteenth-century Majorcan mystic, was a distinguished early writer in Catalan. In 1478 a Catalan Bible appeared. Then, after a long pause in the development of Catalan culture, poets began to write in Catalan again in the nineteenth century. During the past thirty or so years Catalonia has produced an impressive group of writers, ranging from the fine poet Salvador Espriú to Josep Plá, a grizzled and humorous man of letters who lives in an ancient Ampurdán farmhouse not far from Gerona.

The tragedy of Plá and his fellow Catalan writers is that their works are almost never translated from the Catalan into other languages, either because there are no competent translators or because foreign publishers are unaware of the value of Catalan writing. On the other hand, the literature of the world is available in Catalan. Gabriel Ferreter, a Catalan poet I know, learned Polish for the sole purpose of translating into Catalan some modern Polish poetry that had impressed him in a French translation but that he thought should be translated from the original language to do justice to his exigent readers.

Catalonia has produced in our time the painters Joan Miró, Antonio Tápies, and Salvador Dali and the cello virtuoso Pablo Casals. Miró and Tápies are outspokenly anti-Franco, but they live in Catalonia or visit it frequently. Miró, who has a farm near Gerona and a house in Majorca, contributed beautiful political posters for a 1966 celebration of the birthday of the late Antonio Machado, the great turn-of-the-century liberal poet. The celebration had been organized by antiregime intellectuals and artists and was broken up by the Guardia Civil. Tápies was arrested at least twice in the late 1960's for demonstrating against the regime.

Flower stalls abound along the broad Ramblas in Barcelona.

The Milá apartment house in Barcelona was designed by the Catalan architect Antonio Gaudí in the first decade of this century.

But Miró and Tápies are so important internationally that the Madrid regime has refrained from persecuting them. Dali, who does not get involved in politics, has a summerhouse on the Costa Brava. The nonagenarian Casals, of course, refuses to return to Franco's Spain.

The city of Barcelona is a superb tribute to the many aspects of Catalonian genius and history. As Spain's second largest metropolis and principal port, Barcelona is also an active center of industry and trade. It is a sprawling city that somehow has retained its charm and special identity. Strolling down the Ramblas—the broad avenues lined with flower stands that converge on the Mediterranean waterfront—one is reminded more of France or Italy than of the upland Spain represented by Madrid. This sensation bears out to some extent the Catalonians' claim that "we are Europe."

The city's great Gothic cathedral is one of the Iberian Peninsula's greatest religious edifices. It faces onto the Plaza Colón (Columbus). The cult of the explorer is stronger here than anywhere in Spain, for Columbus traveled overland from Seville to Catalonia to report to Queen Isabella on his first voyage to the New World. The cathedral is built on what was a Roman camp when the city was called Julia Faventia Augusta Pia Barcino. The church was severely damaged by both sides during the Civil War, and then restored after the conflict. Generalissimo Franco makes a point of praying there during his periodic visits to Barcelona. The cathedral's broad steps are used frequently for dancing the *sardana,* a grave Catalonian folk dance set to music played on brass instruments.

The Plaza Colón divides the bustling modern city from the ancient Gothic barrio, or borough. The cathedral and the adjacent archbishop's palace are the guardians of that quiet and still medieval quarter. Under the cathedral the ruins of the Roman camp are slowly being excavated. In Barcelona's other churches and in the museums experts study the polychromatic sculpture and retablo altar art, which was born in Catalonia and spread from there to most of Spain. The city's other cathedral, the immense, gaudy church of the Holy Family designed by Catalonia's favorite architect, Antonio Gaudí, is almost impossible to describe. Still unfinished more than forty years after Gaudí's death, it is a startling blend of Gothic, baroque, and the Catalan version of Art Nouveau. Its tall bell tower looms over the city. Gaudí also designed the amazing Parque Güell, a huge hillside park on the outskirts of the city filled with strange statuary and waterfalls, and many Barcelona buildings with intricate façades. He was killed in 1926 by a streetcar in front of his church as he was soliciting contributions for continuing the construction.

The Monastery of the Virgin of Montserrat is a medieval apparition atop a granite mountain some thirty miles from Barcelona. It was burned by Napoleon's troops in the early 1800's, and many of its Benedictine monks were killed or imprisoned by Loyalist mobs at the outset of the Civil War in 1936. Today the monastery provides much of the leadership for anti-Franco sentiment among the progressive clergy in Catalonia and elsewhere in Spain. It is a citadel of Catalan culture and the home of one of the world's great choirs. A Benedictine monk at Montserrat composed an oratorio in memory of John F. Kennedy shortly after his assassination.

Modern Barcelona knows how to live well. Its hotels include the old-fashioned but luxurious Ritz with huge marble bathrooms,

A narrow street in Barcelona's old quarter, or *barrio gótico*

and the comfortable and traditional Colón that faces the old cathedral. The Teatro del Liceo ranks among Europe's greatest opera houses. Spain's world-famous *haute couture* is centered in Barcelona with the salons of Balenciaga, Pertegáz, and Rovira. The gastronomic specialty of Barcelona is seafood, and the city's restaurants are renowned for their *zarzuelas,* which are fish-and-lobster casseroles. Casa Costa on the waterfront rivals the best Basque and Galician establishments when it comes to seafood. Los Caracoles (The Snails) is a leading Barcelona restaurant and specializes, of course, in snails, which are cooked with even more garlic than those in France. The Ecuestre is a luxurious restaurant with a wide selection of excellent European wines.

A ferry sails every evening from Barcelona to Palma in Majorca, which is Catalonia's island outpost. Nowadays, Majorca is chiefly a tourist paradise—it receives more than one million visitors annually and the city of Palma has over six hundred hotels—and a place of retirement for mainland Spaniards, Englishmen (who first had the idea), and Americans.

Inevitably, Majorca is also a repository of history. Palma's ancient castles and escarpments are a reminder of wars fought against the Phoenicians, Greeks, Romans, Moors, Turks, and Barbary Coast pirates. In 1838–39 Frédéric Chopin and his mistress, the French writer Aurore Dupin, better known as George Sand, spent the winter at the old cloister of the former Carthusian monastery (*cartuja*) at Valldemosa. Chopin sought the warmth of Majorca so that he might better resist the tuberculosis that was slowly destroying him. On the island he composed most of his piano preludes, the two great polonaises, two nocturnes, a mazurka, a ballade, and a sonata.

I visited Valldemosa during Easter, 1967. Though it has now been turned into a museum in Chopin's memory, the monastery, the cloister, and Chopin's austere cell are today as they were in his time. Rising high over the surrounding countryside, the monastery commands a superb view of what was a mass of pink-and-white flowering almond trees when I was there.

Unfortunately, Chopin and George Sand spent a chilly and humid winter on Majorca. Mme Sand wrote that "the cloisters of the *Cartuja* were full of ghosts and horrors for him." But, she went on, "it was whilst he was there that he wrote the loveliest of those

Modern Barcelona stretches out below Gaudí's
unfinished church of the Sagrada Familia,
one of whose astonishing ornaments is in the foreground.

Los Caracoles restaurant in Barcelona

brief works which he so modestly called Preludes, and they are true masterpieces. . . . Some of them bring to mind a vision of departed monks and their funeral dirges, which haunted him; others are sweet in their melancholy, conceived in hours of sunshine and good health, with the sound of childish laughter underneath his window, a distant strumming of guitars, and birds singing in the dripping foliage of the garden. Others again are of a sadness so bleak that it pierces one's heart, even as it charms the ear. And one of them, which came to him one desolate and rainy evening, produces a terrifying depression in the hearer's heart. . . ."

Virtually every great musician in the past hundred years has made the pilgrimage to Valldemosa, as the photographs on the walls of the *cartuja* cell and the signatures in the guest book testify. But as Chopin struggled with his "ghosts" and his "pitiful piano" (which is still in the cell), the people of Valldemosa were somewhat skeptical. According to a contemporary account, the Valldemosa parish priest said of George Sand: "This French lady must indeed be a strange person! Just think of it: she never speaks to a living soul, never leaves the *Cartuja,* and never shows her face in church, not even on Sundays, and goodness only knows how many mortal sins she is amassing! Furthermore I have it from the apothecary, who also lives in the *Cartuja,* that *la señora* makes cigarettes like nothing on earth, drinks coffee at all hours, sleeps by day, and does nothing but smoke and write at night."

While on the island I drove from Palma to Formentor on the rugged north coast along what is unquestionably one of the world's most perilous mountain roads. It clings to the hillside over a drop of hundreds of feet to the waves breaking against the rocks below. I saw the endless olive groves, visited the prehistoric caves on the east coast, toured the miniature Spanish town in Palma, with replicas of Toledo, Granada, and Seville, and watched deft women make the famous Majorca synthetic pearls. I had a brandy at Andraitx, a fishing village and one of the best yachting harbors in the Mediterranean. My only regret was to have missed Robert Graves, the great English poet, who was away from his Majorca home that week.

Valencia, the route of conquerors, the fief of El Cid, and the birthplace of two popes, is the fourth region in this survey of Spain, and like the others, its geography has determined its history. Valencia extends from the mouth of the Ebro at Tortosa to Cape Gata, and thus it links the dour northeast to Murcia, Alicante, and sunny Andalusia. It is a coastal region where pungent oranges are grown in the eternal spring that prevails. In Valencia the Spanish character changes to a softer, meridional tone.

The Greeks colonized Valencia in the seventh century B.C. while Greek emporiums were being established in Catalonia. In 219–218 B.C., just north of the present city of Valencia, Hannibal besieged and took Saguntum. (Now known as Sagunto, it is the site of both a modern steel mill and the ruins of a Greek fortress.) It was the first of the great sieges in Spanish history. The Iberians heroically resisted a Roman siege a century later at Numantia; Christians besieged Moors and Moors Christians; Catholic Kings besieged Granada to end the Moorish conquest; Napoleon's armies besieged Saragossa in the nineteenth century; and during the Civil War the Republicans besieged the Toledo Alcázar and the Nationalists besieged Madrid.

The oranges for which Valencia is famous

The Arab influence was strong in Valencia and is today evident in the art of irrigation and in the many lush orange groves. However, Arab rule there lasted only from the eighth to the eleventh century, compared with nearly eight centuries in some parts of Andalusia. Alfonso VI of León and Castile captured Valencia from the first Moorish conquerors in 1086, then lost it to the Almoravide invaders from North Africa. But in 1094 Rodrigo (or Ruy) Díaz de Bivar—the legendary El Cid—appeared from the north. Rather more of a sword for hire than the romantic Christian warrior of the legends, he set out to capture Valencia for the Moslem king of Saragossa. Instead, he kept it for himself, was crowned its king, and in effect created the Kingdom of Valencia as a separate realm under Christian rule. When El Cid died in 1099, his wife ruled for a while in his stead.

In 1238 James I, the Conqueror, captured Valencia and incorporated it into the Aragonese state, giving it the cultural and linguistic characteristics that prevail there to this time. Catalonia was already a part of the House of Aragon, and Valenciano, the language of Valencia today, is a Catalan dialect. Valencianos have the Spanish passion for individualism, however, and many of them insist that their language is purer than Catalan.

In the late sixteenth and early seventeenth centuries Valencia gave the world two of the great masters of the so-called tenebrist style of mystical religious art that influenced painting in Spain and elsewhere for generations. The first was Francisco de Ribalta, who lived and worked in Valencia although he was born near Lérida in northwestern Catalonia. His disciple, the Valencia-born José de Ribera, later moved to Italy. Art historians believe that these two painters paved the way for Murillo and Zurbarán. In the field of modern painting Valencia is known for its young artists working in teams, such as the Crónica Group that was highly regarded by Spanish critics in the late 1960's.

Among Valencia's more controversial figures was Alfonso Borgia, born in Játiva, who became Pope Calixtus III in 1455. He is chiefly remembered for ill-conducted diplomacy and for his nephew and fellow Valenciano Rodrigo Borgia, who was known as Pope Alexander VI. Having already provided two Roman emperors—Trajan and Hadrian, both born in Itálica near Seville—Spain could thus boast of having exercised considerable reverse influence on Rome, so long its colonizer.

Like every important Spanish city (some of which are important for that reason only), Valencia has an imposing cathedral with a rococo façade. It was completed early in the eighteenth century from designs by the famous German architect Conrad Rudolf and two Valencians, Francisco Vergara the Elder and his son Ignacio. It is dedicated to the two Valencian popes and the two Valencian saints, Vincente Ferrer and Luís Beltrán.

On a more mundane level Valencia is the location of the year's first major Spanish bullfight. It is held early in March in Castellón de la Plana, north of the city, and when it is over the bullfighters fan out through Spain until the season ends late in October. In mid-March Valencia celebrates the *Fallas*, the feast of Saint Joseph, with the burning of huge papier-mâché figures. In August the city has its "Battle of Flowers." It opens with a parade of floats bearing mammoth floral arrangements and concludes with a joyful free-for-all in which flowers of all kinds serve as missiles.

One of Valencia's contributions to the pleasures of living is *paella,* a dish of seafood, chicken, and sausage stewed with rice in an enormous metal pan. It may be noted in passing that the Sinai restaurant in Madrid, the only Israeli restaurant in Spain, features kosher *paella* that contains no seafood.

Thtml coastal provinces of Alicante and Murcia are in the orange belt and belong to subtropical Spain. Altea, a rapidly growing town on the Alicante coast, has become in recent years a tourist-oriented artists' community. Previously, it was a sleepy little town crowned by Moorish houses and a medieval church atop a hill. Benidorm, immediately west of Altea, is one of the noisy resorts favored by the Spanish middle class, moderately well-to-do western Europeans, and bearded and barefoot visitors from everywhere. It has an English pub and warm ale.

Andalusia proper sprawls across the entire south of Spain. Its eight provinces stretch from Almería in the east to Cádiz in the west. It is bordered on the north by Murcia, La Mancha, and Estremadura. For almost eight centuries it was the stronghold of Moorish rule in Spain, and to this day it is reminiscent of Moorish Africa in landscape, architecture, culture, music, and the physical appearance of its six million inhabitants.

Andalusia's grandiose cities—Córdoba, Granada, Seville, and Cádiz—are rich in history, yet the region is poor in resources and impoverished in human terms. Its annual per capita income is only slightly more than half the Spanish national average, which in turn in Continental western Europe is higher only than that of Portugal and Greece. Since the mid-1960's the Costa del Sol has thrived thanks to tourism, but in the mountains and isolated villages not much has changed since the days of the Moors. In fact, many historians believe that Andalusia never had it so good as under *El Andalus*—the rule of the Moors. Today its people leave for the industrial labor markets of Madrid, Barcelona, Bilbao, and western Europe because the parched soil seamed by dry rivers does not produce adequate food or income and there are not enough jobs to go around. It is a land of abandoned villages—a southern version of the worst of Castile—and of vast estates owned by a select group

A Malagueño takes the air in his native city.

of the rich and the titled. Feudalism at its most pernicious survives in Andalusia as it does nowhere else in Europe. Authority for this statement comes not from radical agitators but from the Bishop of Cádiz, who year after year issues passionate pastoral letters on the subject.

The fascinating story of the Moorish sway over Andalusia has filled many volumes. But a few general points must be made to correct the false impressions that are commonplace not only among foreigners but also among Spaniards. First, the Moorish occupation was not precisely Moorish. It was an occupation by Arabs and Berbers. Moors (inhabitants of the area that today is Morocco) appeared in Spain quite some time after Tariq, a Berber, crossed the narrow straits from Africa in 711 to launch the conquest of the Iberian Peninsula. The first Moslems to land in Spain were Sunnites (or Sunnis) from Yemen and Shiites (or Shiahs) from Persia. These groups represented the two main branches of Mohammedanism, a religion that was less than a century old. Later there came to Spain

95

Moorish Arabs, Berbers, Almohades, and Almoravides, among other tribes and sects. Despite this fact, the Arab-Berber period in Spain is known in popular parlance as the Moorish period, presumably because the Christians of the day identified all Arabs and Berbers with the inhabitants of what is now Morocco, the nearest African land to the Peninsula. The flamenco laments have helped to perpetuate this historical inaccuracy, since the word *morería,* which roughly means "Moorish captivity," occurs in almost every song. One of Madrid's principal flamenco night spots, in fact, is called the Corral de la Morería.

A second point worth making is that Arab rule over Andalusia and the rest of Spain was never unified. From Tariq's landing to the fall of Granada in 1492, the Arabs fought among themselves as much as they did with the Christian princes. Their Spanish possessions were broken up into a multitude of separate states, kingdoms, principalities, and fiefs. As in the case of El Cid, the Moslem rulers often employed Christian warriors to fight their battles.

The third point to remember is that the Moslem occupation was not generally oppressive, although Arabs and Christians did occasionally indulge in mass slaughter. Particularly in Andalusia, there was a rather extraordinary degree of peaceful coexistence between Moslems and Christians. The Arabs allowed the Christians to practice their religion, and this produced Arab converts to Christianity. Christianity's exposure to Islam resulted in the emergence of the Mozarabic mass, softer, not to say merrier, than the contemporary Roman Catholic rite. Solo singing by men and women was allowed, and the services usually ended with the burning of incense. Mozarabic rites can still be seen almost daily in Toledo and in a number of Andalusian churches. The evening Mozarabic mass at the church in Mojácar, an Arab town atop a steep hill in the Province of Almería, is an outstanding example.

Integration of Arabs and Iberians was so complete that Andalusia was bilingual. The inhabitants spoke Arabic and Romance, a Spanish medieval idiom with its roots in Castile. As Salvador de Madariaga points out, the linguistic division was cultural rather than religious. In Andalusia Arabic was the language of the educated nobles and of the great scholars, scientists, and artists who were established at the Caliphate of Córdoba, which the Arabs made into one of the world's greatest centers of learning. Romance

The spectacular Moorish palace of
the Alhambra dominates Granada.

was spoken by the lower classes, both Iberian and Moslem. The Arabs are gone today, but the Spanish language remains deeply touched by their influence, especially in place names. As a rule, it can be assumed that the names of all cities, towns, villages, and rivers that start with *Al* are of Arabic origin, for example, Alicante, Algeciras, Albacete, Alhucemas. Among the many proper names influenced by Arabic are Alcudia and Almodóvar, both dukedoms. Because the Arabic word for water has the root *gua,* Spanish rivers are named Guadalquivir, Guadiana, or Guadiaro. The Guadarramas are mountains from which rivers run, Guadix is a town with water, and a well-irrigated province is Guadalajara. The great castles built by the Arabs in Seville, Toledo, and Segovia (to name just a few) are the alcazars.

Anthropologically and culturally, the Arab influence persists. The dark, roundheaded Andalusians are descended largely from the Arabs or Moors. Their language is softer and more musical than that of the upland Castilians. The Andalusians are even more courteous than other Spaniards, and this too may be a legacy of ceremonial politeness of the Arabs. When one leaves a restaurant or a filling station in Andalusia, the waiter or attendant invariably says, *"Vaya con Dios"* (Go with God), a farewell no longer heard elsewhere in Spain. Flamenco laments are only a step removed from the sad desert sounds of the Bedouins. The *cantaor*—the man who, so to speak, calls the tune—begins with a lament, usually about his beloved girl having fallen into the *morería,* and the fiery dance that ensues, including the incredibly precise *zapateado,* a sort of tap dance, is reminiscent of the Arab warriors' desert dances. An old *cantaor,* by the way, is usually better than a young one. It takes years to develop the vocal modulations peculiar to flamenco singing. With rare exceptions, such as Rosita Durán and Lucero de Tena in this generation, a middle-aged and even corpulent woman makes a better flamenco dancer than a girl, for it takes time to develop a style that obeys the most precise rules.

Gazpacho is the great culinary contribution of Andalusia. It is a cold soup (important in a region where summer temperatures can rise to 130°) made basically from tomatoes, cucumbers, and water-soaked bread. *Gazpacho* has become a national soup, but purists will argue that Estremadura *gazpacho* is too thin and Madrid *gazpacho* too thick.

Agriculture is the economic mainstay of Andalusia.

The great sights of Andalusia are the cities of Cádiz (founded by the Phoenicians under the name of Gades), Córdoba, Seville, and Granada, which are as impressive today as they were in their heyday. In the 1820's Washington Irving, the first American minister to Spain, rode from Seville to Granada on horseback and installed himself at the Alhambra to write. The road between Seville and Granada has probably not improved greatly since his day, and a motorist still encounters men on mules and donkeys. The vast Alhambra, in whose shadow gypsies still live, and the gardens of the Generalife are the focal points of Granada. Seville was headquarters for the conquest of the New World. Columbus sailed from Huelva, some fifty miles from Seville, and the Archives of the Indies, the greatest collection of manuscripts and books pertaining to the American conquest, are at Seville. At Córdoba, once the capital of the caliphate, the cathedral is built around a mosque, but the original Moorish colonnade is still intact inside the cathedral. Maimonides, the great Jewish philosopher, was born there, as was Manuel Benítez, whose bullfighting name is El Cordobés.

The Costa del Sol, the tourist playground of Andalusia, extends from the old city of Málaga to Gibraltar. The high points of the

Apartment houses have mushroomed in Torremolinos, on the Costa del Sol.

coast are Torremolinos, Fuengirola, Marbella, Estepona, and the new development of Sotogrande (with Continental Europe's best golf course, designed by Robert Trent Jones). Artur Rubinstein, the pianist, recently built two houses near Marbella to which he retreats during the summer to write his memoirs. Gerald Brenan, an English writer who has written better about Spain that most of his contemporaries, has lived in Andalusia for many years.

The inland city of Ronda is the home of great bullfighters. Indeed, the first man known to have fought a bull on foot with a muleta came from Ronda. He was Francisco Romero, an early eighteenth-century matador. Antonio Ordoñez, until his recent retirement the greatest classical bullfighter, was born in Ronda, as was his father, also a famous matador. The best bulls are raised around Seville and Jerez de la Frontera, the city of the world's best sherries.

Gibraltar has been a British crown colony since 1704, but while it is not a part of Spain, it is in many ways a part of Andalusia. The lingua franca among the very pro-British Gibraltarians is Andalusian Spanish, but these same people, who have lived under Greek, Phoenician, Carthaginian, Roman, and Arab, as well as British, rule, have thus far resisted Spain's efforts to regain sovereignty over the Rock.

Ronda is spectacularly situated in an amphitheatre of mountains.

The windmills of La Mancha

L a Mancha (meaning "the spot") is a flat region south of New Castile that is more or less in the center of Spain. Scenically, it is one of the country's least inspiring areas. But such was the genius of Miguel de Cervantes Saavedra that for the past 350 years, La Mancha has had a place on the map of Spain and in the consciousness of men all over the world. For it was over this monotonous landscape that Cervantes's splendid creation Don Quixote de la Mancha roamed; "Our Lord Don Quixote, the Knight of Madness, the Knight of the Faith and the Knight of the Sad Countenance," as the great Spanish philosopher Miguel de Unamuno has called him. Cervantes was born in Alcalá at the time Cardinal Jiménez de Cisneros was opening the university there. He created Don Quixote at the end of the sixteenth century and published the first book of his adventures in 1605. The greatest Spanish prose writer of the Golden Age, Cervantes molded his marvelously mad Don Quixote into a personality so real that one is convinced he *must* have lived, must really have loved Dulcinea del Toboso, must really have carried on dialogues with his squire Sancho Panza, and must really, lance in hand, have ridden his tired nag Rocinante to do battle with the windmills of La Mancha. Not only has *Don Quixote* been a steady best-seller in Spain since 1605, but to an important degree the knight has become an economic mainstay of La Mancha.

La Mancha nowadays is largely a wheat- and olive-growing area that remains lush except during times of drought. Quail and hare and rabbits are still hunted as they were in Don Quixote's time. The region produces the bland *manchego* cheese from goat's milk (cheese, incidentally, is a major gastronomic fiasco in Spain), and wines of no particular distinction when compared with the great Rioja wines of the north. Albacete and Ciudad Real, the capitals of the two rather poor provinces of the same names that comprise La Mancha, offer little to interest the traveler. But then, La Mancha has Don Quixote.

Over the years, many hundreds of thousands of visitors have come to La Mancha to inspect the windmills, stay at innumerable inns and eat at innumerable restaurants named after Don Quixote, and buy millions of carvings and clay figurines representing the tall thin knight and the paunchy Sancho Panza. So real has the myth of Don Quixote become that for years La Mancha towns and villages have been arguing, in all seriousness, over which one of them was his home. Cervantes made a point of giving his readers no clues. The novel tauntingly begins with the words: "Somewhere in La Mancha, I do not know where. . . ."

But Don Quixote was—and is—vastly more than an astonishing literary success and a source of revenue for the present-day Manchegos. The mad knight is both every one of us and the quintessential Spaniard—courageous, romantic, mystical. As Unamuno wrote, "his madness saves our sanity." Although Cervantes was satirizing the chivalric novels popular in the sixteenth century, he did realistically portray the Spanish penchant for fantasy and vagabondage. In his famous essays on "Our Lord Don Quixote," Unamuno finds mystic depths in the foolish knight and compares him with Saint Ignatius of Loyola, the founder of the Jesuit order.

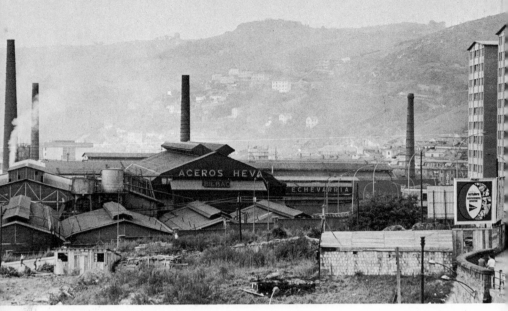

A steel mill in Bilbao, at the heart of the Basque country

The Basque country, like Catalonia, is both a boon and bane to the present government of Spain. Most of the country's banking power, most of her steel and heavy industry, most of her shipbuilding, and much of her agriculture are located in the Basque country. At the same time, the fiercely independent Basques are considerably more separatist than the Catalans.

The Basque language bears no relation to the Hispanic tongues, and it forms a special barrier between the Vascongadas (as the Basque country is called in Spanish) and the rest of Spain. The origin of the Basques and the etymological roots of their language are still unknown. According to one theory, the Basques came to their present home from Asia thousands of years ago. Salvador de Madariaga sees some validity in the belief that Basque was spoken by the Iberian populations of Spain before the Roman conquest. Curiously, Madariaga notes, there is some similarity between Basque and Hebrew pronouns and between Basque and Aztec verbs. There is no known explanation for this. In any event, Basque is mainly a spoken language and has produced no literature worth mentioning.

The Basques occupy the two northern coastal provinces of Vizcaya and Guipúzcoa and the inland Province of Álava just to the south. Culturally, the adjacent mountain Province of Navarra is part of the Basque country. The Navarrese, who established their own kingdom early in the tenth century, speak a dialect of the Basque language. As in Catalonia, Basque is spoken chiefly in the back country villages, where Spanish is often barely understood. In the big industrial cities—Bilbao, San Sebastián, Eibar, or Vitoria —Castilian predominates, in part because of massive migrations in recent decades from the south and west. However, within the past ten years the younger intellectuals and students have increasingly been learning Basque to show their nationalist spirit. As in Catalonia, harsh and inflexible treatment by the Madrid regime has served only to strengthen Basque nationalist sentiments.

In their efforts to assert their identity, the Basques have gone much further than the Catalans. Their terrorist underground organization has successfully defied Franco for years. In 1970 it helped to produce a major political crisis in the country. An illegal but very active Basque Nationalist party is linked to a Basque government-in-exile, which has bases in Paris and just over the French-Spanish border between Bayonne and Biarritz. The terrorists are independent of the exiled government, which is the successor to the autonomous Basque government of the Second Republic and the Civil War, when both Vizcaya and Guipúzcoa were Loyalist provinces. Álava and Navarra, however, favored Franco's Nationalists. Navarra, in fact, provided Franco with some of his toughest and best fighters.

The centers of virulently anti-Franco feeling in the Vascongadas, then, are the rich and dynamic provinces of Vizcaya and Guipúzcoa. Their traditional *fueros* (the Spanish version, dating from medieval days, of states' rights in such matters as trade and internal taxation) were taken away from them by the Franco regime as a result of the Civil War, though Álava and Navarra were allowed to retain theirs. The opposition ranges from the relatively peaceable Nationalist party to the bomb-throwing terrorists of the ETA organization (*Euzkadi Ta Azkatasuna,* "Freedom for the Basques") and the Basque Roman Catholic priests who lead underground workers' movements. Under the slogan of *"Aberi Eguna"* ("Free Basques"), the nationalists have become so active that hardly a week passes

without the Court of Public Order in Madrid sentencing groups of Basques to stiff prison terms for "illegal assembly" or propaganda, bomb-planting, and even armed attacks on police stations. Several Basque priests have been tried for refusing to say mass in their churches in the presence of the Spanish flag.

When the Basques attempted to celebrate their national day in San Sebastián on Easter Sunday, 1968, the regime sealed off the city and placed thousands of policemen in the streets to prevent demonstrations. The Burgos trial of alleged ETA terrorists in December, 1970, led to the gravest Spanish political crisis since the Civil War.

The Basques have been fighting outsiders throughout their history. When Charlemagne invaded Spain around A.D. 778, his rear guard was smashed by the Basques in the battle of Roncesvalles Pass in the Pyrenees. The episode was immortalized in the famous, but inaccurate, French medieval epic poem called the *Song of Roland*. Roland, a Frankish knight, was fighting, not Arabs as the "song" claims, but the very Christian Basques.

Over the centuries the Basque provinces have suffered the protection of Castile, Navarra, and the Kingdom of Asturias. Rafael Altamira, the noted Spanish historian, has said of Basque history: "It is true that no conqueror ever stamped out the indomitable spirit and the customs of the people, but the land was rarely independent."

When they were not busy fighting invaders and meddlers, the Basques dedicated themselves to building a powerful economy and to enjoying the pleasures of life. Although it is mountainous, the Basque region is a major food producer, chiefly because of its rainy climate. The sheep pastures around the old stone villages and the green forests and fields of grain are exhilarating after the dryness of southern Spain. The Basques are sturdy, hard-working, and conscious of the value of money. These qualities probably account for the disproportionate concentration of banks and corporate boards of directors in Bilbao, the capital of the industrialized Province of Vizcaya. It is the province with the highest annual per capita income in Spain—nearly double the national average. Guipúzcoa comes fourth in income, after Madrid and Barcelona. The Nervión River valley, which connects Bilbao with the Bay of Biscay, is one of Spain's great industrial centers. Smoke hangs eternally over its sooty factory towns—Baracaldo, Sestao, Portugalete, and Santurce. The two Bay of Biscay provinces also have what is probably the largest fishing industry on the Peninsula.

In addition to being independent and hard-working, the Basques are possibly the most religious people in Spain. Their deep-rooted tradition of mysticism has produced Saint Ignatius of Loyola, the founder of the Jesuit order, and the monk and renowned theologian Francisco de Vitoria. Miguel de Unamuna and Pío Baroja, both philosophers and men of letters, came from the Basque country, although their humanism tended to soften the harsh mysticism

A Basque shepherd and his flock

characteristic of their strange land.

The Basque joy of living finds expression in formidable physical exercises that range from the game of *jai alai,* an immensely violent version of squash, to boulder-pulling and ox-dragging contests. The same robustness has also led them to develop a fine and intriguing cuisine based chiefly on seafood and offering specialties like codfish and baby eels. Basques are active patrons of "eating societies," which hold periodic contests for the quality and sometimes, it seems, for the quantity of food prepared. The best Spanish restaurants are probably those in Bilbao and San Sebastián.

The little Basque girl dressed like a bride has just received her first communion.

Living along the Atlantic as they do, the Basques have maintained more contact with the outside world than most other Spaniards. Juan Sebastián del Cano, a Basque, has a claim to having been the first man to sail around the world. Miguel López de Legazpe, another Basque, conquered the Philippines, which remained a Spanish colony until the Spanish-American War. To this day, British influence in trade as well as in dress and manners is more powerful in the Vascongadas than anywhere else in Spain. England seems so close to the Basques that a daily ferry service to Southampton has been established.

San Sebastián and the beach areas around it remain the most fashionable summer resorts for highborn and prosperous Spaniards. To them the Costa del Sol is for foreigners and the middle class that has just acquired its Seats. Queen Victoria spent a summer in San Sebastián at the turn of the century, and every summer the Spanish Foreign Ministry moves there for nearly three months, forcing the ambassadors stationed in Madrid to do likewise. One of the compensations, however, is the presence of Basque women, who are among Spain's most beautiful.

Navarra is normally even more austere and mystical than the Basque provinces proper. But every July 7—the feast day of Saint Fermín—the fighting bulls are loosed to run through the streets of Pamplona, the capital of Navarra. This starts the *feria,* a week of top-flight bullfights and astonishing indulgence in the fine Navarra and Rioja wines, usually drunk from wineskins.

Many of the Navarrese are tough, hard-fighting, and deeply devout, leading isolated lives in the mountains. However, thanks to the fifteen-year-old University of Navarra, Pamplona is rapidly becoming a new Spanish intellectual center. The university is operated by the rich and controversial Opus Dei order of Catholic laymen and is probably the most outstanding institution of higher learning in Spain.

West of the coastal Basque provinces lie Santander, a prosperous Castilian outpost on the Bay of Biscay, and the coal-mining province of Asturias.

Santander's historical and artistic fame derives from the Altamira Cave, near Santillana on a hill overlooking the coast. The low ceilings of the cave are rich in polychromatic paintings dating to the Paleolithic Era, perhaps a half-million years ago. Astoundingly well preserved, they depict animals but principally charging, jumping or standing bisons (the forerunners of the Spanish bull?) and deer. The paintings were discovered in 1879 by the Spanish archeologist Marcelino S. de Sautuola. Altamira is now regarded as one of Europe's outstanding archaeological sights.

Asturias supplies most of Spain's coal as well as the tough miners who have fought with dynamite sticks in a long series of Spanish revolutions. Politically, the independent-minded Asturians defied the Second Republic when it was in power, then defended it from the Nationalists in the Civil War. In more recent years, they have turned Oviedo, the provincial capital, into a center of such severe labor unrest that the nearby coal mines periodically close down. Gastronomically, Asturias's gift to Spain is the superb salmon from its rivers. I know of gourmets who rank the Asturias salmon above Nova Scotian and Scottish salmon.

A rural household in Galicia

B eyond Asturias to the west is green Galicia, the eighth region in our tour of Spain. Galicia's four provinces—La Coruña, Lugo, Pontevedra, and Orense—have a per capita annual income that is considerably less than half the Spanish national average. Orense is *the* poorest province in all of Spain. Despite the pleasant greenness of its hills, much of the land in Galicia is mountainous and barely arable. Moreover, it is divided into dwarf holdings that make farming even more uneconomical. Galicia, therefore, has become an exporter of people to the rest of Spain and to the world. In proportion to their numbers at home the Gallegos are the largest group among the Spanish workers in western Europe. There are Gallegos throughout Latin America, much of which was discovered and colonized by Gallego seafarers and conquistadors. The father of Fidel Castro came from Galicia.

Except for the traditionally profitable shipbuilding industry in La Coruña, Vigo, and El Ferrol, Galicia is a depressed region without a bright future. The semiabandoned villages, with old women and children working the land, are reminiscent of their counterparts in Castile and Andalusia. For those staying behind, the difference between survival and destitution is the money that their emigrant men faithfully send home.

The most important Gallegan human export is Francisco Franco Bahamonde. He was born in 1892 at the port of El Ferrol, now known officially as El Ferrol del Caudillo in one of those touches of a personality cult that Franco either quietly enjoys or simply allows his sycophants to keep alive. Although he is not normally a sentimentalist, Franco makes a point of spending a few weeks every summer at a small palace near La Coruña and holding a cabinet meeting there.

Because of Galicia's proximity to Portugal, the Gallegan language is closer to Portuguese than it is to Spanish, though all three belong to the Hispanic group. There is some Gallegan poetry (Rosalía de Castro was the region's most famous lyric poet), but the Galicians are not nearly so culturally aggressive as the Catalans or the Basques. Politically, there is no meaningful Gallegan nationalist sentiment, and this, at least, has the advantage of not embarrassing Generalissimo Franco in his own home region.

The most important event in Galician history was the discovery early in the ninth century of the bones and tomb of Saint James the Apostle near a village that was later named Santiago de Compostela. Santiago (Saint James) has since become the patron saint of Spain. One legend has it that he landed in southeastern Spain after the death of Jesus to bring the gospel to the Iberian tribes and Roman occupiers who then inhabited the Peninsula. How Santiago made his way from Cartagena, the spot where he is believed to have landed, to the diametrically opposite corner of Spain is not known. Just as little is known of his evangelizing activities. But during the reign of Alfonso II, the Chaste, of Asturias, who ruled Galicia in the ninth century, the Holy See authenticated Santiago's bones and tomb. Santiago de Compostela, which is south of La Coruña, became a bishopric and, subsequently, the main center of Christian influence in northern Spain. It also became, and is to this day, the goal of pilgrims from all over the Christian world. The church considers Santiago the equal of Rome or Jerusalem as a pilgrimage destination. For centuries the faithful traveled to the shrine on foot over the "Santiago Routes" that crossed France and the Pyrenees before continuing west along the

113

coast of the Bay of Biscay. Roadside inns and hostels, whose descendants still exist, sprang up along these routes to feed and house the pilgrims, many of whom spent a year or more walking to the shrine.

Around 1100 a baroque cathedral was started in Santiago de Compostela to house the apostle's bones. A famous Galician architect, Domingo Antonio de Andrade, completed most of the construction by 1680 in what has become known as Galician Rococo— an unexpectedly majestic and impressive style. It was Andrade who finished the twin towers that loom over the cathedral. In 1738 Fernando de Casas y Novoa built a new façade. In the best Spanish tradition the cathedral is the product of successive tastes, styles, and generations. On feast days, particularly July 25, the feast day of Saint James and a national holiday, thousands crowd the cathedral for a look at the apostle's tomb. Even now some still come on foot.

Santiago is also the see of one of the three Spanish cardinals and the site of the Pontifical University. The latter is at the Monastery of San Martín Pinario, which was built in 1652 and is considered to be one of the outstanding religious structures in northern Spain.

Galicia is the only place in Spain where people play the bagpipes and make and drink cider. Like the Basques, the Gallegos attach considerable importance to good and plentiful eating. Their cuisine tends to be heavy, but Galician seafood dishes rival those of Bilbao and San Sebastián. Castilians from Madrid customarily look down on the underprivileged Gallegos, but since Franco began to live at El Pardo, the Gallegos have ceased to be the objects of patronizing remarks in the capital's drawing rooms.

E stremadura, our last region, is the poorest in Spain. The name means "extremely hard," and it is not an overstatement. Its two provinces—Badajoz and Cáceres—have together the lowest per capita income in the country. The problem is topographical, for the land is largely mountainous and dry. The villages are poor and often partly abandoned, except west of Badajoz where orange groves abound. That section of Estremadura is beginning to reap the benefits of a government irrigation and land-settlement

program. Along with Andalusia, Estremadura is for some reason one of the gypsies' favorite regions.

During the Roman conquest Estremadura was of strategic importance on the Peninsula. Badajoz was founded in Emperor Augustus's time under the name of Pax Augusta. Mérida's original name was Augusta Emerita. Both cities sprang up around the camps of Roman legions. Estremadura has innumerable Roman ruins, notably around Mérida, ranging from aqueducts to watchtowers. During the eleventh century the Badajoz area was one of the ten principal *taifas,* or states, in Moslem Spain.

Today Badajoz is a city bent on modernizing, but the old town still retains both Roman and Arab architectural influences. In 1808 the city was the center of the brief and pointless War of the Oranges between Spain and Portugal—a by-product of Napoleon's

Living off the land outside Badajoz

campaigns on the Peninsula and his struggle with England. Having invaded Portugal at Napoleon's insistence, the Spaniards quickly came to terms with the Portuguese. Symbolically, the Spanish soldiers in Badajoz handed Queen María Luisa of Spain branches from Portugal's orange groves, and thus gave the war its name. At the outset of the Civil War Franco's Nationalist armies savagely fought through Estremadura on their way north from Seville. In Badajoz the Nationalists, including Moorish units, committed some of their worst brutalities, including the massacre of at least two thousand Republican prisoners. History in Spain tends to repeat itself over the centuries. Estremadura suffered from the Almoravides of Emperor Yusuf-ben-Taxfin in 1086, and in 1936, exactly 850 years later, it suffered from the Moorish units and African legionnaires of Francisco Franco.

BOOK TWO

Spain's Past and Trauma

In the Plaza de España, at the heart of Madrid, a colossal stone Cervantes broods over his famous creations, Don Quixote and Sancho Panza.

1 The First Spaniards

For the past four and a half millenniums the Spaniards have absorbed the best, anthropologically and culturally, from the conquerors who have regularly tramped across their peninsula. They have intermarried and coexisted with Phoenicians, Carthaginians, Celts, Romans, Visigoths, and Arabs. So today Spain has blue-eyed, black-eyed, and brown-eyed people; red- and fair-haired people; longheaded and roundheaded people; long-nosed and short-nosed people; emaciated Don Quixotes and the contented bourgeois that Goya painted. And while many of Spain's conquerors have vanished, the Spaniards have survived to conquer, colonize, and leave their mark on other peoples in parts of the world as widely separated as Africa, California, Tierra del Fuego, and the Philippines.

Archaeological discoveries indicate that the Iberian Peninsula was inhabited in the earliest times by Cro-Magnon man, who may have contributed the Altamira Cave paintings. The late Charles E. Chapman, an American historian, claims that the inhabitants of the Canary Islands, off the African coast, maintained pure Cro-Magnon characteristics until the fifteenth century. Louis Siret, a Belgian archaeologist of the nineteenth century, discovered graves from the late Copper Age and early Bronze Age in the southern Spanish Province of Almería. Ironically, three of the four unarmed hydrogen bombs lost by the United States in an aerial collision in 1966 fell within a few hundred yards of the Bronze Age grave sites. The fourth bomb fell into the sea off the mouth of the Almanzora River where Phoenicians loaded their ships with the almost pure silver they mined from the coastal Cabrera range.

According to one theory that has been neither proved nor disproved, the Iberian Peninsula was once connected to North Africa roughly where the narrow Strait of Gibraltar divides them now. Legend has it that Hercules tore the two continents apart. A granite column east of Tangier is still known as one of the two Pillars of Hercules that in ancient times marked the limits of the known world. The other pillar is presumably the Rock of Gibraltar itself.

Traditionally, the Iberian Peninsula has been a bridge between the continents of Europe and Africa. The Europeans beyond the Pyrenees have always thought of Spain as the gateway to Africa while the Arabs have regarded Spain as the door to Europe. Until

The Pyrenees have long proved a barrier to would-be invaders of Spain.

very recently a Spaniard traveling to Paris, for example, would say, "I'm going to Europe."

Anthropological data does suggest that the so-called Iberians, who apparently settled the Peninsula five or six thousand years ago, may have come from North Africa over a land bridge. There is also speculation that an immense Iberian empire may once have existed around the western Mediterranean, encompassing Spain, North Africa, southern France, northern Italy, Corsica, and Sicily. After defeats at the hands of Egyptians, Phoenicians, and Asia Minor Hittites, this empire is said to have crumbled in the twelfth century B.C. The Iberians are believed to have firmly established themselves on the Iberian Peninsula by 2500 B.C., opening the first contacts with Brittany, the British Isles, Scandinavia, and Germany.

The next full-fledged invasion in Spanish history, following that of the Iberians, came from the north, when the Celts crossed the forbidding Pyrenees. However, scholars disagree by as much as five centuries on the approximate date of their arrival. Salvador de Madariaga places the Celtic invasion at about the ninth century

B.C. Rafael Altamira and Charles E. Chapman believe it occurred between the sixth and the fourth centuries B.C.

While the Iberians held the south and the Ebro Valley in eastern Spain, the Celts settled in what is now Portugal and in the northwest along the Bay of Biscay, where they mingled with the Basques, who are thought to have been there already. In subsequent centuries the Iberians spread north and the Celts spread south. They met in Castile in the center of Spain and on the northern and southern coasts. From this blend emerged the Celtiberians, not a coherent nation but a conglomeration of groups and tribes. These tribes included the Lusitanians, the early name for the Portuguese, the Cantabrians along the northern coast, and the Turdetan people of uncertain whereabouts. Celtiberians mark the beginning of the recorded history of Spain. What Greek and other chroniclers wrote about them can be applied to the Spaniards of today: Celtiberians were said to possess physical resilience, heroic valor, love of liberty, and a formidable lack of discipline.

The Celts and the Iberians left little archaeological evidence of their presence. Spain's career as a land whose history is inexorable began with the appearance of the Phoenicians on the Iberian coast in the eleventh and twelfth centuries B.C. Their contribution was a by-product of their mercantile activities, for they were essentially traders and not conquerors or settlers. They concentrated on the southern coast of Spain and in the Balearic Islands, establishing ports, factories, and trading posts where their ships could unload merchandise brought from all over the Mediterranean and then take on precious minerals from the Spanish mines. The Phoenicians' principal zone of influence stretched roughly from Almería to Gibraltar and then, on the Atlantic side of the Peninsula, to Cádiz and Seville. Later they established posts as far north as Galicia. The Phoenicians' active presence lasted for close to six centuries and had a notable cultural impact, particularly in the south. They also gave Spain her modern name—España. In the Phoenician tongue *Span* or *Spania* meant hidden or remote land.

The Phoenician empire in southern Spain had its easternmost anchor in Almería at the mouth of the Almanzora River, today a dry and dusty riverbed. It was there that the Phoenicians discovered mines that produced almost pure, lead-free silver—an extraordinary rarity. The silver veins ran fairly close to the surface

124

of the soft, porous rock of the Cabrera range, which comes to the very edge of the Mediterranean and then continues underwater in a labyrinth of canyons. Greek chroniclers have written that such was the abundance of silver that the Phoenicians fashioned it into anchors for their ships so that they could take away more of the precious metal on each voyage. The Phoenicians established a port and emporium where the fishing village of Villarico (meaning "the village of the rich") rots miserably under the burning Andalusian sun today. There is no more silver, lead, iron, or copper in these mountains, just bottomless misery. The last mine closed down fifty years ago.

Some of the Phoenician emporiums to the west of the Almanzora have grown into great and prosperous cities. In the eighth century B.C. the Phoenicians founded Málaga, now a major trade, industrial, and tourist center. Then they built what today is Algeciras, the town facing Gibraltar. But perhaps the greatest Phoenician gifts to Spain were Cádiz and Seville on the Atlantic coast. Cádiz is now approaching the end of its third millennium of existence. Seville, on the Guadalquívir River, began as a well-planned port and factory site. Later it was the headquarters for Spain's conquest of the Americas, and today it is a prosperous harbor city and the economic center of western Andalusia.

The Greeks came to Spain from the east about 630 B.C. Chief among them were the Phocians (no kin to the Phoenicians) from Marseilles. The first major Greek colony to be established on the Spanish coast was Emporium, near present-day Gerona in Catalonia. In time Emporium became Ampurias (now known as Castellón de Ampurias) and provided the name for the Catalonian region of Ampurdán. The Catalonians, who evolved into Spain's great merchants, can thus accurately claim Greek origins long before the Carthaginians came from Africa to found Barcelona. The Greeks spread along all the Spanish coast, but the Phoenicians, fearing the competition, eventually chased them back to the region around Emporium.

The Greeks are believed to have introduced to the Iberian Peninsula the cultivation of olives and grapes, thus providing Spain with what continues to be her agricultural mainstays. Olive oil, extracted from the fruit of the millions of gnarled olive trees (some more than a thousand years old), is one of the country's chief exports. Spanish wine today quenches the thirst of most of the thirty-three million Spaniards and earns increasing amounts of foreign currency as the better types become known around the world.

The Carthaginians first appeared in Spain at about the same time the Greeks did. Carthage sent troops to the Peninsula in response to an appeal from Phoenician Cádiz, which was fighting with neighboring Iberian tribes. But in the first of many such situations in the long and tortuous history of Spain, the Carthaginians not only saved Cádiz but kept it for themselves.

Once established in Spain, the Carthaginians devoted themselves to trade and mining. They also set up military garrisons in the cities and demanded tribute in men and money. At the end of the First Punic War, when Rome wrested Sicily from Carthage, the

The Mediterranean port of Málaga

Carthaginian general Hamilcar Barca concluded that the way to offset this loss was to conquer Spain and challenge the Romans on the European mainland. He landed with a powerful army in southern Spain in 237 B.C. and proved to be a colonizer and a civilizer as well as a soldier. He founded the city of Cartagena south of present-day Murcia; then he established Barcelona, naming it for the Barca family. When Hamilcar was killed in battle, his son-in-law Hasdrubal made Cartagena his capital. Carthaginian architectural vestiges still survive there today. When Hasdrubal was murdered, the reins of command passed into the hands of thirty-year-old Hannibal Barca, the son of Hamilcar.

Hannibal at once set in motion the march that was eventually to take his armies and elephants across the Alps to Italy. His first prize,

however, was Saguntum, the city the Greeks had founded on the Valencian coast. The Iberians defended the city with desperate valor in the great siege of 219–18 B.C. Rome considered itself the protector of Saguntum, and when it finally fell, Hannibal found himself at war with the empire. This, the Second Punic War, set the stage for the Roman conquest of Spain.

As Hannibal, his elephants, and his 100,000-man army (which included pro-Hannibal Spaniards in a typical confusion of Peninsular loyalties) marched across northeastern Spain and France toward the Alps, the Romans sent troops to intercept him. But the two armies somehow managed to miss each other, and in a classic Spanish situation, the Romans stayed on in Spain. They first established their rule over much of Catalonia and Valencia, then captured Carthaginian Cartagena with the aid of the Spanish tribes.

The six centuries that the Romans spent in Spain molded the country's character and institutions, changed its landscape, and propelled it into the mainstream of European history. Only the Arabs were destined to play a comparable role in Spain's evolution.

The concept of a unified nation has haunted the leaders of Spain from the Catholic Kings to Francisco Franco. Until the Romans dislodged the Carthaginians, the Iberian tribes lived (and died) in a succession of wars and alliances based on expediency. But the Pax Romana that was established in Spain around the middle of the second century B.C. made a coherent nation of Spain for the first time. The conquest was not altogether smooth. The Spaniards of the north, of the west, and of the central tableland fought so fiercely that it took the Romans seventy-five years to subdue them. It is probable that guerrilla warfare was born in Spain during the Roman invasion. Fighting the "little war," Spaniards harassed the Roman troops, camps, and cities with their shadowy bands of night raiders. The mountainous terrain and Spanish individualism were ideally suited to this form of combat. Hit-and-run tactics were again utilized by the Spaniards against the Arabs, against the Napoleonic invaders, and against each other in the Civil War. The art of guerrilla warfare, as well as the word for it, has thus become one of Spain's gifts to the modern world. The Spanish guerrilla spirit was best expressed by Cervantes's Don Quixote: "Because you must know that in newly conquered provinces and kingdoms, the spirit of the natives is not so tranquil nor so much in the camp

The eleventh-century walls of Avila, and in the foreground the Four Pillars

of the new master that one need not fear that they may still wish to upset the order and, as we say, to try their luck. . . ."

The sheer power of Rome ultimately asserted itself. In 132 B.C., after twenty years of assaults, the stubborn city of Numantia on the Duero River, in what is today Castile, fell to the Roman armies. Determined not to surrender, the Spaniards decided to burn down Numantia and kill themselves. Cervantes, who understood such things, immortalized their defense in a great tragic play. Today nothing remains of Numantia except a few barely distinguishable ruins on the plain. Two thousand years later, the city fathers of Soria, a cold Castilian town some miles away, are still talking, as their ancestors did, about establishing a Numantia museum.

For years the Romans cruelly suppressed Spanish revolts while Roman leaders used the Peninsula as a battlefield in their own struggles to control the empire. Julius Caesar defeated Pompey at Ilerda (today's Lérida) in Catalonia in 49 B.C. and at Munda in Andalusia in 45 B.C. Octavius smashed last-ditch Spanish resistance in the north shortly before being crowned Emperor Augustus. As Rome's most important overseas possession, Spain flourished under

129

the protection of Augustus, a city builder who left a deep imprint on the Peninsula. He turned his two armed camps in western Spain into the towns of Augusta Emerita (Mérida) and Pax Augusta (Badajoz). He founded Braga in Portugal as Bracara Augusta. In northern Spain his Caesaraugusta became Saragossa. Urbs Septima Legionis is now León, Asturica Augusta is Astorga, Lucas Augusti is Lugo. Nowhere in Spain can one forget Rome.

Many of Spain's present-day highways are former Roman roads. Indeed, some of the mountain roads have not been much improved since the days of the Roman legions. Besides contributing systems of law and public administration, the Romans entered the heart and the flesh of their new possession by intermarrying with the population. The classical synthesis was again at work: the Roman impact was to outlast Spain's link to Rome.

Roman cities in Spain were built with encircling walls, forums, and bathhouses. Their ruins are everywhere. But the Peninsula paid Rome back in human talent. The emperors Trajan and Hadrian, and possibly Theodosius, were born in Spain, as were many of the thinkers and artists of the Roman Empire, including the philosopher Marcus Aurelius. Córdoba, already a major intellectual center, produced the philosopher Seneca, the rhetorician Quintilian, the

The enormous Roman aqueduct at Segovia

ironic poet Martial, and the epic poet Lucan. As Salvador de Madariaga has remarked of Rome, "the literature of the Silver Age is Spanish." Spain was no longer a conquered land but a vital part of a great Mediterranean civilization on the eve of the Christian Era. Christianity reached Spain in the second century A.D. and initiated a religious and mystical experience that has survived the ages. The third century saw the rise of Christian communities throughout the country. During that century alone the contingent of Spanish martyrs included Saint Vicente of Valencia, Saint Eulalia of Mérida, Saint Severo of Barcelona, Saint Leocadia of Toledo, and Saint Engracia of Saragossa.

From the very beginning Spanish individualism made itself felt, and Spaniards lost no time in telling Rome that they would practice Catholicism according to their own lights. First, Spain harbored the so-called Priscillianist heresy, which proclaimed that the devil had created the world. Since then, the country has maintained an extraordinary degree of independence from the Holy See. The Catholic Kings and their successors fought for decades with Rome over the conduct of the Spanish Inquisition. While Spain remains today the "most Catholic" of nations, with Roman Catholicism the state religion, there are fewer and fewer things on which Generalissimo Franco and the Vatican see eye to eye. During my stay in Spain the Spanish church split deeply between liberals and conservatives, and the effect of their struggles on politics became one of my prime concerns as a newspaper correspondent.

F ranks from the north and Arabs from North Africa carried out their first incursions into Spain as early as the first and second centuries A.D. But the Roman domination was not ended until the German Visigoths swept down from the north in 414. The Visigoths completed the eradication of the Roman way of life some seventy-five years later.

If anything, the three chaotic centuries of the Visigothic presence in Spain slowed the country's cultural development. Their contribution did not match that of the Romans, but the Visigoths did give the Peninsula its first capital, which they established at Toledo early in the sixth century. Under the Romans each of the five provinces had been autonomous, responsible only to Rome. Throughout Spain, however, it is the Roman touch that remains hauntingly visible, while the Visigoth influence is imperceptible. Besides the aqueducts and the shells of the forums that dot Spain from Andalusia to Estremadura, there must be a thousand Roman watchtowers still looking with empty eyes at the countryside they once protected.

The Moslem conquest quickly dispersed the Visigoths and had an effect on Spain that was in its own way comparable to Roman rule. When the Berber Tariq landed on the Andalusian coast in 711, a new chapter opened in the cultural and political development of the country. The 781 years of Arab presence not only changed the fabric of Spanish society once more and provided still another infusion of new blood but brought Spain a kind of national unity that had eluded her in the preceding centuries. When the last Arab ruler was toppled from power in 1492, Spain was ready to become a nation in the true meaning of the word and to project her influence across the Atlantic with her own overseas conquests.

Because the Arab invaders often fought one another as well as the Christian Kings (and the Spanish guerrillas who reappeared to harass the new masters), it took the Moslems more than two centuries to achieve a semblance of central government. This was finally accomplished by Abd-er-Rahman III, who in the middle of the tenth century established the Caliphate of Córdoba. The moment represented the apex of Arab glory in Spain—politically and culturally. In 1009, only half a century after Abd-er-Rahman hammered together his great caliphate, Sancho Garcés, the Count of Castile, recaptured Córdoba for the Christians and the Reconquest began. The Moslems were gradually pushed back to the coastal areas of Andalusia and Valencia. Finally, the Catholic Kings completed the Reconquest in 1492 by taking Granada, the last major Islamic stronghold.

The motivating force in the Reconquest was not a holy Christian crusade against Islam but the search for Spanish political unity. The Spanish kings from Sancho Garcés to Isabella and Ferdinand

A gypsy dancing at a small café in Seville

sensed that this unity would not be achieved until the Arabs were gone. Chronicles of the day tell of something akin to sadness on the part of the Christians in expelling individual Moorish princes and communities and of the Moors' heartbreak at being ejected, for Christians and Moors had lived in extraordinary everyday harmony. The Moslem lord of Mojácar in Almería successfully pleaded with the Catholic Kings to be allowed to remain in Spain, for it was home to him and his people. Many Arabs smuggled themselves back into Spain, not to attempt to rule anew, but simply to live in the country to which they felt they belonged.

The Moslem presence provided the final element of the modern Spaniard. From the Moslems' departure until the present day the melting pot has simply gone on simmering with ingredients successively contributed by the Iberians, Celts, Phoenicians, Carthaginians, Greeks, Romans, Visigoths, Arabs, and Jews.

The Jews were very much a part of Moslem Spain. The first of them had arrived at the end of the Roman Era and stayed on as Spaniards. Ironically, the days of Islam brought them new distinction: when Abd-er-Rahman built his caliphate, the city of Córdoba became the world center of Hebrew theological studies as well as the intellectual capital of the West. Not only was the philosopher Maimonides born in Córdoba, but so were many of the great Sephardic rabbis. The Spanish Inquisition was to destroy the Jews as a separate community in the post-Islamic years, but hundreds of thousands, if not millions, of modern Spaniards have remote Jewish ancestry.

Córdoba was the most precious jewel in the crown of the caliphate. Chroniclers tell of the city's two hundred thousand houses, six hundred mosques, and nine hundred bathhouses. The Guadalquívir River was spanned by bridges rich in statuary that rivaled the bridges built earlier by the Romans. The Moorish bridges are still in use today. The palace of Medina Azahara, built by Abd-er-Rahman for one of his wives, was a showplace. Its walls still stand. The great Córdoba mosque, begun by Abd-er-Rahman I, is now the Roman Catholic cathedral. The extraordinary cathedral was literally built around the mosque and is an architectural marvel. It has 49 aisles, 21 gates, and 1,293 columns that were once covered with porphyry and jasper and encrusted with marble, silver, and precious stones.

A street in Pezuela de las Torres

The Alhambra in Granada, where Washington Irving spent long and happy months in 1829, has changed little since the days of the Moors except for the addition of uniformed guides and the peddlers who charge three times the proper price for a copy of Irving's *Tales of the Alhambra*. In Seville the Moors built a 295-foot minaret on top of the main mosque. After the Reconquest the mosque became the cathedral, and the minaret the bell tower known as La Giralda. In hundreds of Spanish towns there are the remains of Arab quarters, usually Casbah-like collections of whitewashed houses on hilltops. Most of the great houses in Andalusia are built on the Moorish pattern around a patio that is cooled by a central fountain. Patios are tucked away even in Toledo, a Castilian city with a Mos-

lem past. The masses of geraniums and other flowers that decorate the façades of the most modest Spanish dwellings from Lorca in Murcia to Pezuela de las Torres in Castile are part of the country's rich Arab heritage.

Working together in Córdoba, the Arabs and the Spaniards perfected the sciences of astronomy, mathematics, and medicine. Jointly, they devised new irrigation techniques that are still used in parched Spain. Under Moslem rule Spain was one of the wealthiest and most densely populated lands of contemporary Europe. But the reign of Islam, like its precursors, came and went. The Arabs returned to Africa. The Spaniards stayed behind, absorbing and preserving what the invaders had willed them.

137

2 The Greatness and the Shame

The pilgrimage church of Santiago de Compostela looms ghostlike in the background.

The Spanish syndrome of greatness and self-imposed defeat that time after time has transmuted glory into shame and power into impotence was never more evident than in the centuries following the Reconquest. And it is my belief that one must begin with the recapture of Granada by the Catholic Kings on January 2, 1492, to understand the sad chain of events that led to the greatest Spanish disaster of all, the Civil War that broke out on July 18, 1936.

Two of the epochal events of 1492 were the formal end of the Moslem sway and Columbus's initial voyage of discovery to the West Indies. Virtually simultaneously, Spain freed itself from a conqueror and launched a conquest of its own. Yet incredibly, in the ensuing years, decades, and centuries Spain proceeded to undo with one hand what it was creating with the other. As Rafael Altamira wrote, the ultimate result "was to prove disastrous to Spain herself if, indeed, there were counter-balancing advantages and glorious memory."

By the middle of the sixteenth century Spain ruled much of the New World, Asia, and Africa. Tragically, the new wealth that flowed in from these conquests was wasted as quickly as it was acquired in the spectacular luxury of the royal courts and in Spain's unending and fruitless European and Turkish wars of the sixteenth and seventeenth centuries. Charles V, the grandson of Isabella and Ferdinand, involved Spain in every conceivable European political adventure, including the Crusades. Philip II, the builder of the austere Escorial Monastery, bled the country white to launch the Armada on its disastrous expedition against Elizabethan England. In the seventeenth century Philip III and Philip IV added their destructive contributions to what Salvador de Madariaga has called "an evolution already determined by a century of masterful errors." The eighteenth and the nineteenth centuries brought their share of disasters: the War of the Spanish Succession and the loss of Gibraltar in the early 1700's; the Napoleonic wars and the occupation of Madrid by the French armies; and the shameful installation of Joseph Bonaparte on the Spanish throne. Finally, there was the trauma of the Spanish-American War and the loss of Cuba, Puerto Rico, and the Philippines.

Between 1500 and 1900 Spain was gradually but ineluctably

ruined. Yet the early years of the sixteenth century were its cultural Golden Age; the beginning of the tortured nineteenth century was the Age of Goya; the catastrophic defeat of 1898 brought forth the luminous surge of the Generation of 1898. These were the tragic contradictions of a nation that simply could not live with its own greatness.

While the rest of Europe developed intellectually over the centuries to emerge with a relative freedom of worship, Spain progressively locked itself into an ever-narrower interpretation of Christianity. The twentieth-century consequence of this religious fanaticism was to transform the Spanish Civil War into a "crusade" for Franco's Nationalists against the "antichrist" of the Republicans.

In internal as in external affairs the rule of the Catholic Kings was a watershed in Spanish history. Spaniards still speak of them as if they belonged to the very recent past, and they are a source of inspiration to Franco and many other contemporary Spaniards who still dream of Spain's greatness. Although they accomplished much that was positive for Spain, the outside world probably remembers these monarchs best for a rapacious overseas conquest and for the Inquisition. Isabella and Ferdinand presided at the discovery of the New World, but they also officiated at the creation of the "Black Legend" that was to plague Spain for centuries. To Spaniards nowadays, especially those of the Franco regime, the Black Legend means everything about Spain that is criticized abroad. When a foreign writer comments unfavorably on some aspect of Spanish life— from mores to politics—the cry of "Black Legend" goes up at once. The Spaniards' sensitivity to it and their related guilt feelings are enormous.

The first Black Legend was the Spanish Inquisition launched by Pope Sixtus IV in a bull of November 1, 1478. Issued under pressure from Isabella, the bull authorized the appointment of Inquisitors by the Spanish crown to investigate all charges of heresy. Isabella in turn had been influenced by Alonso de Hojeda, a Dominican prior in Seville, who preached that only a full-fledged Inquisition could prevent the financially important minority of Jewish converts to Christianity (known as *conversos*) from secretly practicing their former faith. The official explanation at the time (and one still current today in some circles in Spain) alleged that the Inquisition was an unavoidable by-product of the national effort at unification. In

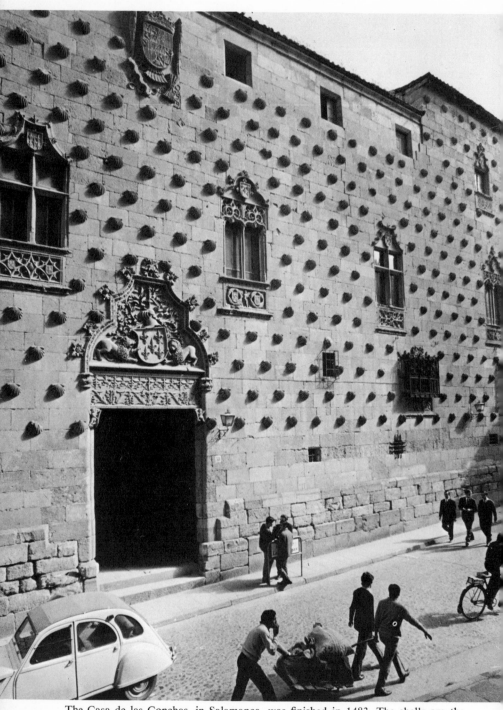

The Casa de las Conchas, in Salamanca, was finished in 1483. The shells are the mark of the builder, not the noble owner.

reality, the Inquisition weakened rather than strengthened Spain, and it bred dissensions that were to plague the nation well into modern times.

By 1480 thousands had been beheaded or burned at the stake, and the Inquisition's excesses had become so great that Pope Sixtus issued another bull accusing the Spaniards of practicing it not out of "zeal for the faith and the salvation of souls, but by lust for wealth. . . ." Indeed, the Inquisition was very much a temporal enterprise, touching upon Spain's economic, social, and political life under the guise of spiritual purification.

Henry Kamen, an English historian, has written that the Inquisition was largely a religious excuse for the economic destruction of the powerful Jewish and *converso* middle class by the Catholic nobility. The Inquisition, Kamen wrote, "was neither more nor less than a class weapon, used to impose on all communities of the Peninsula the ideology of one class—the lay and ecclesiastical aristocracy. . . . Their beliefs and ideals were henceforth to be the norm of Castilian life: at its best this attitude flowered out into heroic spirituality, at its worst it degenerated into the worst of all racialisms —the racialism of a single class." It might be added that the notion of imposing the ideology of one class persists even today, in the Franco regime's abhorrence of all political dissent.

The Inquisition, however, left untouched the Jews who had not been converted to Christianity. To eliminate them, the Catholic Kings decreed in 1492 that all Jews in Spain must either convert to Christianity or leave the country. Spanish and Jewish historians have calculated that of the more than a quarter million Jews in Spain at the time, about 170,000 perferred expulsion to conversion. Over 50,000 accepted Christianity, and more than 20,000 were killed resisting expulsion or conversion. But thousands, if not tens of thousands, of Jews must have converted or "passed" in some way to explain the contention of so many Spaniards today that most of them have Jewish blood in their veins.

Ten years after they decreed the elimination of Jews from Spain, the Catholic Kings broke the treaty they had signed after the fall of Granada that guaranteed freedom of worship to Moslems. Prepared by Cardinal Jiménez de Cisneros, the abrogation ordered all *Mudé- jares* (Moslems living among Christians) to embrace Catholicism or be expelled. Uprisings and bloodshed followed, and in time the

This former synagogue in Salamanca is now an apartment house.

Moslem population of Spain vanished, as the Jewish population had vanished earlier.

Immense as the ravages of the Spanish Inquisition were over the centuries, the Jews found a measure of poetic justice in the end. On Easter Monday of 1966—474 years after the expulsion decree —the head of the Hebrew community of Madrid was invited by the two hundred Dominican fathers at the monastery of Ávila to lecture on the meaning of Judaism. The speaker was Max Mazin, a central European refugee who had come to live in Spain as a businessman after the Second World War and had become a Spanish citizen. As he spoke he stood only twenty yards from the crypt in which Tomás de Torquemada, the most famous Inquisitor General, lies buried. When I met Mazin in Madrid a few days later, I asked him how he had felt delivering an address at Torquemada's own monastery. "It was like spanning the ages," he said. "It was a unique experience for a Jew." One of Mazin's associates in the Madrid Hebrew community is a Moroccan Jew named Samuel de Toledano, the first of his family to return to Spain since 1492. As is the case with thousands of Sephardic families inhabiting the rim of the Mediterranean ever since the 1492 Diaspora, the Toledanos (who came from Toledo) have maintained both the language and customs of Spain. Newspapers written in Ladino—a mixture of archaic Spanish and Hebrew—are still published in Greece and Turkey by Sephardic communities whose members have not set foot in Spain for nearly half a millennium. The exiled communities prospered wherever they went, enriching their adopted countries at the expense of the nation that expelled them. When Sephardic Jews from Spain reached the Ottoman Empire, Sultan Bajazet II said: "Let the kings of Spain impoverish their lands—to enrich ours."

Only in 1967, nearly five hundred years after the royal decree ordering Jews to convert or be exiled, was Spain able to pass legislation establishing freedom of worship for non-Catholics. Although the new law benefited the tiny minority of thirty thousand Protestants and seven thousand Jews then living in Spain—just over one-tenth of one per cent of the population—it was opposed to the very end by a group of religious traditionalists. Sitting in the press gallery of the Spanish Cortes while the law was being discussed, I listened incredulously to a deputy solemnly warn that freedom of worship for the 37,000 non-Catholics would undermine "the religious unity of Catholic Spain."

The sixteenth century in Spain was an era of grandiose enterprises and equally grandiose errors. The first of the enterprises was the discovery of the New World by Columbus. In four voyages made between 1492 and 1502 he sailed to Hispaniola, Cuba, the mouth of the Orinoco River in northeastern South America, and Honduras. Thereafter, Spanish seafarers and conquerors went everywhere. Magellan sailed the treacherous strait between the southern tip of South America and Tierra del Fuego, and Balboa became the first European to cross the Isthmus of Panama to the Pacific. Hernando Cortes arrived in Mexico in 1519 to topple the Aztec Empire with 32 horsemen and 400 foot soldiers. Pizarro undertook the conquest of Peru in 1531 with 227 men and a score of horses. That conquest marked the end of the Inca Empire. Mendoza sailed into the estuary of the Rio de la Plata in 1534 and established the city of Nuestra Señora de los Buenos Aires two years later. Pedro de Valdívia took Chile, and Juan de Ayolas founded Asunción in Paraguay. Florida and Mississippi were discovered in the 1520's, and Spanish explorers ventured inland into Georgia, South Carolina, Louisiana, Texas, Arizona, Arkansas, and Missouri. Later they went to California and even Alaska. The abundance of Spanish geographic names in the United States—from Los Angeles and San Francisco to San Antonio and Nevada—is, of course, the heritage of these Castilian adventurers, while in Latin America the language, institutions, and a mystical sense of Spanishness called *Hispanidad* still attest to their influence.

The Spaniards conquered the New World to claim its gold, platinum, silver, spices, and precious wood for the crown of Spain. Incessantly, the four-deck galleons sailed back from American ports up the Guadalquívir to Seville to deliver their priceless cargoes. They enriched Charles V and the three Philips, their courts, noblemen, and retinues. The spoils from the new colonies fed not only the fierce hunger for luxury among the once austere Spaniards but also paid for their European political schemes. In the end, those riches brought about Spain's ruin as a world power.

To this day the palaces and cathedrals of Spain shine with the gold of the New World. The huge solid gold monstrances (receptacles in which the consecrated Host is exposed for adoration) in the cathedrals at Toledo and Santiago de Compostella are gifts from navigators and viceroys. The nobility created by the Catholic Kings and Charles V to replace the former *ricohombres* (literally, rich men), who had not had precise titles, won great fortunes from the Americas. The naming in 1520 of the eight dukes and fifteen grandees of Spain (who had the right to keep their heads covered in the presence of the king and to visit him unannounced day or night) marked the birth of the wealthy and powerful Spanish aristocracy, which still survives. The great dukedoms and fortunes of the Medinacelis, Albas, Medina-Sidonias, and Infantados date back to the conquest. The lesser nobility—the hidalgos (derived from the word *hijodalgo,* "son of something") and the *caballeros* (gentlemen on horseback) of recognized lineage—likewise came into being in the

This replica of Columbus' ship *Santa Maria* is moored in Barcelona harbor.

euphoric days of the Conquest. Together they are the ancestors of the aristocrats of today, who still proudly display the 2,544 recognized titles that are registered at the Spanish Ministry of Justice.

The Spanish rulers and the nobles of the sixteenth century rapidly squandered the extraordinary wealth won from the Conquest. The magnitude of private fortunes in the late fifteenth and early sixteenth centuries is illustrated by the Marquis de Villena's annual revenue of 100,000 ducats, the equivalent of $2,500,000 today. The Archbishop of Toledo, who personally owned much of Andalusia, received an annual income of 80,000 ducats. The Spanish church had a yearly revenue equivalent to $160,000,000 today. The palaces that began to dot Castile in the early sixteenth century were designed by Italian architects and embellished with solid silver doors and private chapels with marble altars. They show how lustily the Spaniards took to their new and scintillating prosperity.

The Catholic Kings had both wisdom and a keen strategic sense. Machiavelli wrote admiringly that Ferdinand "has continually contrived great things, which have kept his subjects' minds uncertain and astonished." But Ferdinand and Isabella did not dissipate their strength. Spain in their time was primarily oriented away from Europe; King Ferdinand's careful French and Italian campaigns were essentially related to the preservation of his power at home. But Charles V, a Hapsburg prince who became the Spanish king in 1516 and Holy Roman Emperor in 1519, forced Spain's entry into the affairs of Europe. It was a move that carried the seeds of ultimate tragedy.

Before he was twenty the dour and authoritarian Charles had inherited much of Europe, the Americas, and the Orient. From the Catholic Kings he received Castile, Aragon, and Navarra in Spain, the Italian domains of the Kingdom of Naples and Sardinia and Sicily, the Roussillon in France, and the Spanish crown's possessions overseas. From his father, Philip the Handsome, he received northeastern France and the Low Countries. On the death of Emperor Maximilian he acquired the Hapsburg lands in Austria, Bohemia, Moravia, and Hungary, and the title of Holy Roman Emperor. In 1525 he married Portugal's Princess Isabella, which gave him control of the growing Portuguese overseas empire, including Brazil.

During the forty years of his reign Charles sought to hold together his far-flung possessions and as much of Europe as possible. But it was an impossible task, and in the process, the interests of Spain were sacrificed. While he fought the Protestant Reformation, the Ottoman Empire, the papacy, and various French, Dutch, Italian, and other kings and princes who stood in his way, Charles let Empress Isabella run Spain. Signing himself, "I, The King," he sent her a stream of written instructions on Spanish politics and the handling of the New World possessions whose wealth financed his European campaigns. Isabella kept him informed of Spanish court intrigues, her difficulties with the local nobility, and other problems. Being an absentee ruler, however, Charles could not keep pace with events in Spain. The voluminous correspondence between him and Isabella, preserved at the Spanish state archives at Simancas, shows how the emperor gradually lost touch with the country.

After living in retirement as a monk for three years, Charles died in 1558. His empire began to come apart, and Spain found itself the prey of fiercely competitive European powers. The country was entering a period of political decay after less than a century of great-

El Greco's house in Toledo, now a museum

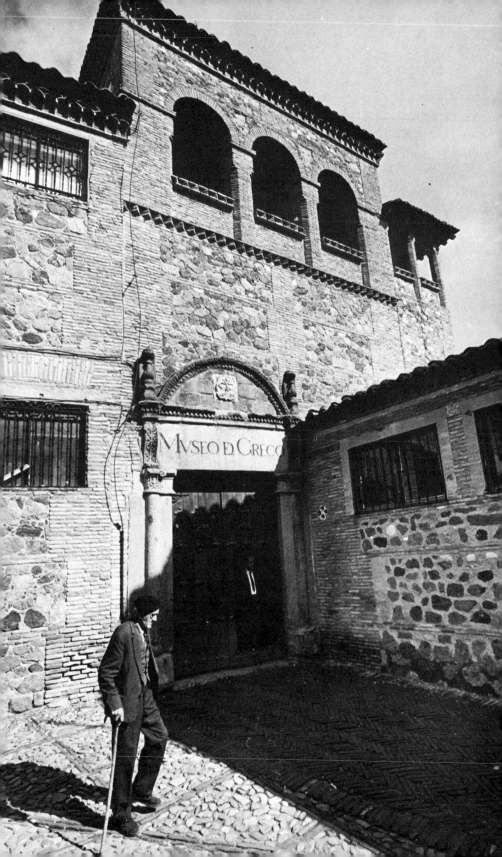

ness, and Philip II, Charles's successor, only aggravated the decline through his errors. Yet, as it began to decline politically Spain produced some of its greatest art and literature.

It was the age of Cervantes, whose left arm was shattered while he served Philip II aboard a Spanish ship in the victorious battle of Lepanto against the Turks. After a life of incredible adventures, Cervantes began to write *Don Quixote* when he was sixty. The era also produced Tirso de Molina, who created the *Deceiver of Seville,* a play about Don Juan, the great lover; Calderón de la Barca and Lope de Vega, the prolific dramatists; Garcilaso de la Vega, the soldier and poet of the American Conquest; and the great Castilian mystics Saint John of the Cross, Saint Theresa of Ávila, and the monk Luis de León.

This golden age was also the time of El Greco, the Greek who appeared in Spain in 1577 to discover in Toledo the incredible hues of the Spanish sky and to paint the great saints and the majestic *Burial of Count Orgaz.* It was the time of Murillo, Ribera, and Zurbarán, and of Velázquez, the painter of the *Forge of Vulcan,* of the common Spaniard at work and play, and of kings, queens, princesses, and cardinals.

Spain's two centuries of cultural flowering paralleled a series of national disasters that culminated in the War of the Spanish Succession at the beginning of the eighteenth century. The trouble, of course, was that Spain had undertaken the impossible: to be the world's leading temporal power and, simultaneously, Catholicism's champion against the Protestant Reformation and against Islam as it was then personified by the Turkish sultans.

Philip II, the son of Charles V, began his reign in the imperial fashion. He intended to reassert Spain's sway after the reverses that had taken place during the later years of his father's life. In fairly quick succession he defeated Henry II of France at Saint-Quentin and the Turkish fleet at Lepanto. At home Philip and his half-brother, Don Juan of Austria, proceeded to impose religious purity —the eternal Spanish theme—by wiping out the rebellious Moriscos (Moslem converts to Catholicism who secretly practiced their old religion) in a series of fierce battles. The climax of this bloody repression occurred when the severed head of Aben-Abu, the Morisco chief, was nailed to the gates of Granada. Terrible vengeance upon defeated enemies is a Spanish reflex action. The Inquisition was another instrument favored by Philip, a religious fanatic, to do away with all heretics of Jewish or Moslem origin and those new foes, the Protestants. Indeed, the king is known to have personally presided at an auto-da-fé in Toledo.

Two years after Saint-Quentin, however, Philip was forced to sign a compromise peace with France at Cateau-Cambrésis, giving up most of Lorraine. As another concession, he married Elizabeth, the daughter of France's Henry II. His first wife, Mary Tudor, had died a few years earlier. After Lepanto the Turks attacked again, and this time Philip could not contain them and had to settle for a dubious truce.

Then the Spaniards were defeated by the European Protestants whom Philip, the "Defender of the Faith," had set out to humiliate. First he lost the northern province of the Netherlands to William the Silent of Nassau; then he lost much of his influence in France. His bitterest defeat, however, was the destruction in 1588 of the 160-ship Invincible Armada that was on its way to invade Elizabeth I's England. The Spanish flotilla was decimated by furious storms and by the more agile English and Dutch warships. Philip then withdrew to his monastery at Escorial in the bleak Guadarramas, to die in agony in 1598. Velázquez was born the following year.

Philip III—another religious fanatic known as the Pious—harvested more tragedies for Spain during his twenty-three year reign. He expelled the remaining 100,000 Moriscos from the kingdom and dissipated what was now only a trickle of wealth from the New World as quickly as it came into the royal coffers.

Philip IV, the worst of the three disastrous Hapsburg Philips, was a cultivated weakling. From 1621, when he mounted the throne at the age of sixteen, to his death in 1665, he allowed his incompetent prime minister, the Count-Duke Olivares, to run the nation. During his reign Spain lost Portugal, Artois, Franche-Comté, Alsace, and the Roussillon. His principal adversary was France's Cardinal Richelieu, who was more than a match for Philip and Olivares.

At home Philip faced the first Catalonian rebellion, led by the *segadores*, the harvesters. While remaining loyal to the church and the person of the king, they rose against the government imposed by Madrid in the first of the interminable Catalonian demands for some degree of autonomy. The Spanish economy was collapsing, yet the king insisted on entertaining lavishly at the Madrid court, and he continued to be the patron of such artists as Rubens and Velázquez. John A. Crow, an American historian, has written that the government and the church became havens for the large number of unemployed: in the mid-seventeenth century 447,000 Spaniards worked for the government and 1,141,000 persons held ecclesiastic or church-related posts. The expulsion of the Moriscos who had inherited the Moors' skill in irrigation, virtually destroyed agriculture in southern Spain. Men of talent left to find fortunes and advancement in the New World colonies.

Matters in general went from bad to worse when Charles II, aptly nicknamed the Bewitched, succeeded his father. He was four when Philip IV died in 1665, and sixteen when he assumed the throne

Philip II built the Escorial monastery and retired there to die.

after a period of regency. Charles had the worst Hapsburg characteristics: he was frail, sick, and indecisive. His adversary was Louis XIV of France, who ultimately prevailed on the childless Charles to name as his successor Louis's grandson Philip of Bourbon, the Duke of Anjou. France thus forced the end of the two-century-old Hapsburg dynasty, and imposed the Bourbons upon Spain when Charles died in 1700.

This move immediately brought on the thirteen-year-long War of the Spanish Succession. The other European powers feared that the accession of Philip of Bourbon, now Philip V of Spain, would tip the delicate balance of power on the Continent in favor of France. Consequently, Austria, England, Portugal, and the Netherlands

joined in an alliance to oust Philip and replace him with Archduke Charles of Austria. The war failed to depose Philip, but the Treaty of Utrecht that ended it provided for the permanent renunciation of all claims to the French throne by the Spanish king. It also confirmed England's sovereignty over Gibraltar, which Spain had lost to English forces in 1704. That clause has been a source of bitter feuds between London and Madrid up to this day. The War of the Spanish Succession established a tenuous alliance between Spain and France and involved the Spaniards in the wars of the Polish and Austrian Succession. The three wars brought Spain to the point of complete political and economic exhaustion.

"The role of Spain as a leading power ends here," Salvador de Madariaga has written. "The main cause of Spain's failure lay in the very task which she had dreamed of achieving. Universality was then impossible, even within the restricted limits of Christendom. . . . Her policy cost her untold sacrifices of money abroad, and of liberty, particularly liberty of thought at home."

The seventeenth century was a time of what the Spaniards call *desengaño,* which literally means "disillusionment" but which in Spanish has an even more poignant sense. Disenchanted and bruised by life, the Spaniards had recourse to fantastic and many-splendored abstractions in literature, architecture, and art. This Spanish penchant for refuge from adversity in the unreal may go far toward explaining the recurrent and peculiarly Spanish phenomenon of artistic flowering in times of crisis. In literature, as we have seen, Cervantes invented Don Quixote to point out the folly of rulers and used satire to restore sanity to his fellow Spaniards caught between the mad imperial schemes of their kings and their own misery. Calderón de la Barca put it succinctly: *"La vida es sueño"* (life is a dream). It could be considered the leitmotiv of the brilliant literary production in seventeeenth-century Spain.

The reaction to the century of *desengaño* was also translated into abstractions by Spanish painters, sculptors, and builders. But because no two Spaniards have ever expressed the same sentiment in the same way, the abstractions run in every conceivable direction. The severe mannerism of Philip II's bleak palaces and monasteries was replaced by the extravagances of the new Spanish baroque, so unlike the Italian baroque that inspired it. The art historian Cirici-Pellicer has described is as a "superfluous elaboration of architectural

154

features, with frames, pediments, pilasters, entablatures, imposts, and openings of various shapes and sizes . . . characterized by broken and twisted lines, projecting and receding surfaces, decorated with parallel mouldings, equally broken and twisted." Prime examples of the new style, which was meant to divert attention from the realities of national catastrophes, are the incredibly elaborate houses on Madrid's Plaza Mayor, the cloister of the Clerecía house of the Jesuits in Salamanca, and the oval church of the Bernardas nuns at Alcalá de Henares. The façade of the small but striking church of the Hospital de la Caridad in Seville, adorned with blue mosaics, is the Andalusian version of Spanish baroque. It is the work of Bernardo Simón de Pineda. The Pilar church in Saragossa, designed by

The Plaza Mayor, in Madrid

Francisco de Herrera the Younger, is reminiscent of a vast Moslem mosque with bell towers resembling minarets. Impoverished as Spain was under Philip IV, the fantastic sum of eleven million reals was nevertheless found to erect in Madrid the church of San Andrés, a grandiose edifice crowned by a cupola and filled with a profusion of stucco ornaments. The money came from Philip, the viceroys of Mexico and Peru, the municipality of Madrid, and several Castilian towns. José de Churriguera, who lent his name to the ornate and flamboyant Churrigueresque style, built the Goyeneche Palace in Madrid, now the Royal Academy of Fine Arts of San Fernando on the Calle de Alcalá.

Velázquez, who at first received a barber's pay from Philip IV, delighted in painting the court jester Calabacillas, known as "The Idiot of Coria," for he was a satirist in the tradition of Cervantes. His portraits of the Spanish nobility make the sitters appear empty and somewhat fatuous, although Velázquez's patrons evidently never became aware of it.

Claudio Coello's painting of the sickly Charles II kneeling at the altar surrounded by his court probably tells more than a history book about the moral decay of the Hapsburg dynasty. It is worth studying the faces of the dissipated and desperate princes and courtiers and the annihilated figure of Charles. This, of course, was no longer abstraction but reality, as Spain prepared to face the next chapter in her history. Yet, nothing in Spain is simple: this realistic school of painting coexisted with the deeply mystical religious abstractions of Zurbarán, Murillo, and Ribera.

With the Bourbons Spain entered the Age of Enlightenment, sometimes known as Enlightened Despotism, which was to last for more than a century, until the Napoleonic conquest of the early 1800's. It was a period punctuated by political reverses and cultural and philosophical advances.

During the forty-five year reign of Philip V the country became more unified than ever before. The customs barriers between the traditional states of the Peninsula were abolished. In 1725 the kingdom abandoned its historical name of Castile and for the first time called itself Spain. Because he was a Frenchman Philip instinctively brought Spain into Europe and opened the country to the intellectual and economic influences of the Continent. The chaos of Hapsburg rule was replaced by the relative efficiency of the French Bour-

The gardens and palace of La Granja

bons. Inevitably, tradition-minded Spaniards resented and resisted the changes. But impoverished and reduced in size, Spain was nonetheless a more viable nation than it had been in the past.

One symbol of the increasing Europeanization of Spain was the summer palace of La Granja built by Philip in San Ildefonso, on the north side of the Guadarramas. It was a throwback to Versailles, and Philip spent much of his time there. La Granja is now a museum, except on July 18, the anniversary of the Spanish Civil War, when Franco somewhat incongruously receives foreign ambassadors there. This, evidently, is one of the links with the Bourbon tradition that the Caudillo likes to maintain.

The second Bourbon king, Ferdinand VI, was crowned in 1747, a year after Francisco de Goya y Lucientes was born at Fuendetodos in Aragon. Ferdinand VI ruled only thirteen years, but during his reign his prime minister, the Marquis of Ensenada, began to build a system of roads and canals throughout Spain, to establish industries, and to reform the corrupt treasury. Ferdinand signed a concordat with the Vatican in 1754 that considerably improved Spain's confused relationship with the Holy See.

Charles III, the third Bourbon, merits special attention. A half-brother of Ferdinand VI, he was the most remarkable Spanish king in the eighteenth century. He called himself an "enlightened prince," though many called him an "enlightened despot." In the context of his time, he was probably both. He persuaded Louis XV of France to cede Minorca, Louisiana, and Florida to Spain. He reorganized operations in the overseas colonies, making South America once more profitable to the crown. He did away with much of the religious persecution, and in the name of religious freedom he ordered the arrest and the deportation of the nearly five thousand Jesuits from Spain in 1767. Six years later, Pope Clement XIV bowed to pressure from Charles and abolished the Society of Jesus everywhere in Christendom. Seemingly to fill the Jesuit vacuum, Charles III authorized the functioning of Freemasonry. An admirer of Voltaire and the French Encyclopedists, Charles III came as close to being a royal liberal as any monarch in his century. With the winds of revolution blowing in France, Charles aligned himself with modern ideas while Louis XVI, his royal relative, helplessly awaited the end of the monarchy.

In a strange way the reign of Charles III anticipated the great conflicts between liberalism and orthodoxy that were to sweep Spain in the nineteenth and twentieth centuries. Needless to say, Charles III is not a hero in the eyes of the Franco regime, which traces its ideological lineage to the Catholic Kings.

Charles IV, who inherited the Spanish throne in 1788, had none of his father's liberalism. Actually, he was only a figurehead. While he dedicated himself to his hobbies of hunting, clockmaking, and eating, the real rulers were his wife, María Luisa of Parma, and her lover, Manuel de Godoy. Godoy was a twenty-five-year-old Estremaduran officer whom María Luisa elevated to the post of prime minister and named, in succession, the Duke of Alcudia, Commander of the Order of Santiago, Grandee of Spain, and Knight of the Golden Fleece. The fatuous, weak-minded king and his leering, corrupt courtiers have been immortalized in Goya's portraits.

After Louis XVI was executed in 1793, the French Convention offered peace to Spain. Instead, the conservative Catholics and officers pushed Charles into war. The king named Godoy "Prince of Peace" to head an expedition against revolutionary France. After two years of inconclusive combat the two countries made peace and Spain sought an alliance with France. When Napoleon became emperor in 1804, he visited Madrid to seal the new partnership. As usual, this latest foreign alliance was to bring disaster to Spain. In 1805 the French-Spanish navy was destroyed by Nelson at Trafalgar. Three years later, Napoleon invaded Spain on the pretext that he was simply en route to battle the British in Portugal. On May 2, 1808, Marshal Murat occupied Madrid. Once again the Spaniards had learned at their cost not to let foreigners help them.

A feud between Charles IV and his son Ferdinand VII initially played into Napoleon's hands. After Charles had abdicated, Napoleon summoned him and Ferdinand, then theoretically the king of Spain, to Bayonne. He informed them that France was assuming the Spanish throne and that their new king would be Joseph Bonaparte, the emperor's brother, who had been brought hastily from Naples. Joseph meant well, but the Spaniards would not have him. The foreigner's presence now served to unite the nation. A rebellion broke out in Madrid, and uprisings spread like wildfire throughout Spain. The Spaniards fought the French not only with regular forces but with their guerrillas. Napoleon countered with brutal repression. The Spaniards fought on. They beat the imperial army at Bailén, but lost Saragossa after a heroic siege. In the end, British forces under the Duke of Wellington helped the Spaniards to expel the French. After the peace of 1813 Ferdinand VII was restored to the Spanish throne. Spain had cost Napoleon half a million men, and as he was to observe later at St. Helena, it was his "undoing." But the conflict also meant near ruin for Spain and the beginning of more than a century of internal strife.

Goya in his canvases and etchings was the great chronicler of the five-year war of liberation that the Spaniards fought against the French. These vivid pictures are preserved at the Prado Museum in Madrid, as if to remind succeeding generations of the meaning of Spanish wars. Goya's warnings were not heeded.

Spanish soldiers on parade

3 The Century of Drama

The nineteenth century belongs more to Spain's present than to her past. The events of the twentieth century—the Primo de Rivera dictatorship, the fall of the monarchy, the Second Republic, the 1936–39 Civil War, and finally, the three decades of the Franco regime—have their psychological and political roots in the awesome internal conflicts and the successive civil wars of the 1800's. The fundamental dispute between liberalism and absolutism not only in the relatively narrow terms of political systems but in the broad sense of the attitude of Spaniards toward themselves and their government erupted in 1812 at the Cádiz Cortes while Napoleon still occupied much of Spain. The dispute remains unresolved in 1971 as Spaniards uncertainly look toward the post-Franco succession. Unresolved, too, is the basic question of whether Spaniards may be safely allowed to rule themselves, without the protective presence of an absolutist regime.

When I first went to live in Spain in 1965, I was astonished to hear politicians discuss the present and the future of the country in terms of nineteenth-century concepts and compare contemporary figures with the men who were in the center of the stage one hundred or one hundred and fifty years ago. My first reaction was that Spain somehow still lived in the nineteenth century, perhaps because of the trauma of the Spanish Civil War. On closer and hopefully more understanding acquaintance with the country, I realized that I was witnessing a continuing drama of such magnitude that a century of history simply did not matter. The terrible inner division of the Spanish nation affected—and continues to affect—everything from the nature of the political regime today and tomorrow to morals and religion. This is why, for example, when a Spanish politician in the 1970's speaks of "military politicians," he may mean General Prim and General O'Donnell during the nineteenth century or General Primo de Rivera and General Franco during the twentieth century. This is also why Franco evidently did not think it an anachronism in 1969 to name Prince Juan Carlos de Borbón as future king and his successor as chief of state. Hadn't the generals of 1874 restored the monarchy after the First Republic?

Since the Cádiz Cortes of 1812 there have been two Spains living side by side, always at war with each other. In 1836, when the nation lay prostrate after that century's first civil war that had ended in the previous decade, the Spanish writer Mariano José de Larra commented: "Here lies half of Spain; it died killed by the other half." A hundred years later, when the nation was torn by another civil war, Larra's comment was again applicable. Franco's long rule may have healed the wounds of this century's civil war, but Spaniards, not really trusting themselves, have not forgotten that it is a part of the Spanish genius to allow "half of Spain" to be "killed by the other half."

The Cádiz Cortes was an outgrowth of the patriotic junta organized to lead the resistance against Napoleon. Actually, the Cortes had fled from Madrid to that corner of Andalusia to keep a Spanish government alive. Its leaders included some of Spain's most enlightened men, and the Cortes eventually drafted a constitution that was one of the most progressive in Europe. The constitution provided guarantees for civil liberties and private property, indirect universal suffrage, freedom of the press, and the irremovability of judges. As a compromise, it recognized hereditary monarchy and proclaimed

The Andalusian city of Cádiz

GONGORA

that Spain's religion "will always be the Catholic, apostolic, and Roman faith." It abolished the Inquisition but banned the practice of other religions. The Cádiz Liberals were sufficiently realistic to know that no government in Spain could be without a deep and exclusive accent on Catholicism.

The flexibility of the Liberals was not enough to make their ideas acceptable. In bringing Ferdinand VII back from exile in France and restoring him to power after the French armies were expelled from Spain, the Cortes's Liberals brought disaster to their cause. Ferdinand VII is described by Spanish historians as a "knave" and the worst king in history. His old-fashioned, fiercely absolutist ideas were reinforced by the crowds that greeted him with shouts of "Down with the Cortes . . . Long live our absolute king!" In short order Ferdinand restored the Inquisition and invited back the Jesuits whom his grandfather had expelled forty-seven years earlier. By 1814 he had suppressed the Cádiz constitution, arrested the Liberal leaders, and banned Freemasonry. The next six years seemed like a return not only to Philip II and the spirit of the autos-da-fé (though none, of course, were held) but also to the Catholic Kings of the fifteenth century. Ferdinand, who indulged in every possible form of intrigue, corruption, and immorality, liked to be called Ferdinand the Desired. His court wallowed in luxury. The rococo elegance of the early Bourbon period was succeeded by the sumptuous neoclassicism of the restoration. It has been said of Ferdinand that during his exile in France "he forgot nothing; he learned nothing." Judging by the way he ran Spain, the verdict is accurate.

In 1820 the pendulum swung the other way. General Rafael del Riego, a Liberal leader, assembled an army at Cádiz, issued a pronunciamento, and marched on Madrid. Riego's pronunciamento marked the beginning of a new style in Spanish politics: when a powerful general disliked the *status quo,* he would issue a statement or manifesto declaring his views on the state of affairs in the kingdom. Then he would launch a rebellion or a *coup d'état.* Riego entered Madrid as his troops sang the Hymn of Riego, the Spanish Liberals' equivalent of the Marseillaise, which was destined to become the national anthem during the republic of 1931–36. The Riego Hymn proclaimed that "If the priests and friars only knew what a beating we are going to give them, they would join in a chorus, shouting: Liberty, Liberty, Liberty!" The anticlericalism of the Liberals was a potent strain in the Spanish make-up, and it was to dominate much of Spain's subsequent history. Riego's troops also sang: "We don't want a whore for a queen and a cuckold for a king." Given the proclivities for sexual licentiousness of Queen María Cristina, a Bourbon, and Ferdinand's blithe disregard of her behavior, the troops were not wrong about their monarchs. Ferdinand was also a coward, for as soon as Riego captured the capital, he agreed to uphold the 1812 constitution and to do away with the Inquisition. He named Liberals as his ministers, withdrew from active political leadership, and pretended to accept the new situation. Meanwhile, he busily plotted against the Liberal government.

This was the start of the vicious circle of Spanish civil wars. Spain was now divided into two camps. The royal supporters, including priests and monks, regarded themselves as "apostolic" warriors and dismissed the Liberals as "atheists." This, of course, was also the political-religious scenario for Franco's civil war more than a century later, for politics and religion are inseparable in Spain. The "apostolic" leaders formed a junta at Seo de Urgel in northern Catalonia and won the backing of the Basques and the Navarrese. By 1823 the nation's first major civil war, accompanied by the usual Spanish atrocities, was in full swing. The following year 100,000 French troops were ordered to Spain by Louis XVIII and the Holy Alliance to save the Spanish throne for Ferdinand. Thousands of Spaniards, including the fighting priests who had led the nation against Napoleon only fifteen years earlier, received the invaders with open arms. Spanish allegiances are fickle indeed. The Liberal government fled back to Cádiz, taking Ferdinand along as a hostage. But the French smashed the constitutionalists and restored the king to power. Predictably, Ferdinand turned to repression, instituting what was known as the White Terror, in which thousands died. Riego was captured and hanged and his body was dismembered. The Inquisition was reimposed, and the Freemasons, many of them army officers, were considered "enemies of the throne and the altar" and put to death. Goya, whose sympathies were with the Liberals as his artistic work clearly shows, escaped persecution by fleeing to France in 1824 at the age of seventy-eight. The pattern of Spanish artists and intellectuals opposing absolutism and going into voluntary exile was established early. Nothing has really changed in Spain in the past hundred and fifty years.

The imposition of an absolutist state did not mean, however, that peace had returned to Spain for long. Although Ferdinand used the last decade of his chaotic reign for positive accomplishments, turning the Prado into a museum, creating the Conservatory of Music, and sponsoring legislation to regulate commerce—his death in 1833 split his rightist supporters and led to still another civil war, known as the First Carlist War. One faction supported Ferdinand's brother, Don Carlos of Naples, for the succession, while the other backed the regency of Ferdinand's widow, Queen María Cristina, and the eventual succession of her daughter, Isabella. Ferdinand had made this legally possible by repealing the ancient Salic law under which the succession could not pass from mother to daughter. The Carlist War lasted seven bloody years and, as usual, had religious overtones. The Carlists thought themselves more "apostolic" than María Cristina's allies. The queen also performed a neat political switch when she turned to the Liberals for support. Though Don Carlos nearly captured Madrid, he lost the war. But the Carlist cause is still so alive, particularly in Navarra, that in 1969 Franco had to exile the Carlist princes to keep them from interfering with his plan to name Prince Juan Carlos, a member of the Alfonsist branch of the Bourbons, as Spain's future king.

Having defeated the Carlists, María Cristina and General Espartero, who had led her backers to victory, aligned themselves with the "Progressivists" among the now divided Liberals. The Progressives preached anticlericalism while the Moderates favored certain privileges for the church. But the Spaniards' deep-seated anticlericalism prevailed. Eighty priests and monks were massacred in Madrid. Monasteries throughout the country were burned or turned into army barracks. The Jesuits were again expelled and diplomatic relations with the Vatican were broken off. In 1840 María Cristina finally abdicated and Espartero became regent. He turned out to be a ferocious dictator who opposed the church as well as the incipient Republicans. Again blood flowed across Spain.

Espartero was overthrown after three years in power, and the thirteen-year-old Isabella II was proclaimed queen. In 1851 Spain signed a concordat with the Vatican that is still in effect today, and confiscated property was returned to the church. Isabella's reign, which lasted until 1868, was a succession of coups and military pronunciamentos. It also was a period of extraordinary debauchery. Isabella's husband, Francisco de Asís, was effeminate, to put it mildly, and the queen developed a love life of her own that was said to resemble that of Russia's Catherine the Great. Her court naturally followed the pattern of promiscuity. José Zorilla, a famous poet and playwright, accurately reflected the mood of mid-nineteenth century Spain in his *Don Juan Tenorio,* a play that overshadowed Tirso de Molina's *Deceiver of Seville* as a study in adventurous love-making.

Finally, in 1868, General Juan Prim (the Marqués de los Castillejos and a hero of the Moroccan and Mexican wars) issued a pronunciamento forcing Isabella to abdicate and flee. By then she had become an absolutist tyrant. Prim and his fellow military politicians seemed to favor a republican solution, and a revolutionary junta emerged in Madrid. But the Liberals lacked the courage to complete the change in Spain's political system. Instead, in 1870 Prim invited Amadeo, the Italian Duke of Aosta, to become king. Amadeo, unquestionably Spain's most forgotten monarch, ruled for three years that were most conspicuously marked by fratricidal struggles among the Liberals. Guerrilla warfare broke out between the workers and peasants and the army, as the newly class-conscious proletariat began clamoring for its rights. A series of violent events led the generals to plot a coup, but Amadeo anticipated them by abdicating. The Cortes then proclaimed the First Republic.

The short-lived Republic of 1873–74 had four presidents, the last of whom was Emilio Castelar, a history professor and noted orator. But the Republic could not cope with the urgent problems of the day: a new Carlist war, dissensions within the military, opposition in the Cortes, and an economic crisis. Consequently, the Cortes abolished the Republic after less than a year, and General Manuel Paría y Albuquerque, the captain general of Madrid, issued a pronunciamento and assumed power. Alfonso de Borbón, son of Isabella II and a sixteen-year-old cadet at Sandhurst, was called back to be crowned Alfonso XII.

The new king inherited a nation exhausted beyond words. His eleven-year rule provided much of the peace that Spain desperately

167

needed. A liberal constitution was promulgated in 1876, and an armistice of sorts prevailed among the politicians. The king died of tuberculosis in 1885 at the age of twenty-eight, just seven years before Francisco Franco Bahamonde, the future Caudillo of Spain, was born in the Galician port of El Ferrol.

Alfonso was succeeded by his wife, María Cristina of Hapsburg and Lorraine, who acted as regent during the infancy of her son, who was born a few months after Alfonso's death. It fell to María Cristina to preside over the virtual liquidation of the Spanish empire that had been founded by the Catholic Kings four centuries earlier.

Spain's South American colonies had already become sovereign republics. In 1895 Cuba declared her independence, and three years later the Spanish-American War erupted. In short order the American navy defeated Spanish squadrons off Cuba and the Philippines. The Treaty of Paris in 1898 gave the United States Puerto Rico, the Philippines, and Guam. Cuba was given nominal independence under *de facto* American tutelage.

Spain's fortunes had never sunk lower. Yet from the ashes of military defeat and political chaos, there emerged the extraordinary Generation of 1898, which to this day exercises a powerful influence on Spanish thought. This "generation" was not a cohesive group but a collection of individuals who surged forward simultaneously, as if to demonstrate to the world the degree of Spain's vitality. Francisco Giner de los Ríos, often called "the first modern Spaniard," was one of its great luminaries. In 1876 he founded the *Institución Libre de Enseñanza* (Free Institution of Learning), Spain's first free university. He did as much or more for Spanish education as John Dewey did for American education. He established the concept that young people should learn in an environment of freedom—something that the venerable state- or church-supported universities had never recognized. Other noted members of this Generation were Dr. Santiago Ramón y Cajal, who was to win a Nobel Prize in physiology; the Basque philosopher Miguel de Unamuno; Joaquín Costa, the prophet of Spain's "Europeanization"; the Nobel Prize-winning poet Juan Ramón Jiménez; Antonio Machado, another great poet; the novelists Pío Baroja and Benito Pérez Galdós; the philosopher José Ortega y Gasset; the political philosopher Ramiro de Maeztu; the essayist Angel Ganivet; and

Galician housewives stop for a gossip.

the composers Manuel de Falla, Enrique Granados, and Isaac Albéniz.

What all these men had in common—and this is a very incomplete list—was the desire to lift Spain from the moral debasement of past centuries and bring it into the modern world. The impact of the Generation of 1898 on contemporary Spanish politics, art, and culture continues to be enormous. It is toward Unamuno, Ortega y Gasset, and Maeztu that today's Spaniards turn for inspiration as they seek to chart their country's future.

The throne room of the Royal Palace in Madrid

Spain's last king, Alfonso XIII, ascended the throne in 1902. His twenty-nine-year reign spanned the First World War, Spain's costly and interminable Moroccan wars, a long military dictatorship imposed on the country in his name, the Great Depression, and the unceasing internal turmoil that brought on the Second Republic and, ultimately, the Spanish Civil War. Alfonso was an amiable and rather ineffectual king, but he must be remembered as the man who in a sense made Francisco Franco by singling

him out for favor and rapid promotion.

Alfonso was stubbornly determined to hold on to Spanish territories in Africa, where France was making increasing inroads. But the Moroccans defeated his army in 1909. Franco was then only seventeen and a third-year cadet at the Toledo military academy, but, it is said, this defeat made a profound impression on him. It may have marked the beginning of his overwhelming obsession with Spain's greatness.

The African fiasco led to serious troubles at home. Calling up the Catalan reserves to reinforce the army resulted in an explosion of Catalan separatism. Barcelona and the other industrial centers had become highly organized and politicized by Anarchists, Syndicalists, and Socialists, and Alfonso's move was met by a general strike, rioting, and bloodshed. In one of those ghastly errors that Spanish governments are prone to make, the king sanctioned the execution of Francisco Ferrer, a Catalan Anarchist who had been accused of directing the Barcelona resistance to the draft. The Ferrer affair led to the fall of the royal cabinet and the naming of a Liberal government. In 1912, however, the Liberal prime minister Canalejas was assassinated by an Anarchist. This act ended all hopes that Spain under Alfonso XIII might develop into a viable constitutional monarchy. Canalejas was the last outstanding Spanish politician before the advent of the Second Republic in 1931.

Spain weathered World War I as a neutral. Madrid was an espionage center for both sides, and Spaniards made huge profits from the war. Internally, there were only crises, each worse than the one before. In 1917 army troops killed hundreds of barricaded workers who demanded a democratic republic or, at least, a democratic kingdom. Rightists were in power, and they chose to drown this movement in blood. The army, it was said, "saved the country from anarchism." Even in the twentieth century the "two Spains" were clearly ready to destroy each other.

Franco personally participated in the quelling of the rebellion in Asturias, the tough coal-mining region of northern Spain. As a twenty-three-year-old major (the youngest in the Spanish army) he commanded a machine-gun company that killed seventy miners before the uprising in Oviedo was put down. Franco had spent the previous five years as a combat officer in Morocco, where he was seriously wounded in 1915. During the Asturias rebellion he

Not a Moroccan mosque, but the Alhambra in Granada

discovered at first hand the explosive character of Spanish politics. As his biographer Brian Crozier has observed, "1917 was a turning point in Franco's life. Two disconnected strands in his professional training came together in his conduct of operations. He had learned the art of war and military leadership and lately he had been studying the civil arts of government. Now, faced with revolutionary violence and disobedience, he became the instrument of order and authority in a civil conflict. . . . Franco took a fundamental decision at the time of the Oviedo crisis: no matter what happened, and wherever it lay within his power, he would never permit revolutionary disorder in Spain. Within a few weeks, the Bolshevik Revolution in Russia and the widespread violence that came in its train, confirmed him in his view and created what was to be a lifelong hatred of Communism." Franco had decided once and for all to which of the two Spains he belonged.

In 1921 Spain's African army was destroyed by Moorish tribesmen and between fifteen and twenty thousand Spaniards were killed. Subsequently, the Spanish Foreign Legion under Franco's leadership reconquered most of the territory taken by the Moors, but revulsion against the Moroccan war, the generals, and the politicians spread across Spain. Strikes, uprisings, and the collapse of cabinets became a way of life. Finally, in 1923, General Miguel Primo de Rivera, the captain general of Catalonia, issued a pronunciamento and established a dictatorship, retaining King Alfonso XIII as a figurehead. It was a replay of the nineteenth-century pronunciamentos inasmuch as, in the words of Salvador de Madariaga, "the ambition of every Spanish general is to save his country by becoming her ruler." But it was also a portent of things to come: military politicians were back in vogue. In tones that were to sound familiar a decade later, Primo de Rivera promised to free the nation from "the professional politicians, the men who for one reason or another are responsible for the period of misfortune and corruption which began in 1898 and threatens to bring Spain to a tragic and dishonorable end." Spanish rhetoric never changes.

Primo de Rivera's dictatorship lasted for seven years. It was reasonably efficient—the Moroccan war was ended victoriously and the country's economy began to improve—but Spain paid the price of political liberty. The 1876 constitution was abolished, severe press censorship was established, and the Catholic Church was returned to full favor. The famous philosopher Unamuno was expelled from the University of Salamanca, arrested, and exiled to the Canary Islands for his outspoken opposition to the regime. Curiously, the dictator enjoyed considerable popular support, at least in the beginning. Spaniards are unpredictable, and the same workers who fought on the barricades for a democratic republic in 1917 now pliantly accepted the dictatorship. In the end, Primo de Rivera fell when the army turned against him and students rioted in the streets of Madrid.

During this period Franco's career continued to advance. When the king promoted him to brigadier general at thirty-three, he became the youngest general in Europe. A year later, in 1927, Franco was named commandant of the new military academy at Saragossa. He was Alfonso's favorite general, but he made no move to defend the king when the monarchy fell on April 14, 1931, and the Second Republic was established. Franco obviously did not favor the Republic, but he accepted it because the transition was orderly. Alfonso XIII left the country voluntarily after the Monarchists appeared to have lost the municipal elections held early in April. In a speech to his cadets General Franco said that with the proclamation of the Republic "the duty of all at this moment is to cooperate with discipline and solid virtues so that peace may reign and the nation be guided into normal judicial channels." Although it may appear paradoxical in retrospect, Franco's initial support for the Republic was a logical consequence of his preoccupation with peace and order. Only when he concluded that "discipline and solid virtues" were threatened did Franco take matters into his own hands—at the last moment.

The pediment surmounting the building in Madrid where the Cortes meets

4 Enter the Republic

The Second Republic, which lasted five years, three months, and three days, was a tissue of awesome errors, contradictions, inconsistencies, betrayals, and misunderstandings that inexorably led to the Civil War. As so many other institutions in Spain have done, the Republic willfully destroyed itself even before the Nationalists, let alone Franco, began seriously plotting against it. The country was rapidy torn asunder by the rivalries between the political parties that formed the loose Republican coalition, as well as by the personal rivalries of their leaders. The Socialist party, with one million members at the beginning of the Republic, split between the moderates of Indalecio Prieto and the radicals of Francisco Largo Caballero. A second schism divided the Madrid Socialists from the Barcelona Socialists. The Anarchists, also with a million members, defied the Socialists. Right-wing and Centrist Republicans, who should have formed the solid core of the Republican government, refused to collaborate. Not only was the Cortes in a state of permanent chaos, preventing rational lawmaking, but the same political struggles were presently taken into the streets, and there were incessant uprisings, strikes, riots, and killings. Finally, only the extremes survived: the Republican radicals opposed the anti-Republican radicals made up of extreme rightist generals, orthodox Catholics, monarchists, and the fascist Falangists. Each Spain screamed for the blood of the other, and finally, blood was what they both got.

A historian as sympathetic to the Republic as Salvador de Madariaga (he was its ambassador to the United States and France and, briefly, its minister of education) has concluded that the Republican government failed "first and foremost because of the unyielding and absolute nature of the Spanish character." He wrote that this character "is the psychological root cause of all Spanish troubles. . . . It determines all that happens in Spain, and explains the periodical failures of parliamentary government and the periodical rises of dictators; as well as the separatist movements, whose leaders, be it Basques or Catalans, are blissfully unaware of the fact that the less tractable they are the more Spanish they reveal themselves to be."

The fall of the monarchy was not the result of a powerful radical movement. It came about because of a typically Spanish misunderstanding. In the municipal elections of April, 1931, the Monarchists won 41,224 councilors' seats, compared with 39,248 seats for the pro-Republicans. At best it was a standoff, if not a minor Monarchist victory. But because they had failed to score an overwhelming triumph, the Monarchists considered themselves badly beaten. General José Sanjurjo, chief of the Guardia Civil, told the king that he could no longer guarantee the loyalty of his troops, and the monarchy folded without a sigh and without a drop of blood being spilled. It was a political comedy of the kind that Cervantes or Calderón de la Barca might have conceived.

The prime minister of the provisional government, Alcalá Zamora, and the interior minister, Antonio Maura, were leaders of a new party of Republican Roman Catholics. Alcalá Zamora was a former monarchist and a minister of the crown. Manuel Azaña, the war minister, headed the middle-class Republican Action party. The Radical party of Alejandro Lerroux, a Catalonian demagogue, formed the right wing of republicanism. The Socialist factions led by both Indalecia Prieto and Largo Caballero had limited influence in the first government because of their poor showing during the election.

The new Republican regime, therefore, had all the characteristics of a European progressive bourgeois undertaking. It had the support of the Spanish middle class and of the great intellectuals of the Generation of 1898—Unamuno, Ortega y Gasset, and Gregorio Marañón. Most of these men were well-meaning idealists anxious to modernize Spain through evolution.

But the new enterprise immediately began falling apart. Alcalá Zamora could not get along with Azaña, and Azaña could not get along with Lerroux. Had they been able to work together, wrote Salvador de Madariaga, Spain might have been spared the Civil War altogether. The constitution of December 9, 1931, was a prime example of errors stemming from the pressures within the Spanish body politic. It succeeded in antagonizing almost everybody. It proclaimed the separation of church and state, thus alienating millions of Spaniards who otherwise might have supported the Republic. The Jesuit Order was dissolved (for the fifth time), and the government stopped paying priests their salaries. Divorce was legalized. Official anticlericalism reinforced the ever-present popular anticlericalism to the extent that the police watched passively

179

as a crowd set fire to Madrid's San Francisco de Borja church. Other churches, monasteries, and convents were burned throughout the country, and priests, monks, and nuns were beaten or sometimes killed. To have unleashed anticlericalism in a nation where religion has always played such a crucial and mystical role was a fault from which the Republic never recovered. It touched a raw nerve and caused Spanish society to split along religious as well as political lines.

Alcalá Zamora, the prime minister, quit over the issue of anticlericalism and was replaced by Azaña. But Azaña had already antagonized the army by drastically reducing its overblown bureaucracy. He was undoubtedly right to do so, since there were 800 generals for 200,000 troops—a general for every 250 soldiers. He even kept the retired officers on full salary. But the loss of prestige—more important to Spaniards than a loss of income—created a continent of potential plotters. Franco himself was a victim of Azaña's demilitarization: his military academy at Saragossa was closed down, and he was in effect removed from a position of influence by being transferred to the command of a brigade in La Coruña in his native Galicia, as far as possible from Madrid. But when General Sanjurjo issued a pronunciamento in Seville in August, 1932, Franco turned down an invitation to join the conspiracy. Either he still believed in discipline, or he was too realistic to become involved in what he judged to be a premature move doomed to fail. Sanjurjo's revolt was quickly put down, although this was not the last that Spain would hear of him.

The government's other problems included an agrarian reform program that was foundering because the regime had neither the experience nor the money to make it work. The backlash of the worldwide depression was painfully felt in Spain as foreign capital fled the country. There were also familiar separatist troubles. When the Republic was first proclaimed in Madrid, the Catalonians proclaimed a Catalonian Republic in Barcelona. An agreement was later worked out by which Madrid granted Catalonia a considerable degree of autonomy, but not independence, under a commonwealth status known as the *Generalitat*. The Basque provinces also received a measure of home rule.

Elections in December, 1933, brought the right wing of the Republicans into power. Alejandro Lerroux, the rightist head of the Radical party, became prime minister. The ensuing two years of rightist rule became known as the *Bienio Negro,* the Black Biennium, because of the degree to which leftist elements were repressed. But to an important extent, the Socialists, Anarchists, and Communists brought the repression upon themselves through the acts of violence that they had directed at each other and at the regime. It was at this point that Franco became a force to reckon with. Azaña had sent him from La Coruña to Palma, Majorca, as military commander of the Balearic Islands. With the accession of the Lerroux government he was brought to Madrid, promoted to general of division (major general), and named special adviser to the war minister, Diego Hidalgo. At about this time, Franco paid a visit to Berlin, where Hitler was already in power.

In October, 1934, leftist revolts erupted throughout Spain. In Aragon "Libertarian Communists" seized farmlands; Andalusia seethed with rebellion; thousands of Anarchists were being jailed for provoking disorders; blood ran in the streets of Barcelona. Largo Caballero, the leftist Socialist, accepted the Communists in his *Alianza Obrera* (Workers' Alliance).

For all practical purposes, Franco was the Republic's military chief, and from the War Ministry in Madrid, he directed the suppression of the leftist revolts. In Asturias close to thirty thousand miners had risen against the government. Eight thousand of them, armed with dynamite, had taken Oviedo, the provincial capital. Franco considered the situation so serious that he ordered Moorish regiments from Africa brought to Asturias aboard ships. Under the command of General Juan de Yagüe Blanco, a tough Foreign Legion officer, the Moors crushed the revolt with incredible cruelty. Then Yagüe let his Moors pillage and rape at will. Thousands of Asturians were killed in battle or executed. Franco, who was personally involved in putting down another Asturian rebellion seventeen years earlier, is not known to have held Yagüe in check.

The rightist government quickly rewarded Franco for his role in defending the Republic. Early in 1935 he was named commander-in-chief of Morocco, where he had fought the Moors as a young officer. In May José María Gil Robles, the new war minister and leader of the CEDA (Spanish Confederation of the Autonomous Right), appointed the forty-two-year-old Franco chief of the army's central general staff.

181

Meanwhile, the Spanish Falange was emerging as an antirepublican force. Founded in 1933 by José Antonio Primo de Rivera, the son of the old dictator and a spellbinding orator, the Falange was modeled on fascism but had elements of Spanish mysticism, orthodox Catholicism, equalitarian populism, and hunger for the revival of Spain's imperial greatness. José Antonio, as he was and still is commonly known, merged the Falange, initially formed by middle-class youths and some intellectuals, with the JONS, a militant and likewise fascist-oriented labor organization in the north of Spain. Now, blue-shirted Falange and JONS toughs fought in the streets against both the leftists and the regime's police. José Antonio wrote Franco telling him a civil war was "inevitable" and offering him the Falange's services. Franco, whose feelings about the Falange have always been ambiguous, advised him in vague terms to remain ready to defend the motherland. Then as later, Franco was not about to turn himself into the military chieftain of a political movement he never quite trusted. When the time came, *he* would use the Falange.

At the elections of February, 1936, the pendulum swung back to the left. The Popular Front won, the rightists came in second, and the Center third. Alcalá Zamora, for the two previous years the president of the Republic, named Azaña prime minister. Azaña, in the context of the time, was a moderate, although his party belonged to the Popular Front. It was too late, however, for moderates or moderation. Azaña tried desperately to pacify the nation by freeing thousands of political prisoners. Then he and Prieto, the Socialist moderate, sought to achieve a semblance of national equilibrium by building up a political Center. This, too, failed. A civil war was now almost inevitable: it was only a question of which side would set it off.

Everybody in Madrid suspected that two conspiracies were simultaneously in progress: one by the extreme left headed by Largo Caballero that was aimed at establishing a revolutionary state in Spain; the other by the army, the extreme right, and the fascists that was aimed at doing away with the Republic. Azaña took precautions against a rightist coup by shifting Franco from his post as chief of staff to the faraway Canaries and by having José Antonio arrested in Alicante. But the prime minister was powerless to control the left. Besides, there was no proof that Largo Caballero actually was preparing a coup. The left was visibly plunging Spain into a chaotic situation that was compounded by the bloody rivalries within its own camp. Azaña knew that this would ultimately bring a violent reaction from the military and their allies. In May he resigned the premiership to replace the fatigued Alcalá Zamora as president. Santiago Casares Quiroga, a former interior minister, became prime minister.

But salvation was no longer possible. Chaos, terrorism, and arson swept the Peninsula. In an often-quoted speech he made in the Cortes in mid-June, Gil Robles reported that since February 160 churches had been totally destroyed and 251 set afire or attacked; 269 Spaniards had been murdered and 1,287 injured; 69 headquarters of political parties had been smashed; and 341 general or partial strikes had taken place.

The final pretext was provided by the murder on July 12 of a Madrid police lieutenant by three Falangists. At dawn the next day the police retaliated by assassinating the Monarchist leader José Calvo Sotelo. This triggered a military rebellion. The Spanish Civil War exploded five days later.

The Valle de los Caidos, a grandiose basilica tunneled through a mountain to celebrate those who fell in the Spanish Civil War

5 The Civil War

Why was the Spanish Civil War fought? Why did a nation of twenty-five million people engage in a fratricidal conflict that cost it more than half a million lives (Spaniards nowadays tend to round out the toll and speak casually though inaccurately of "one million dead"), close to a million wounded and sick, and untold destruction? How could so much hatred have arisen between the "two Spains" that Spaniards not only happily died in battle but indulged in mass executions and other acts of savagery unbelievable in the twentieth century?

Politics, even politics as practiced in Spain, do not provide the answer. The conspiracy by a group of generals determined to restore order, and the resistance of the followers of a duly constituted government, do not tell the whole story either. In retrospect, what appears to have hit Spain with the force of a cyclone was an unleashing of passions far transcending reasons of state. Spanish mysticism and romanticism and unreasoning hatred kept the fires of war burning for nearly three years. The war stopped in 1939 not because either side had concluded that enough blood had been spilled but because the losers, the Republicans, were simply too exhausted to go on fighting. Had they commanded more resources the war would have gone on and on.

When I came to live in Spain in 1965, a thoughtful Spanish historian remarked to me that the Civil War was an overwhelmingly negative phenomenon. Though he admitted that this was somewhat of an oversimplification, he insisted that in broad terms each side had fought *against* an idea rather than *for* an idea. The Nationalists went to war *against* what they considered the Communist atheistic peril. They regarded all Loyalists as Reds and called their campaign against them a "holy crusade" against antichrist. The Spanish church quickly gave its blessing to this crusade, and the Nationalists fought under the sign of the cross for the restoration of Spain's "Catholic unity"—a mystical regression to the days when the Catholic Kings reconquered the country from the infidel Moor. The Loyalists, on the other hand, battled *against* "fascism," although despite the direct assistance given them by Hitler's air force and Mussolini's expeditionary forces, many Nationalists were not really fascists. The Loyalists claimed that they fought for democracy, although the Republic they were defending had actually long ceased to be a democracy and Soviet-supported Communists were making deep inroads into the Loyalist camp. To be sure, the Spanish Civil War rapidly became part of the wider struggle between ideologies that erupted as the Second World War only five months after the Nationalist victory. In the end, the Peninsular conflict involved much of the outside world, militarily as well as emotionally. Once more, the world could not leave Spain alone.

At first, many true Spanish democrats supported the Nationalist cause in the hope that the Civil War would end the homicidal chaos of the last days of the Republic. It is also important to bear in mind that many of Franco's Civil War supporters and comrades in arms —from the royal pretender Don Juan to scores of postwar cabinet ministers, diplomats, and politicians—are today in fierce opposition against his rule.

The Civil War, then, was a clash of mystiques rather than political ideologies. The battle cry of the *requetés,* the Navarrese militiamen steeped in medieval Catholicism, was "Long Live Death!" Nationalist priests, crosses around their necks, led battalions into battle in the name of Christ. Thousands of anticlerical Loyalists, equating the church with fascism, tortured and killed priests, monks, and nuns and burned churches, monasteries, and convents. Both sides fought to the last, dying rather than surrendering, in a fantastic display of courage and, often, heroism. For months the Nationalists held out in the besieged Alcázar in Toledo. Their commander, Colonel José Moscardó, preferred to see his son executed by the Loyalists rather than capitulate and save the boy's life. Madrid, surrounded by the Nationalists for two years except for a narrow corridor to Valencia, did not surrender to Franco until 1939. The enemy was so close to the capital that Loyalist soldiers often took city streetcars to reach the battle lines, and Loyalist guerrillas harassed the Nationalists from their hide-outs in the forests of the Guadarramas barely an hour's drive from Madrid.

A measure of the mysticism inherent in the Spanish Civil War may be gleaned from the fact that many modern historians refer to the period as the Age of José Antonio and García Lorca. The two young men, executed at the outset of the war, became the romantic symbols of the conflict. José Antonio, the founder of the Falange and a political romantic of a kind that only Spain could have produced, was imprisoned and shot by the Republicans in

187

The past is ever present in Spain.

Alicante in November, 1936. Federico García Lorca, the great romantic poet, was killed by the Nationalists near Granada in August, 1936. His body, buried in a common grave, was never found. After the war José Antonio's body was moved to the Escorial Monastery.

Inevitably, the Civil War attracted romantics and idealists from the outside world. Young foreigners flocked to Spain to form the International Brigades, which, appropriately enough, had their headquarters at Albacete in Don Quixote's home territory of La Mancha. André Malraux was a pilot for the Loyalists; Ernest Hemingway, who came as a war correspondent, turned into a fiery advocate of the Loyalist cause. In *For Whom the Bell Tolls* he caught the essence of the Spanish spirit and character as no other foreign writer has done since.

One day in 1966 I drove toward Segovia from the Navacerrada Pass in the Guadarramas looking for the country that Hemingway described. The dense forests where the *guerrilleros* hid have not changed in thirty years. The trees, mostly pine, must still hold the old secrets of the guerrillas. There is a stone bridge almost in the precise spot where Hemingway's fictitious American hero, Robert Jordan, blew up a metal bridge to cut off the Nationalist advance and gave his life for the Spanish Republic. I left my car by the roadside and climbed the mountain to the ledge, hidden by trees, from which Jordan and his *guerrilleros* had watched the movement of the Nationalists' trucks and armored cars rolling toward Madrid. I found the clear spring from which Jordan had drunk. I drank from it, too. It was a warm spring afternoon and reality began to melt into the remembered fiction. I recall thinking that I would not really have been surprised if Jordan or Pablo had come out of the thick foliage to keep me company and to survey the military traffic below. Such is the impact of Spain that one may easily lose the sense of present-day reality and slide over into the ever-present reality of Spanish history. When I lived at the old Benedictine mill at the foot of Pezuela de las Torres, I took a walk one day across the fields that stretch far into Guadalajara Province along the Tajuna valley. I met a shepherd with his flock, and we exchanged grave Castilian salutations. Has anything of importance ever happened here, I asked. "Oh yes," the old shepherd said. "You are walking over a battlefield." Here the Republicans had launched a counter-offensive in 1937. The shepherd told me about it in great detail, remembering how the Loyalists had established their rear echelons there in preparation for the Jarama River attack. He spoke in the present tense, as if thirty years had not gone by.

The Franco regime insists that it would like Spaniards to forget the Civil War except for the terrible lessons about national disunity that it should have taught the country. Yet, Spain is one vast reminder of *who* won the war. The Valley of the Fallen memorial, built by Republican war prisoners, is the most ostentatious example. Every Spanish city, town, and village has a Generalísimo avenue, plaza, or street. And in Madrid the three top plotters of the 1936 uprising—Franco and generals Mola and Sanjurjo—all have broad avenues named after them. Gran Vía, the traditional shopping thoroughfare that is dotted with outdoor cafés, was renamed after the war Gran Vía de José Antonio in tribute to the founder of the Falange. Inscriptions on the walls of many Spanish churches proclaim in black letters "José Antonio—Present!" suggesting that he always answers the roll call of patriots. In official speeches he is mentioned as *El Ausente* (the absent one). Ironically, Franco has thus honored the men who might have been his rivals for power had they lived.

Franco was not the leader of the military conspiracy that began to develop in earnest early in March, 1936, although he did attend some of the generals' meetings in Madrid and he remained in touch with them after his "exile" to the Canaries in mid-March. The revolution was prepared by General Mola, who had served as King Alfonso's chief of police and had been recently demoted by Azaña from the command in Morocco to the provincial garrison in Pamplona. His small group of associates included Lieutenant Colonel Valentín Galarza, who was in charge of organizing the garrisons throughout Spain through his secret Unión Militar Española. Mola's ranking political partner was General Sanjurjo, who had lived in exile in Portugal after his ill-fated attempt at a *coup d'état* in 1932. The other top conspirators were General Manuel Goded Llopis, the commander in the Balearic Islands; General Joaquín Fanjul Goñi, the officer responsible for Madrid; and General José Enrique Varela, a veteran of the Moroccan wars.

Franco met with this group and with José Antonio Primo de Rivera a few days before his departure for the Canaries. Crozier, who has had access to considerable background material on the generals' plot, claims in his biography of Franco that at the time of the Madrid meeting "Franco adopted an entirely non-committal attitude." My own investigations of the origins of the Civil War bear this out. Why Franco should have been noncommittal at that point in the conspiracy will presumably remain unclear forever—unless the Generalissimo chooses to leave his account of the war for posterity. But this seems unlikely, for he has always been a man who keeps his own counsel and confides in no one. It may be that he refused to become identified with the plot until he was absolutely certain of its success—his entire military and political life has been characterized by extreme caution—or that his deep sense of discipline prevented him from conspiring against the government he served, or both. As late as June 23, in fact, Franco wrote a letter to

Prime Minister Casares Quiroga urging him to act to preserve peace and order in Spain.

The curious thing is that although he did not actually launch the uprising, Franco immediately began to behave as though he were its natural leader. The rebellion exploded during the night of 17–18 July on the Peninsula and in the African garrisons. Franco was then in Las Palmas, in the Canaries, preparing to fly to Morocco to take over the African army according to a prearranged plan.

At 3 A.M. on July 18 he was advised that the garrison of the Moroccan fortress town of Melilla had seized it in the name of the uprising. Two hours later, the troops in Las Palmas also rose against the government. Simultaneously, the radio stations in the Canaries broadcast the text of Franco's proclamation, which he had written some time earlier, announcing the start of a "war without quarter on the exploiters of politics, on the deceivers of the honest worker, on the foreigners and foreign-oriented people who openly or deceitfully endeavor to destroy Spain." Curiously, this was the only pronunciamento to emerge from the uprising. Although Franco appeared to be addressing Spaniards as the chief of the revolution, he was merely one of its military commanders. On the other hand, neither of its political leaders, Sanjurjo and Mola, seemed to find it necessary or convenient to quarrel with Franco's delivery of his manifesto. There is no question that Franco intended this pronunciamento to be his bid for over-all leadership of the rebellion, and its phrasing shows that he was already a masterly politician. He carefully refrained from committing himself to any of the groups that comprised the Nationalist movement. He did not promise the restoration of monarchy or the transformation of the Republic into a Falangist state. Because he pledged nothing, he had no political debts to pay later. This is the pattern Franco has followed ever since; he has never aligned himself with any political group. Understanding Spain better than his fellow Spaniards, he has realized that the only way to keep power is to make each faction within his camp compete for his favor without allowing any one of them to receive it fully.

In less than three months Franco had asserted himself as the undisputed head of the Nationalists. By then, most of his potential rivals were dead.. Calvo Sotelo was assassinated in July. Sanjurjo was killed in a plane crash on August 2 as he was taking off from

Lisbon for Burgos, the headquarters of the uprising, to assume the command of the revolution. General Goded was caught by the Republicans in Barcelona and executed. General Fanjul was executed in Madrid. José Antonio was lingering in prison awaiting his death. On October 1, 1936, the National Defense Committee in Burgos issued a decree naming Franco "head of the government of the Spanish State" and "Generalissimo of the National Land, Sea, and Air Forces." General Mola sought to block what was in effect a *coup d'état* carried out by Franco within the Nationalist camp, but he was no match for the Generalissimo. So effective was Franco's political legerdemain that later that day his title was changed from "head of government" to "chief of state"—a crucial subtlety—and the proviso that he would hold his office only "for the duration of the war" was dropped. At forty-three Franco had assured himself of what was to be lifelong rule over Spain. As for Mola, he died in a plane crash nine months later.

Photographs of Franco taken during the Civil War tend to make him appear somewhat ridiculous. He was short, slightly paunchy even then, and his small mustache gave him a pompous and fatuous air. He usually wore a legionnaire's forage cap with a tassel hanging over his face. He had a high-pitched, almost squeaky voice. In sum, he seemed like the satirical creation of a Cervantes or a Goya. The error of so many of his enemies in those days was to take Franco literally at face value.

In truth, Franco was both a formidable military leader and a political artist directing what at first sight was an implausible alliance of monarchists of all stripes, army generals who preferred a republic of their own making to a restored kingdom, mystical Catholics, and fascist Falangists. One of his political miracles was to fuse the Carlists, who considered themselves traditional Catholics, with the Falange and the right-wing labor groups into a loose political party called the FET, an acronym for Traditionalist Spanish Falange. The Carlist traditionalists wore red berets and the Falangists wore blue shirts. Franco's solution was to order FET members to wear blue shirts *and* red berets. The closest Franco ever came to an ideological pronouncement was in the summer of 1937 when in separate statements he said that "we shall not base the future regime on democratic systems which, decidedly, are not convenient for our people" and that "Spain will follow the structure of totalitarian regimes, such as Italy and Germany . . . but with clearly national characteristics. It will be a suit cut to the Spanish measurements." Though this commitment may have been chiefly intended for the benefit of Hitler and Mussolini, whose military aid was vital to the Nationalists, Franco kept it deliberately vague to avoid antagonizing his monarchist allies. In any event, neither the Falange nor the FET was ever elevated to the status of the ruling political party on the Nazi model. Instead, Franco used his native fascists for his own ends. When a top Falangist leader rebelled against Franco's policies, the Caudillo did not hesitate to imprison him. The chief of the traditionalist Carlists, who provided some of the best troops for the Nationalists, was exiled to Portugal when he questioned Franco's wisdom. Unity on his terms was always Franco's obsession, because he believed that no other form of unity was possible in Spain.

Militarily, Franco had his work cut out for him when he assumed the post of Generalissimo. The first thrust of the rebellion gave the Nationalists control of most of northern Spain—except for the Basque country and Asturias—and much of the central plateau north and west of Madrid. Franco's African army had been able to cross the Strait of Gibraltar from Ceuta to Algeciras and join up with the northern army in Estremadura. The Moorish regiments were commanded by the same General Yagüe who, acting on Franco's orders, had crushed the Asturias rebellion with such incredible cruelty in 1934. The Nationalists also held Córdoba and Granada, and subsequently, the Italians captured Málaga for them. But Franco controlled only the poorest and least-populated half of the country while the Loyalists held the great cities of Madrid, Barcelona, Bilbao, Valencia, and Oviedo, along with their industries and their millions of workers highly organized for the defense of the Republic. They also commanded the leftist revolutionary-minded rural areas of Andalusia and virtually the entire Mediterranean coast except for Málaga. When Franco set up his headquarters in Salamanca, he predicted correctly that Spain faced a long war.

Largo Caballero, the extreme Socialist allied with the Communists, became prime minister of the Republican government two months after the Civil War broke out. However, he could not dominate his strange political coalition as effectively as Franco dominated his equally peculiar alliance, and the Republic continued to undermine itself from within as it had before the war. The Republican camp was composed of Socialists who did not see eye to eye with each other, Anarchists who detested the Socialists and the Communists, and Communists who were out to get the Trotskyites. The Catholic Basques, who supported the Republic to protect the autonomy they had been granted in November, 1936, could not abide the anticlerical leftists who burned churches and killed priests. General Mola invented the term "fifth column" to designate the secret Nationalist sympathizers in Madrid (four Nationalist columns were advancing on the city from the outside at the time), and anyone suspected of "fifth columnism" was imprisoned or shot. When the government left Madrid for Valencia, the police simply executed all the inmates of the Model Prison rather than take them along. I know scores of people in Madrid today whose fathers, brothers, or sons simply vanished during the Civil War.

The Republican government was also conducting a violent social revolution. Farms, factories, and homes were being taken over and given to the people. Though few objective observers could quarrel with the need for profound social reform in Spain, the timing seemed most inappropriate. Energies that might have been channeled into the war were being wasted on the chaotic revolution. With pro-Communists increasingly in command of the regime (Largo Caballero had placed two of them in key cabinet posts), the Republican army fell into the hands of political commissars. Except for a few first-rate generals like José Miaja and Vicente Rojo, the Loyalists lacked top commanders, for the officers' corps had largely gone over to Franco. As a result, Republican military decisions were often made on political grounds. Lacking a unified military command, individual units frequently undertook operations that appealed to them, sometimes with success and sometimes with catastrophic results.

The Republic survived nearly three years of steady Nationalist attacks on the ground and bombardments by German and Italian pilots only because of the courage, determination, and idealism of the Loyalists. Regardless of their political persuasion, Spaniards are not quitters, and their tenacity and heroism made blood baths of the battles for Madrid, Teruel, Toledo, Bilbao, Gijón, and a hundred other places. Guadalajara, the Ebro, the Basque country, and Andalusia were scenes of combat so savage as to defy imagination. Both sides took awesome losses without a moment's hesitation. Spaniards fought in bitter blizzards around Teruel and under the burning sun of Andalusia. The Loyalists went to war with wild enthusiasm to defend Spain from fascism. The Nationalists were convinced that they were saving the nation from antichrist and Communism. They prayed, took Communion, and crossed themselves before going into combat. This twentieth-century war was sometimes reminiscent of a medieval crusade.

The Loyalists were aided by International Brigades formed of volunteers from all over the world. The volunteers, some forty-six thousand of them, may have been directed by Communists or pro-Communists, but for the most part they fought for the democratic ideal against the fascism that was already preparing to engulf the world in a global war. There were Frenchmen from across the border and Oxford and Cambridge students from across the Cantabrian Sea and Americans of the Abraham Lincoln Brigade from across the Atlantic. There were Socialists and Communists from eastern Europe. Curiously, many of the veterans were to become leaders of liberal Communism in Yugoslavia, Hungary, Poland, and Czechoslovakia. In a strange way, their youthful romantic and idealistic experiences in Spain made them reject Stalinist excesses and totalitarianism in their mature years.

Foreign intervention in its many forms prolonged the Spanish war, perhaps by years. Left to themselves, the Spaniards might have come to the limit of their strength earlier, and uncounted thousands of lives might have been saved.

From the outset Franco had the support of Germany and Italy. Their planes ferried the first troops of his African army from Morocco to the Peninsula. Later, Mussolini sent Black Shirt divisions to fight alongside the Nationalists, although this assistance was of dubious military value. With few exceptions the Italians lost the battles they fought. Then Hitler provided Franco with the Condor Legion of planes and airmen. This gave the Nationalists superiority over the small and battered Loyalist air force of French- and Soviet-made planes. It also gave the Germans the opportunity to practice dive-bombing and other techniques they were to employ shortly thereafter in World War II.

The most famous instance of Nazi use of air power in Spain was the raid on Guernica in the Basque country on April 16, 1937, in support of the attacking Nationalist ground forces. The town, which is the holy shrine of the Basques, was destroyed as the Loyalists withdrew. There are conflicting versions of what really happened at Guernica, and the truth may never be known. The Nationalists claim that the German air assault caused minimal damage and that the Loyalists blew up the town as they retreated. When I visited Guernica, I asked the older residents what they remembered of that day. I was met with stony silence. Spaniards prefer not to discuss the Civil War with total strangers. But, inevitably, Guernica will live forever in mankind's thoughts as the scene of the Nazi raid. When Picasso painted his unforgettable *Guernica* canvas, he created history.

The Republic fought an uphill struggle from the start. Franco enjoyed German and Italian support principally for political reasons, although he had to pay for some equipment with exports of stra-

On the road to Pezuela de las Torres

tegic ores. The Loyalists, on the other hand, had to scrounge funds to buy arms from whomever they could and then smuggle them into the country. The Nonintervention Agreement of 1936 effectively prevented the Western democracies from providing extensive aid to the Republic. This was probably shortsighted, because a pro-Allied Spain might have been a major asset during World War II. The Germans and the Italians, of course, ignored the agreement, knowing that the West was in a mood of appeasement. And in the end their help to the Nationalists was decisive.

The strangest role of all was played by the Soviet Union. The Russians sent the Loyalists enough aircraft, tanks, and artillery to continue the fight but never enough to gain the winning edge. It almost seemed as if Moscow simply wished to prolong the war without allowing its Loyalist protégés to win it. Moreover, Soviet aid was not free. The Republic paid for it with nearly $500 million in gold—one-half of its total reserve.

No serious historian believes that a Republican victory would have turned Spain into a Communist state. Although the number of Communists in the country rose from some fifty thousand to an estimated three hundred thousand between 1936 and 1939, a viable Republic would probably have held them in check. When Communist leaders finally succeeded in assuming most of the power in Republican Spain, the war was already lost and there was little left of the Republic. In this sense, then, the Communist ascendency was largely irrelevant. This is not merely a Republican view: I have heard it in Madrid from men who held high posts in the Franco regime both during and after the Civil War. But during that war it suited the Nationalists to portray their campaign as a crusade against the *rojos*, and a whole mythology was born. Today, few Spaniards think of the Republic as a Communist phenomenon, and if they still speak of the *rojos*, it seems more idiomatic than political.

By the end of 1937 the Republic controlled only fifteen of the fifty provinces and less than half of the population. But it still occupied Madrid and Barcelona, and the capital was moved to the latter city from Valencia after the pro-Communist Dr. Juan Negrín replaced Largo Caballero as prime minister. Bilbao, Oviedo, and Santander had fallen after long sieges. In December the Nationalists captured Teruel following an unsuccessful Loyalist offensive. In July, 1938, Franco split the Republican territory in Catalonia by fighting through to the Mediterranean at the mouth of the Ebro in a four-month-long battle that was one of the bloodiest of the war. Ten thousand Republicans died during it. On January 27, 1939, Barcelona, severely damaged by aerial bombardments, fell to the Nationalists. Franco flew to Barcelona for a victory parade on February 21, as Nationalist social workers tried to feed the starving population. Azaña resigned the presidency and fled to France followed by three hundred thousand defeated Loyalist soldiers and civilian refugees. Negrín returned to Valencia for a last stand that never took place, for the resistance collapsed. On February 27 Britain and France recognized Franco's regime as the government of Spain.

Now only Madrid stood between Franco and final victory. Having resisted for nearly three years, the city was taken on March 28 in two days of fighting. The last moments of Madrid were grimly in keeping with the whole history of the Republic: for three weeks be-

A street photographer in Barcelona

fore the city fell its defenders fought each other. The Communists battled the forces of Colonel Segismundo Casado, a moderate Republican who had formed a National Defense Council to negotiate peace with Franco. Casado won but he could no longer resist Franco's troops as they surged through the Ciudad Universitaria, where year after year the Loyalists had kept the Nationalists in check.

Then Franco sent out a communiqúe: "Today, the Red Army having been disarmed and captured, the National troops have reached their final military objectives. The war is over.—Burgos, April 1, 1939, the Year of Victory—Generalissimo Franco."

On May 8 Franco stood on a reviewing stand on Madrid's Paseo de la Castellana to watch the victory parade by 120,000 troops. The ceremony has been repeated annually since 1939 lest Spain forget who won her bloodiest war. The next day the Generalissimo went to the church of Santa Barbara for a victory *Te Deum*. This was his prayer:

Lord, graciously accept the effort of this people which always was Thine and which with me and in Thy name has with heroism defeated the enemy of truth of this age.

Lord God, in whose hands is all righteousness and power, lend me Thy help to lead this people to the full liberty of Dominion, for Thy Glory and that of Thy Church.

Lord, that all men may know that Jesus is the Christ, the son of the Living God.

By all accounts, it was a moving moment as the Catholic warrior placed his sword before the altar to mark the end of the war.

All Spanish wars are terrible, but in Spain peace can be even more so. No sooner had the celebrations ended than a frightful wave of repression swept the country. Under laws approved by Franco in the closing months of the war, tribunals of political responsibilities and special military tribunals were established to punish the Loyalists. The resulting blood bath was probably greater than those that took place during the French Revolution or the White Terror of Spain's earlier days. Executions were held daily between 1939 and 1941, and the best estimates place the number of deaths at about 200,000. Added to those killed on the battlefield, the cost in lives of the Spanish Civil War approaches a million. Brian Crozier has written that, in addition, there were more than 250,000 prisoners in Spanish jails on December 31, 1940, twenty-one months after the war ended.

The postwar terror obviously is an indictment of Franco as a ruler. There are thousands of Spanish families who will never forget or forgive his awesome vengeance. But in a profounder sense, that vengeance is also an indictment of the Spaniard's infinite cruelty and a capacity for hatred matched only by his capacity for heroism. I have asked Spanish friends what would have happened had the Loyalists won the war. Almost invariably, Franco's admirers and foes alike have answered that the Loyalists would have taken the same vengeance on the Nationalists. "It's in our blood," said a Barcelona intellectual who was on the Republican side in the war.

Memories of the Civil War cannot really be erased, even if Spaniards of the present generation know the war only from history books or from the remembrances of their parents, to whom the conflict must still be a living reality. The new Spain that has grown up in the past three decades, therefore, has to be understood in the context of the trauma caused by the Civil War.

BOOK THREE

The New Spain

1 The Great War and Spain

A high-ranking Spanish army officer views maneuvers near Madrid.

W hen the Civil War ended, Franco proceeded to build his regime on the four pillars of the army, the church, the National Movement, and the civilian bureaucracy. This program was a throwback to the Catholic Kings—in its reliance on an extraordinary blend of temporal and spiritual powers mutually supporting each other to preserve the newly won *status quo*. Its modern ingredients were the fascistlike Falange and the National Movement, but Franco fitted them into the special Spanish context by requiring that even the fascists submit to his personal authority and to Spain's militant Catholicism. For Franco was more than just an imitator of Hitler and Mussolini. As usual, Spain was different.

The Falange was not permitted to acquire real political weight because Franco never believed in sharing power with any individual or any group, and he was much too pragmatic to engage seriously in ideological or doctrinaire experimentation. He paid lip service to the Falange, and he found it useful as a political instrument and, curiously, as a vehicle for Spanish mysticism and romanticism. During the Civil War these traits had stimulated each side to feel that it was fighting a crusade. Now, in sudden peace, there was an emotional void. There was a need to re-create a sense of Spanish greatness to compensate for the daily drama of life amidst destruction and near famine.

The Falangists thus dreamed aloud of recapturing the empire that had made Spain so formidable a power in the fifteenth century. Such serious men as Fernando María Castiella y Maíz, who later rose to be foreign minister, and José María Areilza, the Count of Motrico, who was Spain's leading diplomat before becoming Franco's opponent in the 1960's, wrote in those postwar days books propounding a totally unrealistic Spanish Irredentism. The National Movement organized a nationwide campaign urging every Spanish municipality to join in a national gift of gratitude to Generalissimo Franco. The gift was a sword identical to what was believed to have been the sword of El Cid. Franco, meanwhile, had awarded himself the Laureate Cross of San Fernando, Spain's highest military decoration, named after Ferdinand III, the Saint, a thirteenth-century Castilian king. All previous governments had refused to award Franco the cross he thought he had earned in the African campaigns. To this day, the red sash of the Cross of San Fernando is the only military decoration Franco wears on his army uniform. Another romantic gesture ordered by the Caudillo was the exhumation of José Antonio's body from its grave in Alicante and its removal to a new resting place at Escorial Monastery. The casket was carried along Spain's highways by relays of torchbearing Falangists in a mystical display of the Spanish cult of death. Official propaganda promptly created the national myth and legend of the *Niño de Jaén,* the Child of Jaén, referring to the Andalusian city in which José Antonio had been born. Franco had kept José Antonio and his Falange at arm's length before the young man was killed in 1936, but he officiated at the stark reburial ceremony and listened to the massed Falangists answer "Present!" in chorus when their dead chief was named in the roll call.

But post-Civil War Spain could not live on mysticism alone. Franco faced an awesome task of reconstruction, aggravated by a terrible shortage of food and the flight abroad of tens of thousands of Republicans—including some of the country's most talented men and women—who preferred exile in France, Mexico, and South America to life (or death or imprisonment) under the new regime. Then, exactly five months after the end of the Civil War, the Second World War erupted on September 1, 1939.

When I traveled through Spain in the summer of 1940, the outside world tended to believe that Franco was virtually, if not actually, an ally of Hitler and Mussolini. The reasoning was that he had won the Civil War largely because of fascist military help; he had often publicly expressed his admiration for the Axis and his contempt for the "rotten" democracies of the West; and in the first year of the world war Spain showed considerable official sympathy for the fascists. Moreover, the day before the Civil War ended, Spain and Germany had signed a treaty of friendship.

However, as Hitler was soon to learn, one should not jump to conclusions when dealing with a man of the amazing political cunning of Francisco Franco. Above all, Franco was the classical Spanish patriot, to whom the best interests of Spain overrode all other considerations. In retrospect it is easy enough to think of Franco's wartime diplomatic acrobatics as pure and successful opportunism. The truth is more complex. Franco had made up his mind from the outset of the war to keep Spain neutral. He knew that the Peninsula could not once more become a battlefield if his nation was to survive at all. He resisted the promises of retaking Gibraltar and re-creating a Spanish African empire, which Hitler and Mussolini vaguely dangled before him as rewards if he entered the war on the side of the Axis. He also carefully refrained from alienating Britain. Most of his advisers were convinced that an Axis victory was imminent after the fall of France, but the Caudillo preferred to go on practicing his policy of "skillful prudence."

Even as he signed treaties with the Axis and let Nazi diplomats, agents, and spies operate freely in Madrid (I still vividly remember the swastikas on the Puerta del Sol), Franco was hedging his bets. Before the outbreak of the war he signed a treaty of friendship and nonaggression with Portugal that committed each party not to allow its territory to be used for aggressive purposes against the other. This move alone should have alerted his Axis friends that Franco intended to remain neutral. Then, in March, 1940, Spain signed a trade agreement with Portugal's ally Britain that provided for extensive British credits to help rebuild the battered Spanish economy.

On June 27 German troops reached the French-Spanish border at Hendaye and at other spots along the Pyrenees. My mother and I had only a few days earlier fled to Spain from France, and I remember our fear that the Caudillo would invite the Germans to enter Spain and that we would be trapped there. Britain feared for the safety of Gibraltar, for had the Germans marched through Spain and taken the Rock, they could have closed the Mediterranean to the British fleet, and themselves crossed to Africa. But Franco did not let the Germans in, and he even fired a general who had toasted Hitler at a border reception for German officers. He made refugees from Nazi-occupied Europe feel welcome in Spain, as my mother and I found out, and he did not allow them to be harassed or sent back to France.

During much of the summer and autumn of 1940 Spanish diplomats, acting on precise instructions from Franco, so exasperated the Germans with their refusals to commit Spain to the war that Von Ribbentrop, the Nazi foreign minister, finally warned Ramón Serrano Suñer, the Spanish foreign minister, that Germany might have to occupy the Peninsula for strategic reasons. Serrano Suñer, a Falangist and Franco's brother-in-law, did not take kindly to this suggestion despite his pro-German sympathies. When Ribbentrop requested permission to establish German bases in the Canary Islands, Serrano Suñer icily informed him that the islands "are a province of our fatherland."

Every time Hitler pressed him to declare war on Britain, Franco invented new evasive tactics, including the presentation of military and economic "shopping lists" he knew the Germans could not fill. At one point he announced that Spain would enter the war only after the German invasion of Britain, which he already realized was not likely to take place. On another occasion he requested delivery of seven hundred thousand tons of wheat in a single year and the complete re-equipping of the Spanish army by the Germans. He demanded a firm pledge that Spain would receive all of French Morocco after the war, knowing perfectly well that Hitler wanted it for himself.

In October, 1940, Franco arrived an hour late for a meeting with Hitler at Hendaye. Some historians claim that the delay was deliberate, but Crozier has written that it was due to the deplorable state of the Spanish railway system. In any event, Hitler failed to make the stubborn Franco go to war. When Hitler pressed him to let Nazi troops take Gibraltar, Franco advised him that Spaniards would not tolerate the idea of foreign soldiers reconquering the Rock for them. Instead, he said, Germany should arm Spain for such an enterprise. In passing, he also mentioned Spain's great need for food. According to Crozier, Hitler later said he would rather have his teeth pulled than to have to confer again with the little Caudillo. Looking back at the Hendaye interview, one can only believe that Franco had mastered the oldest lesson in Spanish history: that whenever Spain invited foreign armies to help her against an enemy, the foreigners tended to stay on and become occupiers themselves.

Franco continued to stall Hitler about the war and about Gibraltar, and he kept raising the ante: at one point he asked the Germans for a million tons of wheat annually. When the Germans proposed January 10, 1941, as the date for an attack on Gibraltar, the Spaniards demurred. As emissary after emissary arrived in Madrid with messages from Hitler, Franco maintained his quiet refusal to set a date for what was known as Operation Felix. And while he pleasantly reassured Hitler by letter that he was "completely and decidedly" on his side, Spanish diplomats in London were busily negotiating for economic aid from Britain.

When Hitler thought of arranging Franco's overthrow, he was promptly dissuaded by his own advisers. In the summer of 1941, he conceived the notion of invading Spain and from there taking both Gibraltar and North Africa. Franco found out about these plans and deployed his best troops in the Pyrenees. He made it clear that Spain would fight a German invasion.

At the same time, Franco sent a group of eighteen thousand volunteers—the Blue Division commanded by General Agustín Muñoz Grandes—to fight alongside the Germans on the Russian front; he secretly allowed Nazi submarines to use Spanish facilities; and he supplied Germany with strategic minerals like wolframite, lithium, and beryllium, as well as with great quantities of iron ore. The dispatching of the Blue Division was an expression of Franco's deep hatred of Communism, while the other acts were designed to cover Spain's bets in the event that the Axis won the war after all.

On the other hand, Franco may have made it possible for the Allies to win the war by first refusing to let the Germans cross Spain to capture Gibraltar and by subsequently failing to interfere with the invasion of North Africa that the Allies launched from Gibraltar. In retrospect it is difficult to believe that Franco was unaware of the preparations for Operation Torch as the Allied navies massed in Gibraltar Bay for the landing in North Africa. The Spaniards could observe it from across the bay in Algeciras, and they were within several hundred yards of the Gibraltar landing strip on the other side of the land frontier at La Línea de la Concepción. Some Spaniards claim that Operation Torch had Franco's tacit approval, although he obviously was not consulted by the British and Americans. A high-ranking Spanish diplomat, who was a junior official in the Madrid Foreign Ministry at the time of the invasion, told me in 1965 that a British aircraft carrying secret plans for Operation Torch had crashed on Spanish territory near Gibraltar a few days before the North African invasion took place in November, 1942. According to my friend, the documents were retrieved by the Guardia Civil, flown to Madrid, and immediately submitted to Franco. The Caudillo, the story goes, ordered the documents destroyed and never breathed a word of what they contained to the Germans or the Italians. Whether or not the story is true, the fact remains that the North African landings were a complete surprise to the enemy. Franco received a personal message from President Franklin Roosevelt on the morning of the invasion assuring him that Operation Torch was not aimed at Spain, and he never created the slightest problem for the Allies. The 150,000 Spanish troops in Spanish Morocco didn't move.

In the spring of 1943 Hitler once more thought of invading Spain, for he felt that Franco's neutrality was becoming dangerously pro-Allied. Preparations for an attack had actually begun, but the Spaniards again made it clear that they would fight the Germans to the death, and Hitler's generals warned him against storming the Pyrenees. In the end, as Crozier has noted, the irony of it all was that Spain "missed being the West's gallant ally . . . by the hair's breadth of Hitler's failure to invade Spain, which would have met with fierce Spanish resistance." The Blue Division notwithstanding, it was the Allied cause that benefited the most in the long run from Franco's artful neutrality. He engineered a nationwide campaign for "Spanish Gibraltar," but he never did the slightest thing to make it come true. Periodically, he organized anti-British demonstrations in Madrid, but the British were quietly told in Madrid and London not to take them too seriously.

Franco was also responsible for unpublicized humanitarian acts that one would not normally expect from a dictator who had ordered the execution of tens of thousands of his fellow Spaniards for having been on the losing side of the Civil War. As I have already mentioned, he never interfered with the flow of European refugees through Spain. Halfway through the war he persuaded Hitler to spare the lives of thousands of Sephardic Jews held in camps near Salonika, Greece. Was it because Franco has Jewish blood in his veins, as some allege? Was it a periodically recurrent display of Spanish guilt feelings for the Inquisition four centuries earlier? Franco, as usual, has not made his motives clear. It seems likely, too, that Franco's tacit consent was necessary for the successful operation in Spain of a wartime "underground railroad" that brought downed Allied aviators out of France and sent them back to Britain. Several friends of mine, who served in the American Office of Strategic Services and in British intelligence, told me in great detail how they ran their "railroad" with invaluable assistance from pro-Allied Spaniards and what amounted to collusion on the part of many Spanish officials. But Franco has never claimed credit for any of these actions.

In October, 1943, Franco withdrew the Blue Division from

Russia. Then, early in 1944, both the United States and Britain demanded that Spain immediately cease shipping wolframite to Germany. The proud Franco refused to agree under pressure. The result was an Allied ban on oil shipments to Spain that was a painful blow to the limping Spanish economy.

After the Allied victory public opinion in western Europe and the United States demanded that Franco, too, be done away with. His public image was that of a fascist dictator, and it appeared incongruous that Franco should remain in power with Hitler and Mussolini gone. Simultaneously, Spanish refugees in France—the defeated Loyalists of 1939—beamed vociferously anti-Franco broadcasts into Spain from Toulouse. Spanish security forces warned the Caudillo that the Americans were arming Spanish Communists in North Africa and landing them in Spain to launch a revolution, but there is no evidence to support this charge. Several thousand Spaniards entered the country from France to overthrow Franco. But contrary to their expectations, they received little support from the local population, which often denounced them to the army and the Guardia Civil instead. The invasion quickly petered out.

Meeting in Potsdam in July, 1945, President Truman, Prime Minister Clement Attlee, and Stalin announced that they would not support United Nations membership for "the present Spanish government which, having been founded with the support of the Axis powers, does not, in view of its origins, its nature, its record and its close association with the aggressor states, possess the necessary qualifications to justify such membership."

It is a matter of opinion whether the Allies were wise to isolate Franco. If they wanted to force a change of regime in Spain, they failed. It has been argued, and I believe with reason, that the error of the democracies was to assume that a frontal attack on Franco would unite domestic sentiment against him and lead to a *coup d'état* or a revolution. The effect was precisely the opposite. Spaniards, including many of Franco's enemies at home, took the attacks on the Caudillo to be attacks on Spain. They rallied around him for reasons of *Spanish* pride. Franco himself issued a typically Spanish proclamation announcing that Spain "will not beg a seat in international conferences and would not accept any position that would not be consonant with her history, her population and her services to peace and culture."

The outside world had once again misjudged the Spanish character. It could even be debated that if the world had refrained from attacking Franco at that juncture, he might have fallen sooner or later for internal reasons. Ironically, then, Franco may owe the length of his reign and his subsequent international vindication to his enemies.

On December 12, 1946, the United Nations General Assembly approved a resolution banning Spain from membership in the organization and its specialized bodies. It also warned that if "within a reasonable time" a democratic government did not emerge in Spain, the United Nations would consider other "adequate measures." The General Assembly then recommended that all member states withdraw their ambassadors from Madrid. Predictably, the response in Spain was an outpouring of support for Franco, who felt that he had received a mandate to continue building the New Spain according to his own lights and without regard for international opinion. In a way, this suited him fine. The ensuing quarter of a century has been marked by the consolidation and then evolution of the Franco dictatorship. During this time a new generation of Spaniards has come on the scene to prepare for the transition, inevitable in this decade, to a new Spanish order and, presumably, a new system.

Shopping at El Corte Inglés, a large Madrid department store

2 A New Generation

Spaniards of the 1970's are markedly different from their parents and grandparents in economic status and in social and even political outlook. They have shared in the relative prosperity of the late 1950's and the 1960's, and they have ceased to be isolated from the rest of Europe. To be sure, Spain still has many pockets of heartbreaking poverty, and the contrast between the affluent cities and the often destitute countryside is shocking. But for the first time since the end of the sixteenth century Spaniards are no longer part of a society in decomposition. In many ways, theirs is now one of Europe's most vital and dynamic societies, as if to make up for centuries of neglect and fratricidal conflicts. Spain has been an active member of the United Nations since 1956 and is influential in international politics in the Middle East, increasingly in Europe, and especially in Latin America. How did this change come about?

When in 1964 the regime blanketed the country with posters saying "FRANCO—TWENTY-FIVE YEARS OF PEACE," it was doing no more than stating a fact. This was the longest period of domestic peace in Spain in this century.

Franco has exacted a high price for this peace—from the mass executions, imprisonments, and repression of the years immediately following the Civil War to the continuing denial of basic political rights to his fellow Spaniards. The old Caudillo, of course, does not trust the Spaniards' political instincts or maturity any more today than he did thirty years ago. In communicating to the nation his obsession with law and order, he has constantly harped on the evils of representative parliamentary democracy, which, he believes, was behind all the past convulsions of Spain, including the Civil War. He anticipates challenge by declaring majestically that he is responsible only before "God and history," which is perhaps an unconscious throwback to the Catholic Kings in its blithe disregard for the people of Spain.

Still, three decades of peace have allowed the Spanish nation to repair the ravages of the Civil War under the most adverse possible conditions and to create a fairly viable society. Hopefully—but not necessarily, given the Spanish temperament—this new society will be able to weather the almost inevitable crises of the approaching post-Franco succession.

A Madrid workman washes down his lunch with wine from a goatskin flask known as a *bota*.

Spain's per capita income in 1970 was nearly $700 annually, or almost double that of 1950. Even though it is the third lowest in western Europe (ahead of Portugal and Greece), its growth is an important measure of Spanish economic and social progress. I think it is erroneous to call this an "economic miracle" and to ascribe it entirely to Franco's wise policies. It would be more accurate to say that prolonged domestic peace has permitted the average Spaniard's creativity and capacity for hard work to bring about this recovery from the devastation left by the Civil War.

Relative prosperity has changed Spain physically and socially, up to a point. The change is amply visible in Madrid, Barcelona, Bilbao, and a half-dozen other cities where industries have enriched their owners, given a boost to commerce and the middle class, and created jobs and reasonable living standards for the workers. Rural migrants are being transformed into a new urban proletariat, and the traditional proletarians—the families that have belonged to the large Spanish working class since the turn of the century—are joining the ranks of the middle class. Yet, this evolution is slow because of the limitations and rigidity of Spanish society. Despite industrial development, there are not enough jobs for all the men and women forced to flee from the impoverished countryside. Hundreds of thousands of Spaniards, therefore, must emigrate to western Europe or South America in order to survive. Between 1960 and 1962, 400,000 went to work abroad. So great are the pressures on the *campesinos,* the rural peasants, that in 1963 alone an estimated 450,000 Spaniards were involved in internal migrations. The movement leveled off in the latter part of the decade—the countryside was squeezed dry of able-bodied young people—leaving uncounted Spanish villages either deserted or inhabited only by old people or by one or two families.

By contrast, new housing projects encircling the large cities, wide avenues and highways, the profusion of little automobiles and noisy motor scooters, and the forests of television antennas are evidence of rising social standards. Even in the smaller cities and towns— Soria in Old Castile, Lorca in Murcia, or Albacete in La Mancha— one finds rows of neat new houses on the outskirts and well-stocked shops. At dusk on warm evenings, the hour of the *paseo,* the streets and plazas are filled with well-dressed young men and women slowly

Motor scooters are an increasingly popular means of transportation in Spain.

strolling arm in arm with children who always seem to be wearing their best clothes. But the old women are still classically stern and silent studies in black. The old men, berets on their heads and cigarettes hanging from the corners of their mouths, squint at the passing parade of the new generation from the little tables of the cafés.

That Spaniards in the big cities have money to spend is demonstrated by the crowds in the big department stores, like Galerías Preciados and El Corte Inglés in Madrid, which sell everything from clothing and furniture to television sets and refrigerators. Spanish men are careful and sophisticated dressers—this, too, is pride—and the clothes they can buy are of excellent quality. There is a minor controversy about whether the custom tailors are better in Madrid or Barcelona; I personally favor the Barcelona style which is reminiscent of Savile Row's. Basque men of substance, particularly in Bilbao, tend to dress like Englishmen, and the sight of a furled umbrella is not uncommon there. Everywhere, modern self-service supermarkets are gradually replacing the traditional neighborhood *bodegas.* Specialty shops, including boutiques, do a brisk business along Madrid's Goya and Serrano avenues and Barcelona's Ramblas. Attendance at bullfights, soccer games, and the movies is at an all-time high. Madrileños stream en masse to the vast uptown Santiago Bérnabeu stadium to watch the Real Madrid, one of the capital's two main soccer teams. On days when there is a game, the police are obliged to cordon off traffic along the adjacent streets to accommodate the rushing crowds.

But Spanish society is still highly stratified. Money, political influence, and often, titles rigorously define the upper classes, which remain more isolated from other social groups than in most European countries. The separation can be very subtle. For example, an upper-class Spaniard automatically addresses his presumed equal of roughly the same age with the familiar *tu* ("thou") on the first encounter. But he will address his presumed social inferior as *usted,* the impersonal "you," no matter how long he has known him. Working-class and even middle-class Spaniards shy away from the *tu* form except within the family or among close friends.

In the provinces family palaces are still inhabited by those bearers of famous old names who have managed to preserve or increase their fortunes by becoming directors of banks and industries or who live on the income from their immense estates. The dukes of Alba, for example, reported an income of $236,000 from their estates in 1970, and their palace in Seville is a good example of their continued opulence.

In Madrid, the hub of Spain, the more traditional rich cling to their downtown mansions, some of which are splendid palaces, or to their old, high-ceilinged apartments that face Retiro Park or line the Paseo de la Castellana. Other members of the upper classes have fanned out to luxurious apartment buildings in stylish and expensive residential districts on or near the Avenida del Generalísimo and to attractive and sometimes very grand villas in elegant suburbs. Puerta

At the *feria,* or spring fair, in Seville

Breakfast on the cobbles in Andalusia

de Hierro, past the university campus, is the preserve of Spanish millionaires, foreign diplomats, foreign movie makers and stars (among them Ava Gardner and Orson Welles for a while), and well-heeled exiles ranging from dethroned European royalty to Argentina's ex-dictator Juan Perón and Cuba's Fulgencio Batista. The deposed dictators apparently make the friends of the Franco regime uncomfortable, and they are neither accepted nor do they seek acceptance. But royalty is very much in demand. Ex-King Simeon of Bulgaria is a pleasant, bearded young man who is happily married to the daughter of a leading Madrid banker and works for his father-in-law. Madrid royalty also includes former Queen Geraldine of Albania and her son, a daughter of Italy's ex-King Umberto (who prefers to live in Portugal), a Hapsburg duke who writes foreign-policy commentaries for a Madrid newspaper, a pretender to the Portuguese throne whose title of princess is questioned by some people, and the former king of Burundi. The most recent arrivals were King Constantine of Greece, who commutes between Rome and

Madrid, and his mother, Queen Frederica. Constantine's sister Sophia is married to Prince Juan Carlos. His other sister, Irene, a concert pianist, is often in Madrid.

Puerto de Hierro adjoins the very exclusive Puerto de Hierro Country Club, which offers golf and polo and is one of three such clubs around Madrid. The suburb is on the way to Franco's El Pardo Palace and Prince Juan Carlos's La Zarzuela Palace. Further along the highway to La Coruña are the suburbs of Aravaca and La Florida, the latter virtually a private village guarded by special policemen. On the other side of Madrid, on the way to Burgos and past some of the capital's worst slums, is the private village of La Moraleja, where the rich and powerful live in splendid seclusion.

International jet-setters move freely in Spanish society when they visit Madrid, the resorts of Marbella, Torremolinos, or Sotogrande, or participate in the great Spanish fiestas. One year during my stay in Spain Princess Grace of Monaco and Mrs. Jacqueline Kennedy (before her marriage to Aristotle Onassis) vied for social supremacy at the *Semana Santa* (Holy Week) celebrations in Seville. Photographs of the two ladies at the Seville ball dominated the Spanish press. The upper class and even the younger middle class have so thoroughly absorbed international customs that every self-respecting Madrid bartender can mix a first-rate Bloody Mary and Scotch whisky has become the accepted evening drink. A Spanish newspaper cartoon once depicted a waiter in a Madrid café ordering drinks from the bartender. "Three Scotches-and-soda, a gin-and-tonic, two Bloody Mary's—and one sherry for that *foreigner* in the corner," the waiter was saying.

S pain's economy is a peculiar blend of free enterprise—often archaic, and in the case of agriculture, almost feudal—and extensive government intervention. Because the Franco regime has ultimate control over the economy, major decisions are frequently made on political grounds, and on occasion, national interest may be sacrificed to reward an official favorite. The intimate relations between the regime and Spain's top bankers, industrialists, and landowners have inevitably led to a state of affairs that would hardly be tolerated elsewhere in western Europe. In 1967, for example, a major automobile manufacturer was saved from bankruptcy by a timely official loan that was reportedly authorized by Franco himself. A close friendship was said to exist between members of the Franco family and the auto maker. Knowledgeable Spaniards claim that there have been other such cases, although they are usually kept from the public. Such things are possible, of course, because there is no system of checks and balances in Spain—no independent parliament and no free press—and officials are thus protected from embarrassing inquiries unless Franco himself orders them. By the same token, economic policies are subject only to a very limited degree of criticism or examination from below, although in recent years individual economists and special-interest groups, including regime-controlled labor unions and farmers, have been trying hard to make themselves heard.

In the absence of open discussion, national economic priorities are often related, in the opinion of independent economists, to the interests of powerful financial groups supporting the regime. These economists claim that despite frequently obsolete practices, industry

The little Seat car has gone far toward putting Spain on wheels.

has been heavily favored over small-scale agriculture, which has no political constituency. Franco returned to Spanish landowners the land seized by Republican reformers during the Civil War, and he has made no attempt to break up the huge and often uneconomical estates. Many of these estates, particularly in Andalusia, are largely dedicated to the raising of bulls for the Spanish *corridas*. They produce relatively few cash crops and almost no jobs. Foreign experts have repeatedly advised the regime to consider some form of agrarian reform to stimulate agricultural production, but Franco evidently has chosen not to antagonize the big landowners.

Banks operate virtually as holding companies, controlling or owning most Spanish industry through a network of interlocking directorates. This practice is particularly widespread in the industrial Basque provinces, and the skein of the Basque-based directorates spreads across Spain. According to a confidential government study made in 1965, twenty-three men were each president, vice-president, and director of between ten and thirty-eight separate banks and corporations. My favorite was Pedro de Careaga Basabe, the Count of Cadagua, who was president of the Banco de Vizcaya, one of Spain's leading banks, as well as president of three large power companies, two of Spain's biggest chemical companies, a small steel company, a paper company, an insurance company, and a textile company; vice-president of Spain's biggest steel company, a mining company, a lumber company, a construction company, and a metal-processing company; and a director of three other power companies, a hydroelectric company, two nitrate companies, a plastics company, another insurance company, a coal-mining company, a shipyard, a rubber-products company, another metal-processing company, and a financing company. A Madrid banker of my close acquaintance personally owns an estimated $60 million worth of oil refineries, international petroleum consortiums, arms factories, mines, shipyards, and a book publishing company, among other interests. These are Spain's one-man industrial and banking conglomerates that control most of the economy in close cooperation with the regime. In practical terms, taxation does not threaten these great Spanish fortunes with extinction.

The Spanish aristocracy is enormous by the standards of Europe's monarchies. According to *Grandezas y Títulos del Reino* (Grandees and Titles of the Kingdom), an official publication of the Justice

Ministry, there were 2,544 recognized titles in Spain in 1966. They were borne by 1,849 Spaniards, some of whom had the right to more than one title and in a few cases to as many as five. An additional 84 titles on the books were borne by no one at the time. The Justice Ministry charges a tax of 20,000 pesetas (about $285) for the inheritance of a title. It costs 300,000 pesetas (about $4,285) to renew a title that has lapsed. Those who request the grant of a title to which they consider themselves heir are placed by the ministry on a *Lista de Demandas* (List of Requests). Franco is kept posted and may privately support or deny a claim. Not being king, he cannot officially bestow titles. Franco has never sought a title for himself, but he, and his wife, Doña Carmen Polo Martínez-Valdés de Franco, and his daughter, the Marchioness of Villaverde, are ex officio members of the Spanish aristocracy. Señora de Franco and the Marchioness are leaders of Spanish society and are very much in the limelight for their elegance and good works. Prince Juan Carlos and Princess Sophia rank immediately after the Francos in order of social precedence. Conservative cardinals and bishops belong to this most exclusive Spanish group, but curiously, none of Franco's non-aristocratic cabinet ministers have ever quite made it.

Franco, the monarchist, quite obviously has a penchant for the aristocracy. Over the years, leading aristocrats have served him in a variety of ways: Marquis Juan Ignacio Luca de Tena, publisher of the monarchist Madrid daily *ABC,* financed the charter of a plane that flew Franco from the Canaries to Africa in 1936; the Duke of Alba was his political agent in Britain during the Civil War; the Count of Mayalda was ambassador in Berlin; Count Goméz Jordana was his first foreign minister in Burgos; the Count of Rodezno became Nationalist justice minister in 1938; Infante Alfonso d'Orléans y Borbón was an air force commander in the war; the Marquis of Bilbao was the first president of the Cortes after the war and chairman of the Council of the Realm; the Marquis of Lozoya was president of the Spanish Institute; Juan Pablo de Lojendio, Marquis of Vellisca, was ambassador to Switzerland and Cuba (where he berated Fidel Castro on a live television show in 1959 for insulting the Caudillo); and the Count of Motrico was ambassador to Argentina, the United States, and France. And so on.

The size of the aristocratic establishment is mind-boggling in a country in which both the regime and the liberal and socialist oppo-

The Count of Motrico in the study of his Madrid home

sition ceaselessly proclaim their republican sentiments. Moreover, there is still great respect for the holders of titles, because Spaniards find it possible to reconcile traditionalism with modernism. The young superintendent of the apartment building in which I lived in Madrid never failed to bow gravely to the aging countess from the fifth floor. He did not bow to my American commoner wife.

But monarchists and aristocrats are as divided as everybody else in Spain. One faction still supports Don Juan, the exiled pretender, even though Franco passed him by in selecting his successor. Another faction, which has grown considerably since Franco picked Juan Carlos in 1969, is devoted to the young prince. There is also the unforgiving Carlist faction that holds out for *its* pretender, who lives in exile in Paris.

The social class second in order of importance to the aristocracy is the upper-middle class and the top bureaucracy—the cabinet ministers, the directors general, the principal military commanders, the provincial military and civil governors, and the chiefs of the National Movement. However, since Spanish social groups rarely mix, the members of this group appear in Franco's entourage only when required by official circumstances.

The broad middle class that ranks below the bureaucrats is not seen at the great social functions, and it patronizes restaurants below the level of, say, Madrid's Jockey Club. Middle-class Spaniards spend their summers at small hotels, apartments, or cottages on the seashore and occasionally go abroad. They are avid television watchers. Probably the most creative class in postwar Spain, they also enjoy the greatest mobility. Among them are the artists, writers, intellectuals, architects, lawyers, educators, and doctors. It will be from their midst that new ideas will someday flow in Spain, and it is among them that much of the antiregime dissent is crystallizing.

The quality of life has improved markedly in recent decades for the Spanish working class, and it has profited from the Franco regime's social-welfare policies. But this class could be the most crucial question mark in Spain's future. On the surface the workers appear contented; they obediently and sometimes enthusiastically cheer Franco when he graces them with his presence at the annual May Day celebration at Madrid's Santiago Bérnabeu stadium or pays a visit to San Sebastián, Seville, or Barcelona. Yet, traditions and allegiances die hard in Spain, and nobody knows the extent of the working class's Catholicism or anticlericalism, their latent sympathies for anarchism, socialism, communism, or just plain republicanism, or their attachment to the National cause. Even less is known about rural sentiment, but it would be wise to remember that some of the most potent revolutionary feeling a generation ago came from the parched fields of Andalusia, the Catalonian countryside, and fertile Aragon. The neglect of rural Spain by the present regime may well have unforeseeable consequences.

Considering the vast contradictions in Spanish society, Franco's own attitude is curious. He is the supreme *jefe* of the National Movement, which in its pure form is a populist organization, yet he is clearly more at ease with aristocrats and *noveau riche* millionaires than with the regimented common people. Franco is not a populist demagogue on the pattern of a Mussolini, but none of the Falangist or National Movement leaders is among his very few remaining intimate friends. When the occasion demands it, he may don a National Movement uniform, deliver a short speech praising the mem-

A resident of the province of Badajoz, near the Portuguese border

ory of José Antonio, and allow himself to be photographed with such old Falange leaders as Pílar Primo de Rivera, the sister of the late party founder. But not even his close wartime companions are known to share his private evenings, which he prefers to spend alone or with his immediate family. Official photographs periodically show him playing with his grandchildren.

On the other hand he *does* choose to live in the sixteenth-century El Pardo Palace, to receive ambassadors in the tenantless seventeenth-century Royal Palace in Madrid, and annually to celebrate the start of the Civil War in Philip V's frivolous La Granja Palace north of Madrid. He spends part of his summer near La Coruña in his native Galicia in an elegant little palace that once belonged to a Portuguese noblewoman. His early autumn hunting is done from the Castle of Calahorra that was built around 1500 in the province of Granada, and during visits to Seville he insists on staying at the Alcázar, the splendid royal castle erected during the fourteenth century in the Moorish Nasrite style. The Alcázar is now a museum, but it is closed to the public several weeks before Franco's arrival so that it can be transformed into living quarters.

Franco's favorite relaxations are fishing and hunting. Great Spanish hunts—*cacerías*—are conducted in royal fashion, and this is how Franco enjoys them most. When he travels to the hunt, his route is patrolled at frequent intervals by members of the Guardia Civil armed with rifles and submachine guns. When he reaches his destination, the Guardias cordon off the area as a security measure. Franco and other invited guests—cabinet ministers, foreign ambassadors, dukes, and bank presidents—take positions in the assigned partridge blinds with their bearers, whose job it is to reload the shotguns. Members of Franco's personal bodyguard stand a few steps from him, submachine guns in hand. Then the peasants of an entire village begin to beat the bushes for the birds, driving them toward the hunters. The Caudillo is a good shot despite his age, and he easily bags the day's quota. Lunch is served by waiters in livery and white gloves in a tent erected in the field. Franco relaxes, smiles, and makes small talk in his high-pitched voice.

"*El rey está cazando*"—the king is hunting—a peasant in a Castilian village told me once during a partridge shoot in which Franco was participating. He spoke with considerable awe and no sarcasm. The uncrowned king of Spain was indeed at play in his kingdom.

The alcázar at Segovia was a favorite residence
of the Castilian kings for several centuries.

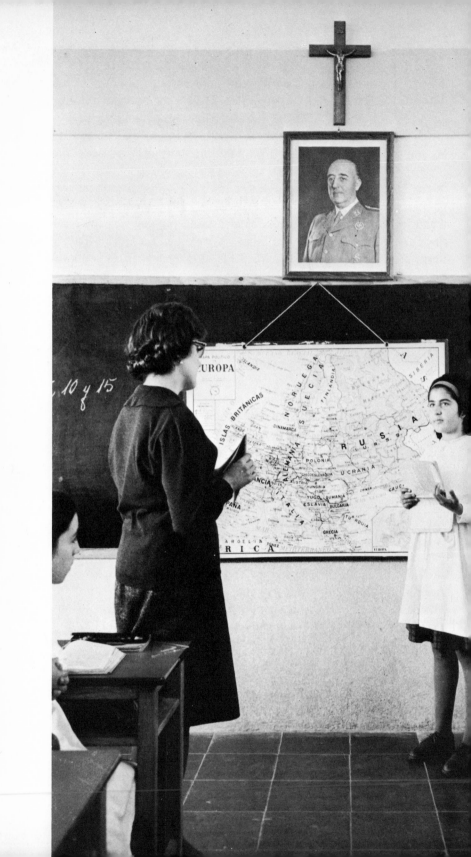

3 Franco Forever?

Church and state—crucifix and Franco—jointly dominate
this elementary-school classroom in Madrid.

In a country where people tend to live to a ripe old age, Galicians have a reputation for extraordinary longevity, and Franco is, of course, a Gallego. His state of health is a matter of intense interest to Spanish politicians, foreign diplomats, and newspapermen. Foreign embassies in Madrid have sometimes sent home long reports describing in detail how Franco looked and acted at his latest public appearance or private interview with a visitor. In one report that I know of everything was noted and analyzed: Was he alert or bored? Did he seem to listen carefully or was his attention wavering? Did he speak at length? Did he have difficulty standing? Was his face twitching?

Rumors of various illnesses affecting Franco have always been rampant in Madrid. He has been said to suffer from Parkinson's disease. He has been reported to be so weak that he dozes off at cabinet meetings. His doctors (his son-in-law, the Marquis of Villaverde, is a noted heart surgeon) have been alleged to give Franco hourly injections to keep him propped up and functioning. A Spanish exile in Argentina even wrote a book some years ago claiming that Franco had actually died and that an army sergeant named Tinoco, his exact double, had been put in his place by a clique of ministers. But every time the rumor mill shifts into high gear, newspaper photographs suddenly appear showing Franco hunting partridges, playing a few holes of golf, or fishing from his yacht *Azor*.

I saw him at close quarters on numerous occasions during my three years in Spain. I followed him as he moved briskly through the Barcelona zoological garden in 1966. I watched him shooting partridges near Toledo and playing golf near Gibraltar in 1967. Three times I watched him as he stood erect for hours, sometimes in the rain, reviewing the annual victory parade along Madrid's Paseo de la Castellana. I observed him at a gala at the Teatro Real listenin, or pretending to listen, to Beethoven's Ninth Symphony. We chatted briefly at a formal audience for foreign correspondents at El Pardo in January, 1968. Protocol required me to wear a morning coat for the occasion. Franco looked paunchy and a bit bloated in his brown army uniform. The last time I saw him was at the Cortes on July 22, 1969, announcing that he had selected Prince Juan Carlos to be the next chief of state. In his speech he used this curious phrase about his own mortality: "I have dedicated my life to the best service to God and Motherland but when due to natural laws my captaincy will be missed by you, which *inexorably must occur,* the decision that we shall take today is advisable. . . . " His justification for the restoration of monarchy, summing up his lifelong blend of Spanish mysticism and pragmatism, was equally striking: "The monarchy of the Catholic Kings, which gave the nation so many years of glory, is a perennial example of its popularity and constant defense of the social rights of our people. . . ." How strange it was to listen to Franco in 1969 invoking the example of a form of government half a millennium old!

Advanced age is the hallmark of power in Spain. Enrique Cardinal Plá y Deniel remained Archbishop of Toledo and Primate of Spain until he died in 1968 at the age of ninety-two. In 1967 the hierarchy of the Spanish church included two eighty-year-old cardinals, the ninety-one-year-old Bishop of Minorca, and seven archbishops over seventy. Twenty-nine out of fifty-nine bishops were born in the nineteenth century. The Vatican finally began pressing the ancient ecclesiastics to retire. Captain General Muñoz Grandes ceased to be vice-president of the government at seventy-one in 1967 —for political reasons—but stayed on briefly as the chief of general staff. His successor as vice-president was Admiral Luís Carrero Blanco, who was sixty-eight in 1971 and who remains one of the most likely candidates for the premiership if Franco ever activates the post. Among the opposition leaders Gil Robles, the Christian Democratic chief, was seventy-four in 1971.

In the past decade Franco has been gradually retiring overage cabinet ministers and replacing them with younger men, including the Catholic technocrats of the Opus Dei. Laureano López Rodó, who is in charge of Spain's economic planning, comes under this heading. Now in his fifties, he is another contender for the premiership and for the job of being Prince Juan Carlos's political tutor.

Women are a powerful element in Spanish society. Often betrayed by their insistently polygamous men, abused by the vicissitudes of a harsh life, and widowed by incessant wars, women are towers of strength in Spain. It is they who really hold together this somewhat anomalous and often savage society. A foreigner's conventional picture of the Spanish woman lies somewhere between the black-clad *dueña* watching over the morals of a virgin damsel, the silent figure in widow's weeds, the unseen presence kept out of sight, Moslem-style, by husband or father, and the sensual flamenco dancer, a flaming rose clenched in her teeth. Those stereotypes are all erroneous. There are, of course, *dueñas,* widows, virgins, hidden wives, and flamenco dancers. But they are neither predominant types nor partial composites of the Spanish woman. Basically, the Spanish woman has always been the realistic and hard-

Dried seafood is on sale at this Galician café.

headed partner in the family. The man, to be sure, is the principal breadwinner, but he also is given in an almost unparalleled degree to gallivanting, bragging, cognac sipping, chess playing, politicking, warring, and arguing with other men about all these topics, as well as about bullfighting, soccer, *jai alai,* cockfights, and the state of the world and the cosmos. It is, then, the strong-willed and practical woman who sees to it that her man stays out of trouble and brings home enough of his pay to assure the family's survival.

Both Moslem and old-fashioned Roman Catholic traditions have combined to keep the Spanish woman out of the limelight. Although more and more women now drive cars and smoke in public, they are not emancipated in the American sense of the word. But in a much more real sense they dominate their men.

When her husband dies, a Spanish widow puts on mourning defiantly, as if to say: "I have defeated you. . . ." Most widows—and there are an inordinate number in Spain—wear their weeds for the rest of their lives, as though they were a badge of honor and accomplishment. Some still force their daughters to dress in mourning until they are married, although in recent decades there has been growing resistance to this practice.

The Spanish scene is peopled with shadowy women in black, fingering rosaries and filling the churches. This does not deter them from pursuing the tasks of life with an energy bordering on violence. While driving through Spanish villages I have been taken aback by the spectacle of elderly women, always in widows' weeds, washing the sidewalks in front of their houses. They empty their water buckets with the élan of discus throwers, and they attack the sidewalk with their brooms as if it were an enemy to be destroyed. And on the impoverished farms it is the widows who till the rocky land with dogged strength.

Relations between men and women are unusual in Spain because of a sexual problem that is evidently unresolved. The problem, amply demonstrated in Spanish history and literature, is that the Spanish woman is much more sensual and sex-oriented than the Spanish man. On the other hand, within the Spanish social order the man must be a full-time seeker of sexual conquests. Spanish history, always immensely colorful, tells us that Prince Juan, the son of the Catholic Kings, literally killed himself through heroic love-making to his young wife. It is not surprising that Don Juan, the great lover, was a Spanish contribution to mankind as well as to literature, the theater, and opera. Polygamy likewise results from masculine pride, as does the ancient Spanish custom of the *piropo*, the risqué remark that a man will address to a woman passing in the street. The *piropo* has been elevated to the status of a fine art, and the female who is not greeted by *piropos* as she strolls along has every reason to feel slighted. The Spanish also invented, and still observe, the time-honored institution of introducing themselves as

A Catalan widow in the streets of Barcelona

"Señor Rodríguez" to women with whom they propose to go to bed while their wife and children are away from town for the summer holidays. Señor Rodríguez is the Spanish equivalent of John Smith.

One fascinating theory links sexual relations between Spanish men and women to bullfighting. Fernando Diaz-Plaja, a noted contemporary essayist and historian, has explained it in his book *The Spaniard and the Seven Deadly Sins* by pointing out that "the bravest and most virile of Spaniards, the *matador*, dresses 'like a woman,' in silks, bright colors. . . . The *matador*—narrow-waisted, graceful in his movements—is the woman. The bull—brutal, direct, following only instinct—is the man. The female symbol moves before him, provokes him with its body and gestures, makes him jealous; when the bull attacks it finds itself frustrated and turns against its enemy, more furious than ever. Just as in coquetry. The *matador* triumphs at the end, and in the death-possession there is always blood. This victory, then, may be a symbol of woman's dominion over man, since Adam and Eve, Omphale and Hercules. In some cases—they are few—the balance has come down on the other side, that is to say with the defeat of the tormentor, the woman."

Vicente Blasco Ibáñez, the great Spanish novelist, clearly linked sex and bullfighting in his book *Blood and Sand*. In a very sensual passage the heroine stages a mock bullfight in which she plays the matador and taunts her lover, who represents the bull, with cries of "*toro, toro.* . . ." Hemingway, who was deeply preoccupied with sex, was a fanatic devotee of *corridas*, and his book *The Sun Also Rises* is rich in bull-ring sexuality. Having attended numerous bull-fights during my years in Spain, I was invariably struck by the sensual sense of excitement on the part of the women spectators, especially at the moment of truth. The men, oddly, were more detached.

Spain has produced a long line of extraordinary women. El Cid's widow ruled the Kingdom of Valencia after his death. Isabella of Castile was one of Spain's greatest monarchs, probably over-shadowing Ferdinand of Aragon, her husband, as an effective ruler and politician. Queen Isabella, the wife of Emperor Charles, governed Spain on his behalf while he fought his wars across Europe. Saint Theresa of Ávila was one of the greatest mystic writers. The Bourbon queens of the nineteenth century—notably

At a popular café in Madrid's Avenida José Antonio

Queen Isabella II—were willful, powerful, and famous for their lovers. Dolores Ibarruri, nicknamed *La Pasionaria,* was among the principal Communist leaders in the Spanish Civil War and has become something of a legend. She was in her seventies when I met her at a Communist party congress in Bucharest in 1969, but I was struck by how fiery she still was. Señora de Franco, the Generalissimo's wife, is said by those who know her to be a highly astute politician in her own right and the only person capable of influencing him. She is also alleged to be a shrewd businesswoman who has quietly amassed a portfolio of important investments. The Spanish government angrily banned the issue of a United States magazine that described these alleged investments.

Perhaps the most astounding Spanish woman I have ever met was Isabel Luísa Álvarez de Toledo y Maura, a distinguished grandee widely known as the Red Duchess. In 1966, when three unarmed U.S. hydrogen bombs dropped near the village of Palomares (and one in the Mediterranean close by), she led the villagers in a march to demand more adequate compensation from the

241

A young receptionist at a Madrid office

United States for the radioactive contamination the village suffered. As a result of this protest she spent a year in prison. She is a petite woman in her early thirties with probably more weighty titles than anybody in Spain: she is the Duchess of Medina-Sidonia, Marquise of Villafranca del Bierzo, Marquise of Vélez, and Countess of Niebla. An outspoken critic of Franco, she is an advocate of radical leftist causes. She has written a novel about the misery of Andalusian peasants, is an expert horsewoman, a passable flamenco singer, the owner of a vast fortune, and the mother of two children by a husband she abandoned.

In 1967 women accounted for 18 per cent of Spain's work force of twelve million. This was quite a jump from a decade earlier, when it was a rarity for a middle- or upper-class married woman to hold a paying job. Nowadays, nobody gives it a second thought because the economics of modern life require it. There are a limited number of women executives, doctors, and lawyers and a handful of women deputies in the Cortes.

Most urban families, even the less affluent ones, still have live-in maids, who are usually young girls brought from provincial villages. But maids are becoming harder and harder to get, for the girls prefer better-paying and more dignified industrial jobs. Spaniards underpay their domestics and tend to treat them with something less than courtesy.

Large numbers of young women in the rural areas still choose to become nuns, either selling their hair or allowing the convent to sell their hair to the agents of wigmakers. In Spain, where so much of life is touched by mysticism, venerated Virgins are expected to perform miracles and intercede for the nation, the region, the city, or the village. The Virgin of Pílar is the patron saint of Spain; the Black Virgin of Montserrat is the patron of Catalonia; the Virgin of Macarena looks after Seville, and the Virgin of Begoña after Bilbao. The shrine of the Virgin of Africa is in Ceuta, and Franco's soldiers prayed to her before crossing the strait to launch the Civil War. The Virgin of Elche, who dates back to the third century B.C., is said to have great miracles to her credit.

The individual Spaniard is probably the most self-centered and the most self-indulgent person in the world. He simply rejects the thought that he lives surrounded by other individuals. This was the dominant trait of Don Quixote, and it remains the dominant trait of every Spaniard in every generation. He is authoritarian beyond words but he rejects all authority. He is enamored of his own liberty but wary of sharing it with others. He is therefore unable to participate effectively in an organized society, because it imposes on him obligations that he would rather not accept. This explains the great and the petty tyrannies of Spanish history and family life, the civil wars, and the anarchist tradition. Spain is the only country in the world in which the ideas of the nineteenth-century Russian anarchist Bakunin took hold in a big way.

Salvador de Madariaga has summed up the Spaniard in these words: "He is neither a citizen of an equalitarian state, nor a partner in a national society, nor a subject in an empire. He is a man. . . . This individualist is an egotist. His person is the channel through which the life-stream is made to pass, thus acquiring a personality polarized along a definite individual direction. The Spaniard therefore feels patriotism as he feels love—in the form of a passion whereby he absorbs the object of his love and assimilates it; that is to say, makes it his own. He does not belong to his country so much as his country belongs to him. . . . In what concerns collective, and particularly political life, the Spaniard is apt to judge events according to a dramatic criterion, singularly free from any practical considerations or intellectual prepossessions. It follows that in Spain, liberty, justice, and free trade matter less than the particular Smith or Jones who is to incarnate them for the time being."

Brian Crozier has written in his biography of Franco that "often a dialogue with a Spaniard is, in fact, not a dialogue at all but two separate monologues." Crozier then quotes the description by V. S. Pritchett, an English writer, of two Spaniards talking: "The whole performance illustrated the blindness of Spanish egotism. The speaker stares at you with a prolonged dramatic stare that goes through you. He stares because he is trying to get into his head the impossible proposition that you exist. He does not listen to you. He never discusses. He asserts. Only *he* exists."

The village elders of Pezuela de las Torres settle the affairs of the world.

Pritchett admirably conveys the frustration of discussing anything with a Spaniard. With rare exceptions I found that an interview with a government official would become a lecture or a proclamation. Once during a talk with the then Information Minister Manuel Fraga Iribarne, an otherwise highly intelligent man, I remarked that I had heard an opinion different from his and I asked him what he thought of it. Fraga blanched with fury, jumped to his feet, and said: "If you want to talk about other people's opinions, go to see other people. . . . This interview is ended." I am glad to say that he recovered quickly from his anger and our relationship survived the incident. On a less exalted level, I once made the mistake of asking directions from two Madrid traffic policemen who happened to be standing together at an intersection. Both saluted me politely, then engaged in an increasingly acrimonious argument with each other about whether I should turn right two or three blocks down the avenue. They were still arguing, oblivious of me, as I pulled away.

The Spaniard has a veneer of courtesy that is genuine but extremely thin. A light scratch draws blood. He can be supremely inconsiderate, but he is never deliberately so, and he would be incredulous if someone brought it to his attention. Time is almost as meaningless to a Spaniard as it is to an Oriental, and he does not think it rude to be up to an hour late for an appointment. Because he likes to be the master of his own time, his prolonged meals do not begin until so late—lunch at two o'clock in the afternoon and dinner at ten in the evening or later. When I once joked about "Spanish hours" to a Spanish friend, he instantly corrected me. "They are *human* hours," he said. High-ranking officials prefer to work when they feel like it. When Grégorio López Bravo, now foreign minister, began to summon people for 9 A.M. meetings, he was immediately dubbed "The Abominable Man of the Ninth Hour," a Spanish play on words on the "Abominable Man of the Snows." The Foreign Ministry, where I transacted much of my business, kept the most peculiar hours in Madrid: it functioned from 11 A.M. to 2 P.M. and then, after lunch and the siesta, from 7 P.M. until dinnertime. The first time I appeared in the morning at the Foreign Ministry and inquired about several department heads, the old liveried porter informed me that "in the morning they don't come and in the afternoon they don't work." This was a bit of poetic license, but it conveyed the mood of official Madrid.

Of the seven deadly sins pride is the most overwhelming for the Spaniard because it affects every aspect of his human, social, and political behavior. He has transmuted it into the concept of honor— every student of Spain has noticed that "honor" is one of the most commonly used words in the language—and in its name he refuses any form of rational compromise with the world, fights exhausting and unnecessary foreign wars, and destroys himself in domestic strife. The Spanish essayist Fernando Diaz-Plaja summarized Spanish pride by quoting from the seventeenth-century writer Baltasar Gracián: "Pride, as the first in all evil, took the lead. . . . It ran into Spain, the first province in Europe. Spain suited its taste so well that it stayed there. There it lives and there it reigns with all its allies: self-esteem, contempt of others, the desire to give orders to everyone and serve no one, pride in being Don Diego, and 'descended from the Goths,' showing off, excelling, boasting, much

The spring fair is a proud time in Seville.

speaking, tall and hollow, gravity, pomp, daring with every kind of presumption, and all this from the noblest to the most plebian."

Whether he is titled or not, every Spaniard's name is prefaced with the title Don, or sir. The correct form of addressing a letter to any man is "Señor Don Juan Pérez" (Juan Pérez is the Spanish John Doe). For women the form is Señora Doña. In short, Spaniards tend to knight themselves. By contrast, Don Juan, the royal pretender, is addressed simply as Señor, which in this context means "Sire."

The distinctive feature of Spanish dress, the long cape, is worn by noblemen, soldiers (dark green for the Guardia Civil), and beggars. Besides its usefulness in keeping out the cold, the cape obliterates all social distinctions. You cannot tell the king from the beggar. This satisfies each Spaniard's proud conviction that he is equal to every other man. And I must say pride is contagious. I, too, feel a bit prouder when I wear my velvet-lined Madrid cape.

The classic example of Spanish pride at its most extravagant during the Civil War was the refusal of Colonel Moscardó to surrender the Toledo Alcázar to the Loyalists even though this cost the life of his son, whom the Loyalists were holding hostage. In the museum at the Alcázar the visitor is shown the telephone over which Moscardó told his son to die for the cause. But Moscardó was not the first Spaniard to sacrifice his son in this way. Late in the thirteenth century Guzmán el Bueno, governor of the fortress of Tarifa on the southernmost tip of Spain, was besieged by an army of Moslem mercenaries led by Prince Juan, the brother of the Castilian king. Juan sent word to Guzmán that he would kill his infant son, whom he held, unless the governor surrendered. Guzmán, in true Spanish fashion, sent Juan his own dagger to murder the baby. Juan promptly beheaded the infant in front of Tarifa's walls, although he failed to capture the fortress. Curiously, no thirteenth- or twentieth-century Spaniard seems to have questioned the notion of executing child hostages. This is how Black Legends are created.

Pride also serves to justify defeats without loss of honor. After the Invincible Armada was destroyed by a combination of storms and England's naval power, Philip II told his court that "I sent them to fight the English, not storms." Admiral Montojo, whose naval squadron was smashed by the United States navy in the Philippines during the Spanish-American War, sent a signal to Madrid that "Spain prefers honor without ships to ships without honor." Rather unbelievably, both remarks have survived in the Spanish pantheon of proud phrases.

The Spaniard is intensely proud of his country, but he seems to forget it entirely when he begins to extol the virtues of his province. I have heard Spaniards in Barcelona remark in the same breath that "say what you will, Spain is still the best place to live in the world," and "we Catalonians want to be separate because we are too good for the Spaniards." The Basques feel exactly the same way. Every town in Spain is convinced that *its* castle, *its* church, and *its* architecture are the best and most beautiful in the country. They look down on one another's Virgins because, naturally, it is their town's Virgin who performs the greatest miracles. Diaz-Plaja recalls the placard at the Palencia bull ring that proclaimed: "Palencia greets all visitors except those from Valladolid." The two are rival towns in northern Castile.

Pride can also result in generosity and hospitality. No matter how

destitute, every Spaniard is a Señor, and he will pawn his last possessions to demonstrate that he is the world's greatest host. A foreigner is still treated with extreme courtesy in Spain, despite annual invasions by millions of tourists who often display something less than good manners. I wish United States Customs Service inspectors were ordered to receive lessons in politeness from the white-gloved border guards who inspect one's baggage on arrival at Spanish airports. Spain may be a dictatorship, but the incoming visitor is not greeted with the visible suspicion that he is a potential criminal, arsonist, narcotics' smuggler, security risk, or enemy of national morals that often appears to be the attitude of American immigration agents.

To make their way through the country's immense bureaucracy, Spaniards have invented the institution of the *enchufe* (literally, a plug). To succeed in Spain, one must be *enchufado,* plugged in, to *somebody* who knows *somebody* in power. An *enchufe* enables one to obtain a telephone in Madrid in a matter of days despite a waiting time of a year or more in some parts of town. All kinds of arrangements become possible—from bank loans to reservations at fully booked hotels—with an *enchufe*. If you tell a Spaniard that you want to buy a pair of shoes, he will insist that you go to the store where he has a friend so that you will get better service. Unlike similar institutions in Latin America, the *enchufe* seldom involves cash payments. It is a matter of pride for the Spaniard to have an *enchufe*. He wants you to know about it, and he wants to be able to do you a good turn.

Spanish pride is responsible for others of the cardinal sins. Lust, for example, is a proof of manly pride; anger is a response to injured pride; envy (since I am better than you are, how dare you have more than I?); and sloth (I am too good to rise early and work hard). The monumental gluttony of Spaniards is part of the national habit of self-indulgence that in turn results from the prideful view that a Spaniard deserves the best. Yet, devoted as Spaniards are to wine, alcoholism is not the problem it is elsewhere in Europe.

Quite illogically, then, the proud and self-indulgent Spaniards have proved themselves to be formidable workers, fierce soldiers, and men of rare and perceptive talent.

The morning loaves are delivered in Santiago de Compostela.

The church casts a long shadow in Spain.

4 The Church–
Old and New

I 'm an atheist, thank God," a Barcelona friend once exclaimed, thus summing up the characteristically ambivalent Spanish attitude toward religion and the Roman Catholic Church. Officially, Spain is the "most Catholic of nations"; statistically, it is overwhelmingly Catholic. Under a 1953 concordat with the Vatican, Catholicism was recognized as the official religion of Spain—the "true one" —and the church was reconfirmed in its prewar privilege of owning property in the country. In 1962 there were 42,129 churches in Spain—one for every 750 Spaniards. There were 33,352 priests and fathers of religious orders, 5,440 convents, 1,427 monasteries, 72,783 nuns, 29,873 monks, 510,077 pupils in 2,954 women's religious educational institutions and 332,052 pupils in 1,698 men's religious institutions. The vast church hierarchy is headed by the Primate of Spain in Toledo, three other cardinals, thirteen archbishops (four of them also cardinals), fifty-one diocesan bishops, fourteen auxiliary bishops, one military archbishop (in charge of the chaplains), and one bishop heading military religious orders. It is a formidable structure that reaches from the village parish to the twelve permanent episcopal commissions (including one for radio and television) and the ruling National Episcopal Conference. Nevertheless, the thirty-three million nominal Spanish Catholics are as deeply divided about their religion as the Spanish church is about itself.

The religious division dates from the late eighteenth century, when anticlericalism first emerged as a militant movement in Spain. This anticlericalism was not born of atheism but of a profound feeling that the Spanish church was not living up to its original spiritual teachings of universal justice. It was a reaction to the alliance between the church, the monarchy, and the oppressive noble landlords. The Spaniard had always believed that he owned God as well as the church, and he simply felt betrayed. When he killed a priest or burned a church, therefore, he saw himself as purifying religion. The Spaniard is the genuine Old Christian, which is why he has rejected Protestantism as a possible alternative.

A clear distinction must thus be made between anticlericalism, which does not question God, and atheism, which does. I do not believe there are many true atheists in mystical Spain. Passengers on Spanish airlines cross themselves before take-off, although the chances are good that most of the men among them are not church-goers. Spanish prostitutes wear religious medals around their necks. The Spanish shout of approval at a bullfight is *Olé,* from the Arabic *Wa-Allah,* which means, "Oh, God!" The bullfighter prays to his favorite Virgin before he goes into the ring. The name of God—*por Dios*—is invoked in every other sentence both by Spanish believers and by those who claim to be atheists.

In Franco's new Spain the church (not the religion) is a major source of national controversy. Times have changed since 1937, when the Spanish hierarchy proclaimed in an open letter to the bishops of the world that the Nationalist "crusade" was "theologically just." Even twenty years ago the Spanish church was an almost monolithic pillar of the regime, along with the army, the National Movement, and the moneyed classes. Today this pillar is deeply fissured. The young clergy, inspired by the Vatican Council, is outspokenly opposed to the Franco regime and its political, economic, and social structure. The younger bishops are quietly siding with the liberals while the conservative hierarchy, unable to put down the rebellion, is hedging its bets and adopting an increasingly neutral attitude. As a Spanish bishop told me in 1968, "We cannot afford to be nailed down to Franco's coffin." In other words, the Spanish church has begun to realize that unless it adopts a more progressive attitude toward national life it may face another anticlerical explosion when the Caudillo is gone. The hierarchy is painfully aware that church attendance has been plummeting and that the priesthood is no longer a desirable career in Spain. In 1961 there were 21,615 men preparing to be ordained at Spain's 64 seminaries; in 1967 the total had dropped to an estimated 15,000. In the latter year the seminaries in Barcelona, San Sebastián, and Seville were unable to graduate their students because of strikes against the superiors.

When I came to Spain in 1965, it was absurd to imagine a priest being arrested by the Franco regime. By 1970 arrests and trials of priests had become commonplace. So has the spectacle of priests and monks leading students and workers in antiregime demonstrations. The progressive clergy today is the nearest thing to an organized anti-Franco underground movement in Spain. Not surprisingly, official repression has been daily winning the movement new converts. The government has been so heavy-handed in dealing with rebels of all kinds that in recent years some bishops and archbishops have issued pastoral letters condemning the regime's repressive practices along with its social policies, or lack of them.

Franco has shown himself singularly unresponsive to this growing rebellion. He has evidently chosen to ignore the profound spiritual considerations motivating what he regards simply as breaches in law and order. Having identified himself politically with the Catholic Kings, he has followed their religious example by punishing the new heretics in a way that has made even the Vatican wince. His own conventional displays of piety also have the royal touch. At the annual rites for the dead monarchs of Spain at the cold Escorial Monastery, Franco sits not with his ministers in the front row of the pews but in a thronelike chair to the right of the main altar—on the same level as the officiants. He seems so far from the reality of Spain's new church.

I was exposed to the new church not long after my arrival in Spain. On May 11, 1966, in Barcelona about a hundred and thirty Roman Catholic priests and monks formed what might have been taken for a Good Friday penitents' procession and marched silently out of the great Gothic cathedral. They crossed the Plaza Colón and went down the short and narrow Calle de Colón to the gray police headquarters building. There they sought to present a letter to the chief of Barcelona's Social Brigade, or political police, protesting the alleged mistreatment of a twenty-three-year-old architecture student named Joaquín Boix Luch. Boix Luch, who was known to be a dedicated Marxist, had been arrested several days earlier for his involvement in riots at the University of Barcelona, where students were demanding the right to participate in organizations other than those approved by the Franco regime. Outside police headquarters a plain-clothes man spoke briefly to Reverend Father Josep Dalmau, a stocky man in his late thirties who was one of the leaders of the procession. The procession was tying up the heavy noontime traffic, and the plain-clothes man ordered the demonstrators to disband. Father Dalmau refused and insisted on completing his errand. Just then, half a dozen Land-Rovers full of uniformed riot policemen—known in Spain as *los grises,* the gray ones, for the color of their uniforms—roared out of a side street and surrounded the priests. With clubs raised, they charged into the crowd, swinging hard at the heads and shoulders of the demon-

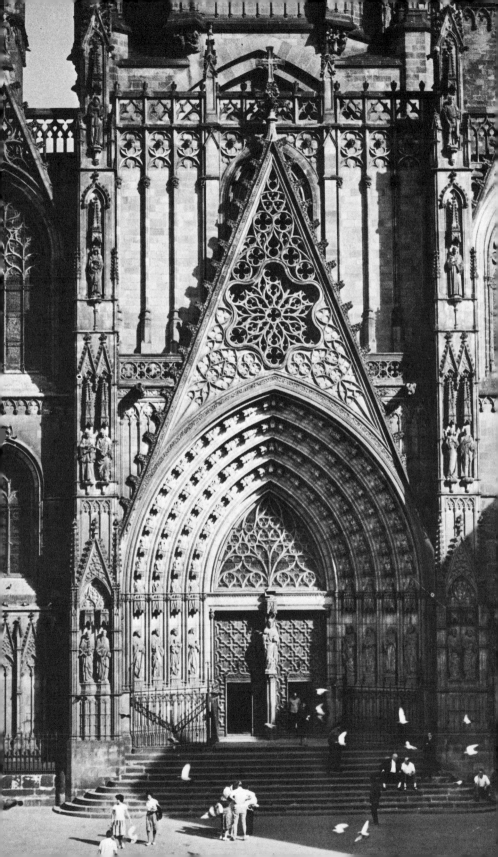

strators and kicking many of them in the groin. When a Capuchin brother's glasses fell to the sidewalk, a policeman deliberately ground them into the pavement with the heel of his boot. Priests wearing trousers were more fortunate than those in cassocks and monks' robes: they could run faster. As the demonstrators fled, pursued by *los grises,* many of them were bleeding profusely.

It was the first open confrontation between the clergy and the regime, and I remember the incredulous looks on the faces of the people on the Vía Layetana as they watched the savage police attack. The action was an unbelievable political blunder on the part of the regime. At first I thought that it had come about because of the stupidity of the police commander on the scene. But neither the police nor the provincial authorities in Barcelona nor the central government in Madrid ever apologized to the prelates. There never was the slightest hint that the Franco government thought the beating to have been wrong. Though the Caudillo has not hesitated to fire cabinet ministers or generals whose actions have annoyed or embarrassed him, he stood foursquare behind his police. When it came to the enforcement of law and order, Franco evidently did not differentiate between students at the University of Barcelona and Catholic priests. Public protest against the regime had to be punished. Otherwise, Franco must have reasoned, the principle of authority would be undermined and God only knew what would happen next in his volatile nation.

Four hundred Barcelona priests marched on the local archbishop's palace to protest the incident. Later in 1966 several hundred university students, some of their teachers, and about forty intellectuals and artists, including Antonio Tápies, locked themselves inside the Capuchin Sarría Monastery in Barcelona to organize a "free" student union. The police besieged the monastery and at the end of forty-eight hours took the artists and intellectuals to jail. With the exception of Tápies, most of these men did not have the money to pay the heavy fines exacted as punishment by Franco's Council of Ministers. To raise the money, a committee of sympathizers in Paris organized an auction. Picasso donated a painting that went for $15,000, and Joan Miró gave one that brought $20,000.

In the years since the Barcelona clash, rebel priests have been beaten, arrested, and tried elsewhere in Catalonia, in the Basque

To effect a cure, or in thanks for one, devout Spaniards will offer replicas of the affected member in their local church.

country, in Andalusia, and in Madrid. In characteristic Spanish fashion, neither side has been willing to retreat.

Franco has dominated the Spanish church since 1939 as he has dominated everything else in Spain. In fact, he made it a part of his regime, directly supporting the church through grants and what amounted to the payment of priests' salaries. (One of the first recommendations made by a group of rebel churchmen late in 1966 was that Spanish priests refuse to accept these salaries.) To further strengthen ties between the church and the state, Franco included the senior cardinal in the Council of the Realm, a hand-picked group without any real authority, which in 1969 rubber-stamped the selection of Prince Juan Carlos to be the future king. Three archbishops are ex officio members of the Cortes, and chaplains have been appointed not only to the armed forces but also to the Falange, the regime-run labor unions, and the schools.

The 1953 concordat with the Vatican in effect guaranteed that any bishops appointed to a see in Spain would be politically acceptable to the Spanish government. But in the late 1960's the question of the pope's freedom to name bishops became a major point of controversy between Madrid and Rome. Even Spanish bishops began to demand a revision of the concordat to eliminate the political clause. However, Franco has followed the Spanish tradition of ignoring the popes' wishes if they do not accord with the views or policies of Spain's temporal rulers. This centuries-long conflict has ranged from the sublime to the ridiculous: the Catholic Kings and Charles V turned a deaf ear to papal entreaties for less passion and cruelty in carrying out the Inquisition, and later, Spanish priests ignored the Vatican ban on their attendance at bullfights by watching them from behind the pillars of the bull ring.

At the time of the Barcelona clash in 1966 the youth and workers' branches of the Spanish Catholic Action movement (a lay organization linked to the church) became centers of protest against the prolonged denial of political liberties, the uneven distribution of wealth, and the government's monopoly on trade unions and student associations. But the conservative church hierarchy, goaded by the regime, silenced these groups in 1967. Since then, protest has become crystallized among younger bishops inclined toward the liberal cause, church intellectuals impressed by the liberal ideas emanating from the Vatican Council, and simple parish

The Sagrada Familia, Antonio Gaudí's fantastic unfinished cathedral in Barcelona

priests from the villages of Andalusia and the slums of Madrid to the factory districts of Bilbao and Barcelona. As a Latin American diplomat I knew remarked to me once in Madrid, "Franco should know better than to take on the church in the world's most Catholic country." The diplomat pointed out that this was precisely the error made by several former Latin American dictators, causing the church to side with the liberals and leading to the dictators' overthrow.

Shortly before the Barcelona incident, the president of a young working people's group within Catholic Action dropped in to my office in Madrid to discuss what he called the rebellion of the "New Church" in Spain. His organization, *Juventudes Obreras Católicas* (commonly known as JOC), had been in the forefront of the rebellion, and its fortnightly tabloid publication, *Signo* (later closed by the bishop's conference after the Information Ministry

261

kept seizing one issue after another), had acquired a reputation for outspoken criticism of the regime. Since the young man asked me to keep his identity secret, I shall call him Ricardo.

He was an intense twenty-three-year-old, slim and dark-haired, with handsome Andalusian features. His father, a construction worker, had moved from Andalusia to Madrid shortly after the Civil War. Ricardo was born in Vallecas, an ugly industrial suburb of the Spanish capital that today has a number of impressive low-cost housing projects along with its old slums. In Ricardo's childhood it was common for the new migrants to live in caves dug out of the sides of the soft sandstone hills. Ricardo's family lived in a dilapidated tenement a stone's throw from the cave dwellers. His father, who sometimes managed to get work two days a week, was an embittered Socialist. In fact, Vallecas was full of embittered Socialists, as well as Anarchists and Communists, all glumly and silently suffering the aftermath of the Republic's defeat. Ricardo was brought up in an atmosphere of hatred and despair. He went to a Vallecas elementary school, then graduated in 1959 from an *Instituto de Enseñanza Media,* one of the very good public high schools operated in Madrid by the Spanish government. Now, he told me, he was studying law at the University of Madrid in the morning, working the afternoon shift at an electronics plant, and spending his evenings on Catholic Action affairs. I asked him to explain how—and why—he had become involved in Catholic Action. He spoke quietly and with conviction. There was nothing of the zealot about him. He was a moderate young man with an idea.

"I am a practicing Catholic, you see," Ricardo said, "and I think that it is the responsibility of Catholics to look after the welfare of our people. I believe in the teachings of Jesus Christ—don't forget he was a carpenter, a worker, himself—and I feel it is our responsibility to work for justice in our society.

"What I see around—ever since I was a child in Vallecas—is injustice. Social injustice. Two years ago I went to visit my grandparents in Andalusia, a village near Jaén, and I really had a shock. More than one-half of the men of the village had emigrated—to Madrid or Barcelona or to jobs abroad, in France or West Germany. Those who stayed behind were old men and young boys. They worked the bad, dry land in the tiny parcels that belonged to

262

individual families. The land produced almost nothing. The women worked, too. They were burned by the sun and exhausted and old before their time. There was not enough food to eat any day of the year. There was no water unless you walked several kilometers to the well. The rivers are dry, you see. There was no school for the children in the village. I went to see the *cura,* the parish priest. He had come from the seminary the year before and had just taken his orders. 'There is nothing to be done here,' he told me. 'The old women come to my church to pray, but nobody else comes. Nobody else cares. Why should they? So, what is the sense of my telling them about religion and the goodness of God and about what Christ taught if I have no way of helping them live like decent Christians?' I came back to Madrid and I thought the priest was wrong. You can't just shrug your shoulders and give up and do nothing. I started talking to people in Vallecas, my old neighborhood, and then at the plant where I work. The official union to which I belong is no good. It is run by old Falangists who have no use for freedom or justice or anything like that. They are just functionaries. Then I started meeting some of the fellows from JOC. They were different and they thought differently. They wanted to do things about this country and make it possible for the people to live like decent Christians and to be decent Christians. I joined JOC. We have a program here and it includes telling the workers and the youth the truth about what is going on. If they don't know the truth, if they don't know what the church in Rome thinks now—the Vatican Council and all that—they can't help themselves nor have any hope. And we have some very good priests working with us, men who understand the problems of Spain and our generation. Do we get into trouble? Sure, we do. I spent three months in jail early this year because we were holding what the police called 'illegal meetings' with some of the workers. Then I was elected president of my group. I'm sure I'll be in jail again. But what can you do?

"If you don't print my name, I'll probably manage to stay out of jail a bit longer," he said a little sheepishly, and laughed.

A few weeks later, I met another active participant in the rebellion of the "New Church" in Spain, a thirty-three-year-old priest who had studied abroad for many years, spoke several foreign languages, and was well known and respected in Madrid's intellectual community. Father Alberto, as I shall call him, was a sophisticated if somewhat cynical man. He expressed the intellectual's contempt for the coarse politicans who made up most of the Spanish hierarchy.

"Unfortunately," he said, "our church is polluted with imbeciles in high places. I mean priests, bishops, archbishops, and cardinals who simply refuse to understand, or cannot understand, that the world and Spain have changed since the Civil War; that we have a new generation of people who are not going to put up with the pious nonsense they are dishing out. The new generation doesn't want to hear about 1936 and the 'Catholic Crusade' of Franco. They don't want to be told that all a good Catholic has to do is go to mass, confess himself once a week, and keep his mouth shut about everything else that is happening around him.

"You must have heard all the lamentations of our bishops in their pastoral letters and sermons about the new wave of anti-clericalism, dechristianization, and alienation from the church. They complain that students and workers are turning their backs on the church and religion. Well, they are right about the backs being turned on the church, but they are wrong that people reject religion. You see, we Spaniards are peculiar people. We can be against the church because it's no good, and still be for religion. When I say that bishops are imbeciles, I mean that they bring on anticlericalism and the alienation from the church by their own actions. They don't think and they don't understand.

"I happen to believe that, particularly with the coming of the Vatican Council, the church in Spain is at the crossroads. Either it will change its ways quickly and survive—or it will remain as it is and die with Franco. Then you'll have a wave of anticlericalism—not as violent, perhaps, but deeper—worse than we had in the thirties, when they burned the churches and killed the priests and nuns. My private opinion is that the church in Spain can and should fulfill a positive and constructive role—a role of leadership—in all the great changes that are occurring in our society."

One of the ecclesiastic centers of the "New Church" rebellion is the ancient Abbey of Montserrat not far from Barcelona. It crowns a volcanic mountain four thousand feet high, and much of it was built by the founders of the Benedictine Order in the year 986. Montserrat became an independent abbey in 1410 and has remained one ever since—in every sense of the word. In the 1960's the antiregime sentiment of the Montserrat Benedictines contrasted

The Abbey of Montserrat

sharply with that of the Benedictines in charge of the great monastery at the Valley of the Fallen, who have the reputation of being reactionary and thoroughly pro-Franco. The Montserrat liberalism was in large measure inspired by Father Aurelio Escarré, the former abbot and a man of independent and original thought. Under him the monks quietly began to encourage liberal attitudes in the Catalonian clergy and to advocate cultural autonomy for the Catalans. The abbey's monthly magazine, *Serra d'Or* (Golden Mountain), which emphasized Catalan culture and was at the time the only periodical regularly published in the Catalan language, was constantly in trouble with censors in Madrid. Early in 1965 Abbot Escarré granted an interview to a Paris newspaper and spoke critically of the regime. Arrangements were made to remove him from the abbey, and he went to live in Milan in virtual exile. But his successors have kept the Montserrat spirit alive. When I visited

265

the abbey late in 1966, the monks were discussing whether the Barcelona civil governor should be allowed to enter the monastery on one of his periodic official calls. The monks wanted him to apologize first for the assault on the priests that had taken place in Barcelona in May.

Among the consequences of that assault was the creation of "truth squads" that secretly traveled across Spain to inform the clergy everywhere of what had *really* happened. The idea was to counterbalance the one-sided reporting in the controlled Spanish press, which had described the protesting priests as *"provocateurs."* Then, a clandestine priests' movement emerged in Madrid. It called itself Action Moses, for reasons I could never discover, and it urged the Spanish clergy to sign a document, drafted by prelates from the Santander diocese, urging the church hierarchy to end its political support of the Franco regime and push for the separation of church and state in Spain. The movement collected hundreds of signatures and presented the petition to the Spanish Episcopal Conference. As anticipated, the conference rejected it. But as a member of the group told me later, the Moses exercise served to awaken the "consciousness" of priests throughout Spain.

When Franco held a nationwide referendum on a new Spanish constitution in December, 1966, the church hierarchy astounded a great many Spaniards (and, presumably, the regime itself) by issuing a pastoral letter urging Catholics to arrive "freely" at their decision on how to vote. The regime had counted either on the hierarchy's endorsement of the constitution or, at least, on its silence. Considering the formidable government propaganda campaign for "yes" votes, the church's stand seemed almost subversive.

In March, 1967, a Navarrese priest named Victor Arbeloa went on trial in Madrid for calumny against the National Movement. He had dared to publish an article in *Signo* saying that the atrocities committed by the Loyalists during the Civil War were no worse than those committed by the Nationalists. Father Arbeloa had mentioned the mass executions of Loyalists by Franco's Moors in Badajoz and the destruction of Guernica—references the regime found blasphemous twenty-eight years after the war's end. I attended the trial because it had struck me that in a sense the whole morality of the Civil War was to be put up for public judgment for the first time. The court acquitted Father Arbeloa in an interesting

266

display of the relative independence of the Spanish judiciary or, perhaps, of that particular judge.

The "New Church" rebellion was quickly echoed in the Basque country. In April, 1967, five thousand workers and students and a number of Catholic priests clashed violently with the police in Bilbao. A few weeks later, some seventy priests staged a silent evening parade in downtown Bilbao to protest "police brutalities." Having some contacts in the Catholic underground, I drove to Bilbao shortly afterward to see for myself what the Basque priests were up to. While I was there a stranger telephoned me at my hotel and told me to be at a certain downtown café at a specific hour. Arriving at the café, I sat down at the counter, ordered a cup of coffee, and buried myself in a newspaper. I went on reading until I felt a tap on my shoulder. "You have dropped something," said a nondescript man who had sat down next to me, pointing to the floor. I picked up the white envelope I saw there. Later, I found that it contained five typewritten sheets describing in detail the role of Catholic groups—including Catholic Action—in raising money at masses in local churches and from industrial workers throughout Spain to help support striking workers in Bilbao. The document provided an account of the priests' demonstration earlier that month and went on to discuss the responsibility of the Catholic church in assuring social justice and freedom.

On another occasion I visited the local Catholic workers' association at a town along the Nervión River valley, one of Bilbao's main industrial areas. There I met a young priest who had graduated from a seminary two years earlier and had been immediately assigned to the association. I asked him about the role of the Catholics in the clandestine labor organizations.

"The Catholics and, to a lesser degree, the Communists are in control of the trade unions around here," he told me. "The Communists are making inroads and we must watch out. Isn't it strange that we must fight both the Communists and the Franco regime? But we don't want an open battle. The truth is that we need the Socialists and the Anarchists. If we split up now, we'll be sitting ducks for the government. So it has to be more subtle, more elegant."

I said that I found it surprising to discover how many priests were defying both the government and the church hierarchy in this region where Catholicism tends to be traditional and conservative.

The young priest waved his hand in deprecation.

"Here in the Basque country," he said, "it's been that way for as long as anybody can remember. The priests—first the village curates and later the parish priests in industrial areas like this one—have lived close to the people. We haven't had the separations and the alienation you find elsewhere in Spain. You see, the Basques are very religious, but they expect—they demand—that the priests be with them, on their side, in all things. In war, in peace, in the defense of the Basque identity, or in the defense of their rights as human beings. So our rebellion, the things we are doing now in a more modern society, is essentially what the Basque priests have been doing for centuries."

On May Day, 1967, priests confronted the police all over Spain. In San Sebastián hundreds of antiregime demonstrators sought and received sanctuary in a downtown church. In the Basque town of Eibar two priests were arrested for marching at the head of a crowd shouting, "Liberty! Liberty!" In Bilbao two priests were detained for disregarding a ban on sermons that dealt with anything but the adoration of the Virgin Mary. They had dedicated their sermons to the need for social justice. At Torre Baró, a workers' suburb of Barcelona, Catalan priests in Windbreakers and boots joined several thousand workers at a picnic that promptly turned into an antiregime demonstration. Following a pitched battle with the police, three priests were arrested. The police alleged that they were carrying copies of a manifesto signed by fifty Catalonian priests proclaiming their "interest" in the fight for freedom of all workers' groups, "be they official, illegal or clandestine." At the Can Oriach suburb of the industrial town of Sabadell, near Barcelona, priests joined workers chanting "Democracy, Yes! Dictatorship, No!" When the police came, three priests and scores of demonstrators took refuge in the little parish church of the Sacred Heart of Jesus. The next day, Barcelona's Archbishop Marcelo González Martín authorized the police to enter the church and arrest the rebels, including the three priests. In all, ten Roman Catholic priests were arrested as a result of the May Day demonstrations. There had not been so many priests in Spanish jails since the anticlerical excesses of the Republic thirty years earlier. During the summer of 1967 the ancient statue of the Virgin of Nuria, a twelfth-century Romanesque masterpiece and the object of great veneration, was stolen from its sanctuary near Caralps atop a six-thousand-foot peak in the eastern Pyrenees. A manifesto signed by a "Commission of Priests and Militants of Catholic Action" announced that "the Virgin of Nuria, faithfully guarded by the people, will be returned only when we have sufficient proof of the freedom and independence of the Church in relation to the state."

The battle between the progressive churchmen and the Franco regime has continued, and by 1971 the Spanish church was as deeply split as it has ever been in modern history.

In September, 1971, the first assembly of Spanish bishops and priests ever held in the country (a larger body than the permanent Spanish Episcopal Conference) recommended the severing of links between the church and the state.

Then the assembly declared by majority vote that it might have acted wrongly during the Civil War, when it issued a manifesto declaring that Franco's uprising was a theologically justified crusade. With the conservative churchmen opposing it, the assembly said: "We humbly recognize, and ask pardon for it, that we failed at the proper time to be ministers of reconciliation in the midst of our people, divided by a war between brothers."

One of the elements of this split is the Sacerdotal Society of the Holy Cross and Opus Dei, commonly known as Opus Dei (God's Work). It describes itself as an organization of Catholic men dedicated to a true Christian life and to good works. It has fifty thousand members in sixty-seven countries, in which it runs scores of schools, student homes, and neighborhood associations. In Spain it also has vast political power. Why Franco handed Opus Dei members such power, including key cabinet posts, has never been explained. In 1971 the Economic Planning Ministry, which directs the entire Spanish economy, was in the hands of Laureano López Rodó, the Foreign Ministry in the hands of Grégorio López Bravo, and the Education Ministry in the hands of José Luís Villar Palasi. All three are full-fledged Opus Dei members. The vice-president of the government, Admiral Carrero Blanco, is believed to be at least an Opus Dei "cooperator"—something like an associate member. The information minister, Alfredo Sánchez Bella, is close to the

society, and his brother, Florencio, a priest, is director of the Opus Dei in Spain.

Full members of Opus Dei take vows of piety and of celibacy (but, apparently, no longer of chastity). They are expected to assign a large portion of their earnings to Opus Dei and to live modest lives. The society insists that its members are not bound in any way by the politics of its directors and that in all temporal matters members enjoy "the greatest possible freedom." This claim is borne out to a considerable extent by the fact that the membership includes both top officials of Franco's regime and some of its strong opponents. A Madrid afternoon newspaper owned by Opus Dei members has been repeatedly seized and fined by the government for its outspoken criticism, and a domestic news agency likewise controlled by members of the society has received similar treatment. Some Opus Dei members have been arrested for antiregime activities.

The society's enemies see it as a sinister organization bent on controlling Spain's political and economic life. Although Opus Dei has no more than twenty-five thousand full-fledged members in Spain, plus perhaps a hundred thousand cooperators and sympathizers, it is considered a formidable force. Catholics of other persuasions ranging from pro-Franco conservatives to opposition Christian Democrats and church rebels—tend to regard it with vast suspicion, if not downright hate. In Franco's camp Falangists and monarchists fear and resent it as a powerful rival. Except for Opus Dei figures who themselves oppose the regime, the opposition thinks of Opus Dei as part of a Franco conspiracy to perpetuate his type of rule after his death. They point to the fact that Opus Dei member López Rodó and Opus Dei cooperator Carrero Blanco are the principal contenders for the premiership whenever that post is reactivated.

The mystically-inclined Spaniards resent mystics whom they do not fully comprehend. And I must confess that after three years in Spain and close friendships with many leading Opus Dei figures, I am still unable to offer a succinct definition of what the society really is. Opus Dei has been variously accused of being a "white Freemasonry," a "neo-capitalist" scheme, a church Mafia, and a latter-day version of the Society of Jesus. The Jesuits and other religious orders abhor it, too, because they see Opus Dei as competition even though it is a secular organization. Being demonologically-minded,

A member of the Guardia Civil, in dress uniform, accompanies a religious float during a Holy Week procession in Seville.

millions of Spaniards are just plain afraid of Opus Dei.

The society remains an exclusive club with members or supporters to be found among the country's top executives, bankers, economists, and publishers. It is also believed to control vast wealth. But how this wealth is amassed, used, or manipulated is among Spain's best-kept secrets. It is known that a former naval captain is Opus Dei's chief financial officer and works out of the society's central office for Spain on Madrid's Calle de Diego de León, but very few outsiders have met him. Well-informed Spaniards have reason to believe that Opus Dei owns or controls at least two major banks in Spain, as well as an unknown number of other profitable businesses. Opus Dei spokesmen readily admit that the society has financial holdings that allow it to run the University of Navarra in Pamplona, as well as schools and other organizations, but they refuse to confirm or deny allegations concerning the magnitude of its portfolio. Spanish businessmen claim, however, that Opus Dei is acquisitive and has a precise program for taking over attractive properties.

The society was founded in 1928 by Monsignor Josemaria Escrivá de Balaguer y Albas, an Aragonese priest who at the time administered a parish in one of Madrid's poorest areas. He has lived in Rome since 1946, but he makes regular visits to Spain. It was during one of these visits, in the autumn of 1966, that the society's efficient director of public affairs drove me to an Opus Dei residence near Barcelona where Monsignor Escrivá was spending that day. The gate to the mansion's garden was guarded by quiet young men who looked like karate experts, and other young men patrolled the grounds and steps of the building.

Monsignor Escrivá was rotund and expansive, but his almost jocular demeanor seemed to conceal powerful inner tensions and a strong vein of mysticism. The monsignor was sixty-five years old at the time, but he looked and acted younger. The only other people present during our two-hour talk were Opus Dei's secretary-general, the Reverend Alvaro del Portillo, a one-time highway engineer, and the public-affairs director. Monsignor Escrivá ordered one of his quiet young men to bring Scotch whisky for me and mineral water for himself. Then he embarked on reminiscences, anecdotes, and explanations of Opus Dei. He spoke of his days as a Madrid parish priest, of his traumatic experience during the Civil War when the Loyalists killed another priest believing it was he. Speaking of his life in Rome, he said with a little laugh that in the basement of his *palazzo* a sarcophagus awaited his death and burial.

He was a skilled conversationalist and successfully avoided revealing his political beliefs or his sentiments about Franco's regime. "Opus Dei has no political or economic orientation in Spain or elsewhere," he said, adding that Opus Dei members "are led by Christ's teachings always to defend personal freedoms and the rights of all men. . . . This includes the right to be treated as befits free men and citizens." He also said that Opus Dei was charged with being political perhaps because of "the subconscious prejudice engendered by a one-party mentality, in politics or in the spiritual realm." Were these criticisms of the Franco regime?

Monsignor Escrivá shed no light on Franco's favoritism of Opus Dei members. Has the Caudillo been attracted by the society's spiritual message (which seems unlikely given his pragmatism), or has he been won over by the professional talents of the administrators who are members of the Opus Dei (which appears more reasonable)? Whatever the explanation, Franco defended some of his Opus Dei men even through the Matesa affair of 1969 that was Spain's greatest modern political and financial scandal.

Matesa, a Catalonian textile machinery company, was owned by José Villa Reyes, who was a close friend of Opus Dei figures. The company had been granted $200 million in export credits by the government before it was discovered that most of its exports were fictitious. Matesa declared bankruptcy, and Franco immediately fired the finance minister, who was not an Opus Dei man, and the minister of commerce and the president of the Bank of Spain, who were. All three were indicted, and Opus Dei's enemies happily anticipated the end of the society's sway in the affairs of state. But surprisingly, Franco kept on Opus Dei member López Bravo, who as the minister of industries at the time was at least partly responsible for extending the credits to Matesa. The education minister and Opus Dei man Villar Palasi, who was close to Matesa's owner and had been his lawyer, also escaped unscathed. López Rodó, Spain's economic czar and Opus Dei's brightest star, was never touched by the scandal. In 1971 the Spanish Supreme Court ruled that there were no grounds to indict Villar Palasi and López Rodó. In the same year, Franco fired the military governor of Granada, for criticizing Opus Dei publicly. So the Opus Dei mystery persists.

A cart driver getting a ticket from a Málaga policeman

5 To Perpetuate Power

By the early 1970's the Franco regime had not only isolated Spaniards from reality by denying them responsibility for their own destiny, but it had succeeded in isolating itself from reality as well. The designation of Prince Juan Carlos as king-to-be is as good an example as any of the curious political sleight of hand with which the government maintains the illusion that all was well in Spain.

When Franco presented the prince's nomination to the Cortes for their approval in 1969, he said that this would simply reinstate the monarchy in Spain. Alfonso XIII had left in 1931 without a formal act of abdication; a plebiscite in 1947 had confirmed that Spain was a kingdom, and the Organic Law, the equivalent to a constitution that was approved in 1966 by another plebiscite, had also recognized monarchy. Franco duly noted that "two generations of Spaniards" had thus expressed their desire to accept the type of succession he was proposing.

The Cortes obediently approved Franco's choice, and on the following day the prince swore loyalty to the principles of the totalitarian-minded National Movement. This in effect obliged him to remain loyal to Franco.

On paper the mechanism of succession looked perfect. At the proper time, presumably after Franco's death, the Cortes would proclaim Prince Juan Carlos the chief of state (assuming that Franco had not exercised his legal right to change his mind and either to name someone else or to leave the succession open). The regime evidently felt that Spaniards truly accepted this painstakingly prepared scenario because 99 per cent of the eligible voters had cast "yes" ballots in the 1966 plebiscite and because the Cortes had unanimously endorsed Prince Juan Carlos. The regime was also assuming that the Spanish armed forces would guarantee the succession. In mid-1971, Franco went a step further when he announced that the prince would be acting chief of state if the Caudillo became ill.

But it was far from certain that Spaniards really wanted Juan Carlos. In the eyes of many, Franco was guilty of a series of artful betrayals to achieve his nomination. He rode roughshod over the monarchists who supported Don Juan (Juan Carlos's father), his wartime Carlist allies, his Falangist constituents, and some of the most powerful men in his regime, who simply preferred a republican but totalitarian form of government to the idea of a monarchy.

In the second place, Franco refused to consult the overt political opposition when he chose a successor. That opposition is made up chiefly of urbane and civilized men who shun violence and who might have sought an accommodation with Franco for the price of minimal political liberties. When they became too outspoken, even in the context of their essential moderation, Franco had them arrested or exiled to the African possessions or to remote Spanish villages. The Guardia Civil and the riot police were allowed to deal with the rebellious students, fiery intellectuals, dissident priests, separatist Basques and Catalonians, activist Socialists and Communists, and illegal "commissions" of rebellious workers that were organized in defiance of the regime-run *sindicatos*.

The Asturias miners' strikes in 1962 constituted the first major jolt the regime had received since the Civil War. Then, in June of that year, the chiefs of the Spanish opposition gathered in Munich and issued a manifesto recommending that Spain be excluded from the European Common Market pending Franco's agreement to domestic democratic reform. The leaders were arrested when they returned to Spain, and then they were exiled. Gil Robles, the venerable Christian Democratic leader, was allowed to go and live in Geneva after his release from jail. Joaquín Satrústegui, a liberal monarchist who was wounded while fighting on Franco's side during the Civil War, was packed off to the Canary Islands. In 1963 the regime executed Julián Grimau García, a top Communist leader, who had secretly returned to Spain in 1959. He was charged with war crimes committed during the Civil War and with other subversive activities. Grimau was executed despite the opposition of several members of the cabinet, clemency pleas from all over the world (including one from Nikita Khrushchev, then Soviet premier), and the fact that he had fractured his skull while attempting to escape from the secret-police headquarters by jumping out the window. The execution became a *cause célèbre* in Spain and abroad, bringing back memories of the Civil War and causing Franco suddenly to lose his carefully constructed image of a Caudillo of peace.

During my years in Spain arrests of the regime's opponents were so frequent that it was almost impossible to keep track of them. Aside from the mass arrests of students and workers at antiregime demonstrations and the imprisonment and trials of separatist

Basques (for propaganda as well as for occasional bomb-throwings), scores of well-known Spaniards went briefly but repeatedly to jail. These detentions were presumably meant to intimidate the regime's critics and disrupt their activities. Lawyers, journalists, artists, and university professors often came under that heading.

A young lawyer I know, the son of a count bearing a famous old Spanish name, was arrested at his Madrid apartment three times in the course of one year because of his involvement with the illegal workers' commissions. In 1967 the regime rounded up virtually the whole leadership of the commissions in Madrid, and thirty or forty men, including my lawyer friend, were sent to Carabanchel Prison for varying periods. Marcelino Camacho, a Communist and probably the most important leader of a workers' commission, was kept at Carabanchel for more than a year without being charged One of those arrested briefly was José Luís Aranguren López, one of Spain's leading philosophers, who is identified with the Christian Democratic opposition.

One day Aranguren told me that he had failed the most brilliant student in his ethics course at Madrid University upon discovering that the youth was an undercover agent of the secret police. It was widely known that the police had infiltrated the university, which was a hotbed of antiregime sentiment, but this particular incident angered Aranguren. "The boy came to me to ask why I had failed him despite his high grades," Aranguren said. "I replied that by acting as an underground police agent in my class he was guilty of highly unethical conduct and, therefore, could not be passed by me in ethics. . . ." Aranguren chuckled as he told me the story; this was one of the few ways the opposition had to get back at the regime. More traditional ways, which the opposition believed had an impact on the country, were the appeals and manifestos continuously issued by lawyers' associations, teachers, and intellectuals demanding democratic rights, the release of prisoners, and consultation with the nation on major political decisions. Sometimes the newspapers were allowed to refer to these documents; on other occasions the papers were impounded for doing so.

Before and after Juan Carlos was approved by the Cortes, Franco purified his cabinet of opponents to the prince's succession. Captain General Muñoz Grandes was retired from the vice-presidency of the government late in 1967 despite his long association with Franco in the African wars and in the Civil War. No reason was ever given for his removal, but informed Spaniards knew that the old general opposed the restoration of monarchy. It was also known that his successor, Admiral Carrero Blanco, was in favor of Prince Juan Carlos, as were most of the Opus Dei figures high in the regime. In 1970 Franco removed Fraga Iribarne from the Information Ministry, thereby depriving himself of one of his most intelligent younger ministers. Fraga had antagonized many hard-liners in the cabinet with his 1966 Press Law that eliminated advance censorship. But his major sin was opposition to monarchy. It was Fraga who told me when I came to Spain that Franco "simply does not share power." Fernando María Castiella y Maíz was replaced as foreign minister because, according to his friends, he favored Don Juan over Juan Carlos. Franco's pretexts were Castiella's failure to force Britain to surrender Gibraltar despite a major campaign that he had directed personally, and his failure to renew the U.S. bases agreement on the same exhorbitantly favorable terms.

But the elimination of a few key men could not still the opposition within the regime to the restoration of monarchy. The Falangists were the most vocal about it, and the left wing of the party— youths belonging to the José Antonio Doctrinary Circles—circulated manifestos accusing Franco of having betrayed the social ideals of the party and "sold out" to business interests.

The moderate opposition saw in the Juan Carlos formula a perpetuation of the Franco system inasmuch as the prince was sworn to observe the principles of the National Movement, which explicitly rule out the existence of political parties in Spain. This sounded the death knell for even a gradual evolution toward representative democracy.

Franco's special—and very un-Spanish—genius for letting rival factions fight it out before intervening to restore the balance has enabled him to govern successfully for thirty years. He has bottled up most of the negative and positive influences in Spanish society and offered the nation a period of policed peace that has allowed Spain to recover from the Civil War and develop economically. But no other man in Spain is known to command the fear and respect that Franco has commanded, and no other man is believed to have the political talent required to control the contradictory forces that divide Spaniards.

Like all dictators, Franco has prevented the emergence of a dominating personality who might succeed him and act firmly in a crisis. Indeed, having ignored the moderate opposition, he may have created a vacuum that more radical elements will rush to fill. A diplomat who returned from Madrid early in 1971 put it this way: "The Spanish crisis is not a crisis of the Franco regime but a crisis of his whole system. You can almost see the hyenas getting ready to set upon the old lion."

Franco's greatest dream was to unite Spain as the Catholic Kings did. Ironically, he may have sown the seeds of a most dangerous polarization.

Prince Juan Carlos, the successor-designate, is a tall, handsome, and pleasant man in his early thirties whose broad education has been directed by Franco since the prince was in his teens. Under an agreement with Don Juan, the prince's exiled father, that was extracted virtually by trickery, Franco sent Juan Carlos to study at Madrid University and then to all three military academies. The prince learned to be a soldier, a sailor, and an aviator. Juan Carlos then spent years in various Madrid ministries to acquaint himself with the problems of governing Spain. He has traveled extensively in all the Spanish provinces and has met local officials, but seldom the local citizenry. Few men in modern times have been so thoroughly prepared for the job of ruler. But many thoughtful Spaniards wonder whether Juan Carlos truly understands the realities of present-day Spain and whether he can handle them.

Perhaps the prince's most serious political problem has been that in effect he has lived as Franco's hostage. He has never been allowed to forget that the Succession Law permits Franco to withdraw his designation at his pleasure should the prince get out of line. Consequently, Juan Carlos has kept very much to himself except for ceremonial appearances, often with Franco. Those who know him well consider him to be intelligent but rather self-effacing and not particularly aggressive. One of his former professors, who had known him for a long time, told me: "I just don't see him putting his foot down when the politicians and the generals and everybody else start pushing and pressuring him." Juan Carlos has not succeeded in electrifying the Spaniards, who usually are responsive to magnetic personalities. *"Qué niño tan simpático,"* I once heard a woman remark as she watched the prince arrive at Madrid's Teatro Real. For Spaniards, "such a nice boy" is not an accolade reserved for the prospective chief of state. After 1969, however, Juan Carlos began hinting in private conversations, especially with foreigners, that he may be a more independent king than people suspect. This was also the impression he quietly sought to convey when he visited Washington early in 1971.

Juan Carlos's immediate political adviser at Franco's death may be Admiral Carrero Blanco, the vice-president of the government since 1967. A brusque man with bushy eyebrows, Carrero Blanco is a classical Spanish rightist and a Catholic in the fifteenth-century mold. It was the old admiral's stubborn personal opposition that is believed to have delayed for years cabinet approval both of the relatively modest law on religious freedom for non-Catholics and of the 1966 Press Law. His close links to the Opus Dei would probably strengthen ever further the society's power in Spanish life should he ever be made premier.

Another possibility for the premiership is López Rodó, the Catalonian Opus Dei member who has managed the Spanish economy for more than a decade. He is a highly intelligent man in his fifties who leads an ascetic private life and enjoys an extremely close relationship with Juan Carlos. Unlike Carrero Blanco, he has a completely modern outlook, and it was thanks to him that Spain's economy was liberalized after 1958. He is, of course, a political conservative, but he is not a dogmatist. I found López Rodó to be an easy conversationalist, and we spent many stimulating hours discussing the present and future of Spain. He is one of the few highly placed Spaniards I have met who is neither domineering nor patronizing.

With the exception of the tough foreign minister, López Bravo, none of the other ministers seemed likely to be made premier. Fraga Iribarne, who was in his late forties when he left the cabinet, may still entertain ambitions, but he has no visible constituency. Now he runs a chain of breweries.

A military *coup d'état* at Franco's death and the imposition of a military dictatorship have never been discarded as possibilities in Madrid political circles. In 1967, when Franco was taken ill during a stay at his hunting preserve near Granada and first reports suggested he might die or become incapacitated, General Camilo Alonso Vega, then interior minister, put the armed forces and the Guardia Civil on alert. Not a word of this emergency was ever made public, but there are sound reasons to believe that Spain may have been on the verge of a military coup. The army today is increasingly restive, and I met no Spaniards who believed that the age of military pronunciamentos had ended forever in 1936.

The commanders of the armed forces have always been completely loyal to Franco, with whom they rose to power during the Civil War. But among the generals there are monarchists, republicans, and even Falangists. It is impossible to predict how any of

Spanish generals at an airfield outside Madrid

them will react during the succession or whether the unity of the armed forces will be maintained. In 1970 it became clear that a number of the colonels and younger officers were pressing for the maintenance of order at all costs and favored taking severe measures against all opponents to the regime. These young officers are mostly men of the middle class who were children at the time of the Civil War. It is not clear at this writing whether they were simply expressing their sentiments or whether they were forming secret associations on the model of the traditional Officers' Lodges of the nineteenth century or of the Unión Militar Española that prepared the 1936 uprising.

The views of these officers became known, and they emerged as a possible political force in Spain, in December, 1970, during the trial of a group of Basque nationalists in Burgos. The Basques were charged with the murder of a police inspector and were tried before a military tribunal. The army prosecutor demanded death sentences, plunging Spain into its most severe political crisis since the end of the Civil War thirty-one years earlier. The defendants were supported even by opponents of Basque separatism who condemned the terrorist activities of ETA, the Basque secret society. Strikes and demonstrations were called throughout the country, and the trial quickly became an issue between the regime and its opponents. Franco even found it necessary to address a hastily organized mass rally from a balcony of Madrid's Royal Palace in order to seek the support of the nation. He had never done this before, and significantly, he had Juan Carlos at his side. The crowd gave him a vast ovation, for many Spaniards make a peculiar distinction between him and his regime, and he still enjoys considerable personal popularity.

When everybody had assumed that the lives of the Basques would be spared, the Burgos military court handed down death sentences. Two of the defendants, in fact, received double death sentences. Many foreign governments urged Franco to reverse the sentences; Pope Paul VI sent a personal appeal. But President Nixon was conspicuously silent, which was instantly noted in Spain. Finally, Franco commuted the death sentences to life imprisonment after a reportedly stormy cabinet meeting.

Many observers in Madrid believe that the Burgos trial was a watershed in the history of the Franco regime. The army was said to have resented Franco's clemency on the grounds that it undermined the army's authority. It may have been to appease the military that Franco ordered the arrest of hundreds of Spaniards throughout the country after the Burgos crisis. This in turn created new resentments in the population. Even ranking prelates protested the arrests and the treatment allegedly given the prisoners.

At this time of crisis the course of Spanish history began to repeat itself. The moderate opposition was demoralized while the radicals gained strength. Yet the moderates have shown themselves to be men of courage and principle, keeping alive the flame of democratic principles under the most trying circumstances. As one of the moderate leaders once told me, "Franco does not seem to understand that we are not out to overthrow him. . . . Nobody wants it, and besides, nobody has the power to do it. If he had realized that all we wanted was a relaxation of the dictatorship and a promise of democratic change in the next period, he might have rendered a service to Spain."

As always, the moderate opposition is divided, despite periodic agreements to cooperate and reasonably good personal relations between its leaders. Oddly, the rebel workers' commissions and the students present a less divided front than the professional politicians of the opposition.

Probably the most important group among the moderates is the Socialist party. It acts quite openly although it does not exist legally. The key Socialist in Spain at this writing is Dr. Enrique Tierno Galván, a university professor, lawyer, and gentle human being whom I have visited often. Tierno Galván and an array of Socialist lawyers spend much of their time defending people on trial at Public Order Tribunal. The Socialist tradition remains strong in Spain, but at one point Tierno Galván was willing to go along with a restoration of the monarchy provided that Don Juan was made king. Franco's opposition has always felt that Don Juan is a more liberal man than his son Prince Juan Carlos. Tierno Galván told me that he felt Don Juan's reign would be a transition to a pluralistic democracy. But there are destructive divisions even within the Socialist party. Rodolfo Llopis, the Socialist chief living in exile in Toulouse, refuses to accept the independence of the "home Socialists," just as Tierno Galván refuses to take orders from abroad. The Madrid Socialists are also at odds with the Catalonian Socialists.

The Christian Democrats are led by old Gil Robles, who was the rightist war minister during the Republic, and by Joaquín Ruíz-Gímenez, a former education minister in Franco's regime and most recently the world president of Pax Romana, a Catholic lay organization. Ruíz-Gímenez, who has by now turned completely against Franco, is also a lawyer who defends the regime's prisoners in Madrid courts and the publisher of *Cuadernos para el Diálogo,* a courageous political and intellectual monthly whose issues are periodically seized by the police.

At this writing the liberal monarchist contingent includes the wealthy Count of Motrico, once Franco's top diplomat and later

Don Juan's chief spokesman in Madrid. The count and Tierno Galván occasionally visit each other, and the count has often received leaders of the workers' commissions at his elegant home on the Paseo de la Castellana. As I quickly discovered, the Count of Motrico is one of the best informed politicians in Madrid. His passport was seized by the government when he and a delegation of Spanish opposition leaders attempted to present a letter to U.S. Secretary of State William P. Rogers during a visit he made to Madrid in 1970. Another important liberal monarchist is Joaquín Satrústegui, who was my next-door neighbor on the Avenida del Generalísimo.

Don Juan has continued to live quietly in exile in Estoril, Portugal, hoping against hope that the army will call him to the throne after Franco's death. He is a gregarious bear of a man who told me during our periodic talks that he believes he could keep Spain united under a fairly liberal constitutional monarchy. He is an enthusiastic yachtsman who once served as a lieutenant in the British navy. During his occasional calls at Spanish ports he is accorded royal treatment by the authorities, who act under strict orders from Franco. Spaniards have always greeted him with a warmth that his son, Juan Carlos, has never seemed to inspire. Franco by-passed him because he considered him too liberal and because he has never forgotten the ringing manifesto that Don Juan issued in Lausanne, Switzerland, in 1945, as World War II was ending. In it, Don Juan said that "the regime established by General Franco, which was modeled on the totalitarian systems of the Axis powers and which is completely contrary to the character and tradition of our people, is quite incompatible with the conditions prevailing in the world as a result of the present war." Don Juan then urged Franco to surrender power.

T he clandestine radical opposition is much harder to identify. But there is no question that it is growing. It consists of students, rebellious workers, and increasingly, dissident priests.

Socialists, especially among the workers, have been involved from the earliest stages in antiregime demonstrations. However, the Communist influence has grown as the regime has become more oppressive. The Spanish Communist party is headed by Santiago Carillo, a party veteran, who spends most of his time in Paris. Clandestine

Police check on a resident of Barcelona.

Communist cells multiplied in Spain during the 1960's, sometimes recruiting surprising candidates. In 1964 the son of the air minister, Lieutenant General José Lacalle Zarraga was arrested as a Communist courier. A powerful weapon in the Spanish Communists' arsenal is Independent Spain Radio. It broadcasts from a strong transmitter at a secret location, long presumed to be Prague. It can be heard clearly across the Peninsula, and it commands a wide audience. The station's two main assets are that it is both credible and very well informed. I heard it broadcast detailed accounts of events that had occurred less than twenty-four hours earlier and that often were news to correspondents in Madrid. Except for deliberate propaganda, its reports were completely factual.

Known radicals include the young and highly respected economist, Ramón Tamames, who admits he is a left-wing Socialist and who is often accused of being a Communist. He is the chief critic of López Rodó's economic policies, especially of his efforts to build capitalism in Spain. He expressed his political views in an interview with Salvador Paniker, the author of *Conversations in Madrid,* a book that the regime rather surprisingly allowed to be published in 1969. Tamames said: "The regime knows that in Spain freedom is the doorway to revolution—in the good sense of the word. I'm not talking about blood baths but about historic change. In Spain we have not had the change that France had in the eighteenth century, or the United States with independence. And since we have not had a revolution to achieve formal freedoms that would channel the demands of the people, there is great fear of more freedom."

Another exponent of fairly radical views is the Reverend José María Gonzáles Ruíz, who was removed from his post as the Canon of Málaga because of his politics but was allowed to keep his title when he moved to Madrid. Father Gonzáles Ruíz, the youngest important Spanish theologian, took part in drafting the Vatican Council's decree on religious freedom, which most of his Spanish colleagues opposed. In Madrid Father Gonzáles Ruíz is a worker-priest, dressing regularly in slacks and a sweater or Windbreaker. When I visited him once at his tiny apartment, he proudly showed me a photograph of Ché Guevara next to the crucifix on his dresser. To Paniker he said: "A Christian can never cooperate with the violence of the oppressor. The violence of the oppressed to free themselves is a struggle which, insofar as it is violent, is wrong and a

Christian cannot give his blessing to it. . . . But the Christian can take his violence upon himself to redeem it. And he can take it upon himself with the advantage that he will never be tempted to deify violence."

After the thirty-odd years of Franco's "peace," changes are bound to come to Spain. The last time I was in Madrid, a Spanish friend said: "This country has already changed more than you realize. It is changing every day. Nothing can stop this change. But I must hope that we, the Spaniards, will change with it. Otherwise we shall again see tragedy."

Special Interest Guide

T his guide section is arranged alphabetically according to pro-
fessions, hobbies, and fields of interest. It will enable the prospective visitor to plan his trip to Spain so as to pursue most
profitably his special interest. The guide is by no means all-inclusive,
but every attempt has been made to include the relevant professional
associations that can provide the visitor with further details.

Contents

Many Spanish wines are sold straight from the barrel.

Agriculture

Because Spain is an agricultural country, the Ministry of Agriculture encompasses many departments. Below are cited only some of the more unusual. For information about the Ministry's other activities contact:

NEGOCIADO DE ASUNTOS GENERALES
SECRETARIA GENERAL TECNICA
MINISTERIO DE AGRICULTURA

Paseo de la Infanta Isabel, 1
Madrid

ANIMAL HUSBANDRY

Artificial and natural insemination of cattle is the specialty of the:

SECCIÓN DE REPRODUCCIÓN ANIMAL
DE LA DIRECCIÓN GENERAL DE
GANADERIA
MINISTERIO DE AGRICULTURA

Paseo de la Infanta Isabel, 1
Madrid

FORESTRY

Information about reforestation is obtainable from:

4A INSPECCIÓN REGIONAL

Republica Argentina, 42
Seville

6A INSPECCIÓN REGIONAL

Plaza de Alonso Martinez, 7
Burgos

SERVICIO HIDROLÓGICO-FORESTAL
DE LÉRIDA

Avenida Generalisimo, 63
Lérida

SERVICIO HIDROLÓGICO-FORESTAL DE
SANTANDER-VIZCAYA

Alameda de Urquijo, 28 (5th floor)
Bilbao

TRAINING SCHOOLS

Forty-seven of these schools have a capacity of 4,250 boarders. Among the subjects taught are agricultural mechanics, forestry, stock raising, grape growing and wine making, pests and pesticides. For further information contact:

DIRECCIÓN GENERAL DE CAPACITACIÓN
AGRARIA

Calle Bravo Murillo, 101
Madrid

WINE

Regulatory councils, known as Consejos Reguladores de la Denominaciones de Origen, control the production of Spanish wines, ensuring their purity and seeing to the maintenance of a consistent quality in the various regional marks. The regions and councils controlling them are:

Alella—Estación de Viticultura y
Enologia, Amalia, 27, Villafranca
del Panadés (Barcelona)
Alicante—Sección Agronómica, Teniente
Alvarez Soto, 1, Alicante
Cariñena—Sección Agronómica, General
Sanjurjo, 10, Zaragoza
Huelva—Sección Agronómica, Gran
Via, 5, Huelva
Jerez—Avenida Alvaro Domecq s/n,
Jerez de la Frontera (Cádiz)
Jumilla—Sección Agronómica, Gonzalez
Adalid, 4, Murcia
Málaga—Sección Agronómica, Córdoba,
10, Málaga

Mancha, Manchuela, Almansa y
    Mentrida—Sección Agronómica,
    Ronda de Santa Maria, 31, Ciudad
    Real
Montilla y Moriles—Sección Agronómica,
    Avenida Generalisimo, 24, Córdoba
Navarra—Sección Agronómica, Avenida
    Carlos III, 36, Pamplona
Panadés—Estación de Viticultura y
    Enologia, Amalia, 27, Villafranca
    del Panadés (Barcelona)
Priorato—Estación de Viticultura y
    Enologia, Paseo Sunyer s/n, Reus
    (Tarragona)
Rioja—Avenida Pio, XII, s/n, Logroño
Tarragona—Sección Agronómica, Real,
    28, Tarragona
Valdepeñas—Sección Agronómica,
    Ronda de Santa Maria, 31, Ciudad
    Real
Valdforras—Sección Agronómica,
    Capitán Eloy, 17, Orense
Valencia, Utiel-Requena y Cheste—
    Sección Agronómica, Plaza del
    Caudillo, 5, Valencia

Archaeology

DIGS

Archaeologists wishing to take part in a dig or visit an excavation site should contact in advance:

Instituto Rodrigo Caro
Consejo Superior de Investigaciones

Duque de Medinaceli, 4 (3rd floor)
Madrid 14

> Twice yearly the Institute puts out a multilingual publication called Archivo Español de Arqueologia. Hours 4 P.M. to 8 P.M.

PREHISTORIC CAVE ART

Archaeologists have distin-guished three types: Cantabrian, Levantine, and Stylized.

Cantabrian cave art is so named because the majority of examples are located in the Cantabrian mountains to the west of the Pyrenees. These ochre and black drawings of bison, deer, mammoths, and other animals date from Paleolithic times. Frequently the artists used the cave contours to enhance the realism of their pictures. The most famous of the Cantabrian caves is the Altamira cave, near Santillana del Mar in Santander Province. It was discovered in 1879 in almost perfect condition. However, the temperature and humidity changes introduced by a constant stream of visitors have caused considerable deterioration in the drawings. A replica of the cave is on view at the National Archaeological Museum in Madrid.

Levantine cave art has been tentatively relegated to the early Neolithic period. Bison and mammoths are gone, and man makes his first real appearance. There is some indication of a primitive agricultural life and domesticated animals. These caves are located near the Mediterranean coast of Spain.

Stylized cave art is less well known. The wildly active and minute figures in these caves are often represented by several lines with knobs for heads and symbols distinguishing male and female. It is estimated that these paintings and engravings date from somewhere between 3000 and 1000 B.C.

What follows is a partial listing, by province, of Spanish caves containing prehistoric art.

Cantabrian
GUADALAJARA

CUEVA DE LOS CASARES

Near the village of Riba de Saelices

MALAGA

CUEVA DE LA PILETA

OVIEDO

CUEVA DE PEÑA DE CANDAMO

CUEVA DE PINDAL

SANTANDER

CUEVA DE ALTAMIRA

Near the town of Santillana del Mar

CUEVA DEL CASTILLO

Village of Puenteviesgo

CUEVA DE COVALAÑAS

CUEVA DE HORNOS DE LA PEÑA

CUEVA DE LA PASIEGA

Village of Villanueva

VIZCAYA

CUEVA DE BASONDO

Levantine
ALBACETE

CUEVA DE MINATEDA

Near the town of Hellín

CUEVA DE LA VIEJA

Near the village of Alpera

ALMERIA

CUEVA DE LOS LETREROS

Near the village of Velez-Blanco

CASTELLON

CUEVA DEL CIVIL

Near the village of Tirig

CUEVA DE MORELLA LA VIEJA

Near the town of Morella

LERIDA

COVACHO DE COGUL

TERUEL

CALLEJON DEL PLOU

Near the town of Albarracín

COCINILLA DEL NAVAZO

Near the town of Albarracín

COCINILLA DEL OBISPO

Near the town of Albarracín

CUEVA DEL CHARCO

Near the village of Valdealgorfa

VALENCIA

CUEVA DEL ARAÑA

Near the village of Bicorp

Stylized
JAEN

CUEVA DE MIRANDA DEL REY

ABRIGO DE LOS CONFOROS

RUINS

Phoenician and Carthaginian

The Phoenician and Carthaginian occupations are commemorated chiefly by the remains of necropoli. The pre-Carthaginian ruins, dating from about the ninth century B.C., are in the south (all ruins are listed by province):

ALMERIA

VILLARICOS

PUNIC NECROPOLIS

CADIZ

Baños de Blanco

Funerary monument dating from the ninth century B.C.

Punta de Vaca

Necropolis dating from the ninth century B.C.

Puerta de Tierra

Necropolis dating from the ninth century B.C.

SEVILLA

Carmona

Necropolis with semiartificial caves and carved marble sarcophagi. There is an archaeological museum at the site.

The post-Carthaginian ruins, dating from about the seventh century B.C., are located in Ibiza:

Puig de Molins

Necropolis with more than 5,000 tombs.

Puig d'en Vallas

Ruins of a Carthaginian monastery.

Iberian
ALICANTE

Alcoy

Ruins of Iberian settlement of La Serreta.

Elche

The Iberian city of Ilice, where the famous Dama de Elche statue was discovered (now in the Prado Museum in Madrid).

CASTELLON

Lucena del Cid

Ruins of Los Foyos, dating from the third century B.C.

GRANADA

Galera

Ruins of the Tutugi necropolis, dating from the sixth and third centuries B.C.

JAEN

Peal de Becerro

Ruins of the Iberian necropolis of Cerro de la Horca, belonging to the anicent Iberian city of Tugia.

Castillar de Santiesteban

Iberian ruins of Despeñaperros.

SORIA

Numancia

Ruins of a Celtiberian city.

TERUEL

Azaila

Ruins of an Iberian settlement destroyed by the Romans in the first century B.C.

Calaceite

Ruins of a large Iberian city dating from the sixth to the third century B.C.

VALENCIA

Ayora

Ruins of the Iberian city of Castellar de Meca.

Cerro de los Santos

Site where bronze Iberian votive statues were discovered.

Mogente

Ruins of the Iberian settlement of La Bastida, dating from the fifth and third centuries B.C.

Greek
GERONA

Ampurias

The old Greek colony of Emporion, with the remains of a city wall, a pier, and other buildings. It dates from the sixth and fifth centuries B.C.

See also **Roman Ruins, Cities.**

Roman

Because the Roman occupation lasted for six centuries, Roman ruins in Spain are almost commonplace. Here are some of the major ones.

Aqueducts

BADAJOZ

MÉRIDA

Ruins of the Milagros and San Lázaro aqueducts.

SEGOVIA

SEGOVIA

This aqueduct, still very much intact, has 128 arches and is 2,500 feet long and 85 feet high. Traffic passes through the arches.

TARRAGONA

TARRAGONA

Aqueduct also called the Puente de las Ferreras.

Bridges

BADAJOZ

MÉRIDA

Two bridges, on the Albarregas and Guadiana rivers.

CACERES

ALCÁNTARA

On the Tagus River.

SEGURA

On the Spanish-Portuguese border.

SALAMANCA

SALAMANCA

On the Tormes River.

Cities

BADAJOZ

MÉRIDA

The old Emerita Augusta colony. Remains of the Theatre of Agrippa, an Augustan period amphitheatre, and other ruins.

BURGOS

PEÑALBA DE CASTRO

The site of the old Roman town of Clunia Sulpicia, with ruins of public buildings and houses.

CACERES

TALAVER LA VIEJA

Site of the old Roman town of Augustobriga, with ruins of a temple, an amphitheatre, and city walls.

CADIZ

SANLÚCAR DE BARRAMEDA

Site of the old Roman colony of Belo, or Bolonia.

CUENCA

SEGORBIGA

Ruins of a theatre, an amphitheatre, and baths.

GERONA

AMPURIAS

On top of and mingled with the ruins of the old Greek colony of Emporion are the remains of a Roman city wall and other Roman constructions.

LUGO

LUGO

The site of the old Lucus Augusti colony, from which the present-day city derives its name. The old Roman walls, over a mile long, are still intact, and one can walk along the road that ran on top of them.

MALAGA

RONDA

Ruins of a Roman theatre.

SEVILLA

CARMONA

Still being excavated. So far a large Roman graveyard has been uncovered.

SANTIPONCE

Site of the old Roman colony of Italica, where Trajan and Hadrian were supposedly born. It was one of the largest Roman cities in Spain. Ruins of a theatre and an amphitheatre are at present being excavated.

VALENCIA

SAGUNTO

Site of the Roman town of Saguntum, with ruins of an amphitheatre and part of the town walls.

ZARAGOZA

CALATAYUD

Site of the Roman colony of Bilbilis.

Moorish

CORDOBA

CÓRDOBA

The ruins of Medina Azahara, the capital of the Moorish empire at the time of Caliph Abderrahman III, lie five miles east of the modern city. The medina was built in 936.

ARCHAEOLOGICAL MUSEUMS

Barcelona

MUSEO ARQUEOLÓGICO

Parque de Montjuich

Córdoba

MUSEO ARQUEOLÓGICO DE CÓRDOBA

Plaza de Jeronimo Paez

Cuenca

MUSEO ARQUEOLÓGICO DE SEGORBIGA

About 5 miles from the city of Cuenca.

Roman sculpture.

Ibiza (Balearic Islands)

MUSEO ARQUEOLÓGICO DE IBIZA

Plaza de Cataluña, 1

Ibiza

MUSEO MONOGRÁFICO

Puig des Molins

Ibiza Island

Madrid

MUSEO ARQUEOLÓGICO NACIONAL

Serrano, 13

Madrid

Seville

MUSEO DE LA NECRÓPOLIS

Carmona

MUSEO ARQUEOLÓGICO DE SEVILLA

Plaza de América

Seville

There are also state archaeological museums in the towns of Burgos, Murcia, Santander, and Toledo.

Architecture

Spain is a land rich in outstanding examples of the architect's art from every epoch. What follows is simply a sampling, organized by province.

Ávila

AVILA

The eleventh-century walls that surround the city are the best preserved in Spain.

Baleares

MALLORCA

The Casa Palacio de Verí is a good example of eastern Spanish architecture during the fifteenth century.

Barcelona

BARCELONA

The Roman walls date from the third century. The city was the home of Antonio Gaudí (1852–1926), a remarkable sculptor, ceramicist, and architect, whose bizarre and ingen-

ious structures are best seen in Barcelona. They are:

The Cathedral of the Sagrada Familia
Calle Mallorca-Provenza y Marina-Cerdeña

> Gaudí lived to finish only the eastern façade, but a model of the whole fantastic building exists and building continues.

Batilo House
Paseo de Gracia, 43

Bellesguard (Figueras House)
Calle Bellesguard

Calvet House
Calle Caspe, 48

Guell Farm
Avenida de la Victoria s/n, Pedralbes

Guell Palace
Calle Conde de Asalto 3 and 5

> Now a museum of theatre arts open to the public.

Guell Park
Calle Larrad

Mila House (commonly known as La Pedrera)
Paseo de Gracia, 92

College of Santa Teresa de Jesus
Calle Ganduxer, 41

Vincens House
Calle Carolinas 24 and 26

MATARÓ

> The remains of a Roman town of the first and second centuries.

Burgos
COVARRUBIAS

> Medieval and Renaissance buildings.

LERMA

> The best example of seventeenth-century Castilian architecture.

Cáceres
CÁCERES

> A medieval and Renaissance city.

Córdoba
CÓRDOBA

> The enormous cathedral (Mezquita) was formerly the mosque of the Moorish Caliphs. It was built in the eighth century and added to until the eleventh century. In the sixteenth century a plateresque cathedral was built in the middle of the forest of 850 marble columns that support the roof of the building.

Coruña
SANTIAGO DE COMPOSTELA

> The cathedral is the finest medieval monument in Spain.

Cuenca
CUENCA

> The old town is most picturesque. The so-called hanging houses are of particular architectural interest.

Gerona
GERONA

> One of the most ancient towns in Catalonia.

RIPOLL

> The Benedictine monastery of Santa Maria, founded in the eleventh century, has a fine, two-storied cloister dating from the twelfth to fifteenth centuries.

Granada
GRANADA

> The Alhambra is one of the most remarkable fortresses ever built. Constructed by the Moorish rulers of the city in the thirteenth and fourteenth centuries, it was partly razed in the sixteenth century to make way for the unfinished palace of Emperor Charles V. The Generalife, the country residence of the kings of Granada, is widely admired for its magnificent gardens.

Guadalajara
ATIENZA

> A medieval town that is practically a fortress.

299

The Escorial

Guipúzcoa
FUENTERRABIA

Notable examples of Gothic architecture are to be seen.

Huelva
PALOS DE LA FRONTERA

The Convento de la Rábida, a Gothic-Mudéjar church, was built at the end of the fifteenth century.

Huesca
SAN JUAN DE LA PEÑA

This monastery, founded in the ninth century, is partly carved into the living rock. The church was built in the eleventh century; the cloister in the twelfth.

Jaén
UBEDA

Contains important eaxmples of Renaissance architecture.

León
LEÓN

The basilica of San Isidoro is largely Romanesque. The royal tomb inside is entirely decorated with frescoes that date from the Romanesque period. The thirteenth-century cathedral is one of the most beautiful Gothic cathedrals in Spain.

Lérida
SEO DE URGEL

The twelfth-century Romanesque cathedral, built of granite, is particularly interesting.

Logroño
SAN MILLÁN DE LA COGOLLA

Notable are the Gothic cloister of the monastery known as Juso (Below) and the tenth-century Mosarabic church in the monastery known as Suso (Above).

Madrid
ARANJUEZ
An interesting royal palace constructed from the sixteenth to the eighteenth centuries.

SAN LORENZO DE EL ESCORIAL

The monastery is in the purest style of the architect Juan de Herrera.

EL VALLE DE LOS CAIDOS (THE VALLEY OF THE FALLEN)

This memorial to those who fell during the Civil War of 1936–39 was carved out of the living rock.

300

MADRID

The grandiose royal palace was built during the eighteenth century; the equally splendid Plaza Mayor is of the seventeenth century.

Málaga
MÁLAGA

The Alcazaba is one of the most powerful fortresses the Moors built in Spain.

RONDA

The picturesque town is divided into two quarters by a gorge nearly 600 feet deep.

Murcia
LORCA

Notable examples of Spanish Baroque architecture.

Oviedo
OVIEDO

The cathedral is a splendid fifteenth-century Gothic edifice. Santa Maria del Naranco, two miles from the town, was the summer palace of Ramiro I, King of the Asturias. It was built in the ninth century.

PRAVIA

San Juan, dating from the eighth century, is the oldest Asturian basilica.

Palencia
PALENCIA

The Gothic cathedral is built over a Visigothic crypt of the seventh century.

FRÓMISTA

The Church of San Martín (1066) is one of the best examples of Romanesque architecture in Spain.

Pontevedra
VIGO

The old quarter contains good examples of Galician architecture from the sixteenth to the eighteenth centuries.

Salamanca
SALAMANCA

The whole town is of the greatest interest for its monuments. Notable among them are the university, dating chiefly from the sixteenth century; the Plaza Mayor, surrounded by Churriguesque buildings; the Gothic "new" cathedral of the sixteenth century; and the Roman bridge of twenty-six arches that spans the Tormes.

Santander
SANTILLANA DEL MAR

One of the most picturesque towns in Spain, its architecture ranges from the twelfth to the eighteenth century.

Segovia
SEGOVIA

The Roman aqueduct of 170 arches is 2,665 feet long and 92 feet high. It is one of the most important Roman relics in Spain.

LA GRANJA

A charming palace built by Philip V during the eighteenth century in the French style.

PEDRAZA DE LA SIERRA

A medieval walled town that is most picturesque.

Sevilla
SEVILLE

The Moorish minaret known as the Giralda was built largely in the twelfth century; the splendid cathedral was begun toward the end of the fourteenth century and is the largest cathedral in the Christian world after St. Peter's in Rome. The alcazar, built between the twelfth and the sixteenth centuries exemplifies the Mudéjar style of architecture.

Soria
SORIA

The cloister of the twelfth-century church of San Juan de Duero denotes a curiously Moorish influence.

Tarragona
TARRAGONA

The remarkable cyclopean walls formed the base on which the Romans built their walls. The Gothic cathedral was raised on the ruins of a mosque, which in turn was built on the foundation of a temple to Jupiter. There are many reminders of the Roman occupation in the town. Two miles outside there is a Roman aqueduct that is almost as important as the one at Segovia.

Teruel
ALBARRACÍN

A well-preserved medieval town that has been declared a national monument.

Toledo
TOLEDO

Among the many buildings not to be missed are the pure Gothic cathedral, the Tránsito synagogue of the fourteenth century, and the house of El Greco.

Valencia
VALENCIA

The Lonja de la Seda (Silk Exchange) has a very ornate façade in the Gothic style and noteworthy galleries.

Valladolid
VALLADOLID

Students of architecture would do well to compare the early plateresque architecture evident here, where Gothic influences abound, with the later, purely Renaissance plateresque of buildings in Salamanca.

Vizcaya
LEQUEITIO

The fifteenth-century church of Santa Maria is an interesting monument to the regional adaptation of the Gothic style.

Zamora
TORO

This town, which flourished in the Middle Ages, is still most picturesque.

CASTLES

Many of Spain's castles are still intact; others have been restored or are restorable. A limited number of them have been turned into *paradors* and *albergues*—comfortable state-owned inns administered by the Spanish Information and Tourism Ministry. You can stay for as long as a fortnight in a *parador*, but only for two days in an *albergue*.

ASSOCIATION

The Society for the Preservation of Castles in Spain, which charges a small membership fee, organizes tours to castles in every part of Spain during spring and fall. For itineraries contact:

ASOCIACIÓN ESPAÑOLA DE AMIGOS DE LOS CASTILLOS

Génova, 23
Madrid 4
Telephone: 4-19-18-29

Following is a partial listing of Spanish castles arranged by province.

Albacete
ALCARAZ

Castle dating from the Arab occupation, added to in the thirteenth and sixteenth centuries.

ALMANSA

Castle dating from the Arab occupation, added to in the fifteenth century.

Almería
VELEZ BLANCO

Castle dating from the fifteenth and sixteenth centuries.

Ávila

ARENAS DE SAN PEDRO

Castle dating from the fourteenth century.

ARÉVALO

Castle dating from the Middle Ages.

EL BARCO DE ÁVILA

Castle dating from the Middle Ages.

MOMBELTRAN

Castle dating from the fourteenth and sixteenth centuries.

Badajoz

JEREZ DE LOS CABALLEROS

Castle dating from the Middle Ages.

MEDELLÍN

Castle dating from the Middle Ages and the fourteenth century.

MÉRIDA

Castle dating from the ninth and eleventh centuries.

OLIVENZA

Castle dating from the fourteenth century.

ZAFRA

Castle dating from the fifteenth and sixteenth centuries. Now a parador.

Balearic Islands

PALMA DE MALLORCA

Castle of Bellver, dating from the fourteenth century.

Barcelona

CARDONA

Eighth-century castle with medieval and eighteenth-century elements.

VILASAR DE DALT

Castle dating from the thirteenth and fourteenth centuries.

Burgos

COVARRUBIAS

Castle dating from the Middle Ages.

Cáceres

TRUJILLO

Castle dating from the thirteenth and fourteenth centuries.

JARANDILLA DE LA VERA

Castle dating from the twelfth and fifteenth centuries. Now a parador.

Cádiz

SANLÚCAR DE BARRAMEDA

Castle dating from the fifteenth century.

Castellón

PEÑÍSCOLA

Castle dating from the thirteenth and fourteenth centuries, in which summer courses for foreigners are now held.

Córdoba

ALMODOVAR DEL RÍO

Castle dating from the fourteenth century.

CAÑETE DE LAS TORRES

Castle dating from the Arab occupation and the Middle Ages.

EL CARPIO

Castle dating from the thirteenth and fourteenth centuries.

MONTEMAYOR

Castle dating from the thirteenth century.

Cuenca

ALARCÓN

Castle dating from the thirteenth and fifteenth centuries. Now a parador.

BELMONTE

Castle dating from the fifteenth century. Now an albergue.

GARCIMUÑOZ

Castle dating from the Arab occupation and the fifteenth century.

UCLES

Castle dating from the Arab occupa-

tion, the Middle Ages, and the sixteenth century. Now a convent.

Gerona
PORT DE LA SELVA

Castle dating from the tenth century.

Granada
LA CALAHORRA

Castle dating from the sixteenth century.

Guadalajara
BRIHUEGA

Castle dating from the thirteenth century.

JADRAQUE

Castle dating from the twelfth century.

SIGÜENZA

Castle dating from the Arab occupation and the fifteenth century.

ZORITA DE LOS CANES

Castle dating from the Arab occupation and the twelfth and thirteenth
centuries.

Guipúzcoa
FUENTERRABÍA

Castle dating from the fifteenth and
sixteenth centuries. Now a parador.

SAN SEBASTIÁN

Castle dating from the twelfth, fifteenth, and seventeenth centuries.

Huesca
LOARRE

Castle dating from the eleventh and
twelfth centuries.

MONZÓN

Castle dating from the Middle Ages,
and the sixteenth and seventeenth
centuries.

Jaén
ALCALÁ LA REAL

Castle dating from the Arab occupation, and the fourteenth and fifteenth
centuries.

BAÑOS DE LA ENCINA

Castle dating from the tenth century.

CANENA

Castle dating from the Middle Ages
and the sixteenth century.

JAÉN

Castle dating from the Arab occupation and the Middle Ages. Now a
parador.

SABIOTE

Castle dating from the Arab occupation and the sixteenth century.

León
PONFERRADA

Castle dating from the twelfth, thirteenth, and sixteenth centuries.

VALENCIA DE DON JUAN

Castle dating from the Middle Ages
and the fifteenth century.

VILLAFRANCA DEL BIERZO

Castle dating from the Middle Ages
and the sixteenth century.

Málaga
ANTEQUERA

Castle dating from the Arab occupation and the Middle Ages.

Murcia
LORCA

Castle dating from the thirteenth,
fourteenth, and fifteenth centuries.

Navarra
JAVIER

Castle dating from the thirteenth century.

OLITE

Castle dating from the fifteenth century. Now a parador.

Palencia
AMPUDIA

Castle dating from the thirteenth and
fifteenth centuries.

AGUILAR DE CAMPÓO

Castle dating from the thirteenth century.

Pontevedra
BAYONA

Castle dating from the Middle Ages and the eighteenth century.

SOTOMAYOR

Castle dating from the eleventh and nineteenth centuries.

Salamanca
CIUDAD RODRIGO

Castle dating from the fifteenth century. Now a parador.

VILLANUEVA DE CANEDO

Castle dating from the Middle Ages. Now a hotel.

Segovia
COCA

Castle dating from the fifteenth century. Now a high school for forestry students.

CUÉLLAR

Castle dating from the fifteenth, sixteenth, and eighteenth centuries.

PEDRAZA

Castle dating from the Middle Ages and the sixteenth and twentieth centuries.

SEPÚLVEDA

Castle dating from Roman times and the tenth and seventeenth centuries.

TURÉGANO

Castle dating from the twelfth, thirteenth, and fifteenth centuries (with a thirteenth-century church inside).

Sevilla
ALCALÁ DE GUADAIRA

Castle dating from the Roman occupation and the fourteenth and fifteenth centuries.

CARMONA

Castle dating from the Roman and Arab occupations.

Soria
MEDINACELI

Castle dating from the Middle Ages.

MONTEAGUDO DE LAS VICARIAS

Castle dating from the fifteenth and sixteenth centuries.

Tarragona
ALTAFULLA

Castle dating from the Middle Ages.

TAMARIT

Castle dating from the eleventh century.

RUIDECAÑAS

Castle dating from the eleventh and twelfth centuries.

Teruel
ALCAÑIZ

Castle dating from the thirteenth century, now being restored.

MIRAMBEL

Castle dating from the Middle Ages.

VALDERROBRES

Castle dating from the fourteenth and fifteenth centuries.

Toledo
ALMONACID

Castle dating from the Middle Ages.

BARCIENCE

Castle dating from the fifteenth century.

ESCALONA

Castle dating from the thirteenth, fourteenth, and fifteenth centuries.

CONSUEGRA

Castle dating from the Roman occupation and the Middle Ages.

GUADAMUR

Castle dating from the fifteenth century.

MAQUEDA

Castle dating from the fifteenth century. Now local police headquarters.

MORA DE TOLEDO

Castle dating from the Arab occupation and the twelfth century.

OROPESA

Castle dating from the fourteenth and fifteenth centuries. Now a parador.

ORGAZ

Castle dating from the fourteenth, fifteenth, and sixteenth centuries.

VILLALUENGA DE LA SAGRA

Castle dating from the twelfth and sixteenth centuries.

Valencia

ALACUAS

Castle dating from the fifteenth century.

GANDÍA

Castle dating from the Arab occupation.

JÁTIVA

Castles Castillo Mayor and Castillo Menor, dating from the Roman occupation and the Middle Ages.

MONTESA

Castle dating from the fourteenth and fifteenth centuries.

SAGUNTO

Castle dating from the Roman and Arab occupations and the Middle Ages.

BENISANÓ

Castle dating from the fifteenth and nineteenth centuries.

Valladolid

CURIEL

Castle dating from the fifteenth century.

FUENSALDAÑA

Castle dating from the fifteenth century.

MEDINA DEL CAMPO

Castle dating from the Middle Ages. Now a high school.

MOTA DEL MARQUÉS

Castle dating from the Middle Ages.

PEÑAFIEL

Castle dating from the thirteenth and fifteenth centuries.

PORTILLO

Castle dating from the fifteenth century.

SIMANCAS

Castle dating from the twelfth and sixteenth centuries. A military museum and archive today.

VILLALBA DE LOS ALCORES

Castle dating from the Middle Ages.

Vizcaya

GÁTICA

Castle dating from the eleventh, fourteenth, and nineteenth centuries.

GAUTEGUIZ DE ARTEAGA

Castle dating from the fifteenth and nineteenth centuries.

Zaragoza

ALMONACID DE LA SIERRA

Castle dating from the thirteenth century. Now an albergue.

CALATAYUD

Castle dating from the Middle Ages.

CETINA

Castle dating from the fifteenth century. Now a barracks.

DAROCA

Castle dating from the fifteenth century.

ERLA

Castle dating from the fifteenth century.

ILLUECA

Castle dating from the fourteenth and sixteenth centuries.

MESONES DE ISUELA

Castle dating from the fourteenth and fifteenth centuries.

NUÉVALOS

Castle dating from the twelfth and fourteenth centuries. Now a monastery.

Art

CONTEMPORARY ART

Artists

BARCELONA

Xavier Corberó (sculptor)
Arabal de San Mateo, 24
Esplugas de Llobregat

José María Subírachs (sculptor)
Carretera de San Cugat, 36

Antonio Tapies
Zaragoza, 57

MADRID

Jaime Burgillos
Virgen de Lourdes, 2

Rafael Canogar
Marcelino Santa María, 6

Juan Genovés
Arandilla, 17

Antonio Lorenzo
Almirante, 7

Muñoz Lucio
Islas Filipinas, 50

Manuel R. Rivera
General Yagüe, 8

Antonio Saura
Hilarion Eslava, 61

Eusebio Sempere
Jose Marañon, 10

Raoul Valdivieso (sculptor)
Escalinata, 3

Manuel Viola
Rio Rosas, 54

Fernando Zóbel
Fortuny, 12

Galleries

MADRID

Galeria Biosca
Genova, 11

Galeria El Bosco
Aranda, 14

Circulo 2
Manuel Silvela, 2

Galeria del Cisne
Eduardo Dato, 17

Galeria Edurne
Monte Esquinza, 11

Galeria Fortuny
Calle Turbano

Kreisler Gallery
Serrano, 19

Galeria Juana Mordó
Villanueva, 7

Galeria Seiquer
Santa Catalina, 3

Galeria da Vinci
Conde de Xiquena, 8

Sala del Prado
Calle del Prado, 21

Sala de Santa Catalina
Santa Catalina, 10

FOLK ART

Once again, this is a selection of the museums that house regional or national Spanish folk art. The museums are arranged by province.

Álava

MENDOZA (near Vitoria)

FOLK MUSEUM

Hours: 10 A.M. to 6 P.M.

Ávila

AVILA

PROVINCIAL MUSEUM

Casa de los Deanes

Plaza Nalvillos, 5

Hours: 10 A.M. to 1:30 P.M.

Balearic Islands
Mallorca Island
MALLORCA

PALACIO RESIDENCIA DE LA ALMUDAÍNA
Plaza Almoina, s/n

Hours: 10 A.M. to 1 P.M.; 3 P.M. to 6 P.M.

SON MARROIG (near Valldemosa)

MUNICIPAL MUSEUM
Plaza Maimónides, 5

Hours: 9 A.M. to 3 P.M. Stays open later in summer.

Barcelona
BARCELONA

MUSEUM OF INDUSTRIES AND POPULAR ARTS

Montjuich

Hours: 9 A.M. to 8 P.M.

PUEBLO ESPAÑOL

Montjuich

This is an assemblage of different streets, showing the architecture of

Fine embroidery from Mallorca

MINISTRY OF INFORMATION AND TOURISM

different parts of Spain. Each building is a faithful reproduction of an actual building. Artisans make regional specialties on the spot. *Hours: 9 A.M. to 8 P.M. The Information Office of the Pueblo (telephone: 223-69-54) offers specific information on outlets for Spanish arts and crafts.*

Córdoba
CORDOBA

In addition to examples of local arts, this museum contains artifacts relating to the history of bullfighting in Córdoba. Hours: 9:30 A.M. to 1:30 P.M. Stays open until 2:30 P.M. in summer.

La Coruña
MUSEO DE LAS PEREGRINACIONES (PILGRIMAGE MUSEUM)

Calle San Miguel, 4

Folk art as it has related to the pilgrimage route to Santiago de Compostela. Hours: 10 A.M. to 2 P.M. Summer: 3 P.M. to 10 P.M.

Granada
GRANADA

CASA DE LOS TIROS

Calle Pavaneras, 19

Hours: 10 A.M. to 1 P.M.; 4 P.M. to 7 P.M.

Madrid
MADRID

MUSEO NACIONAL DE ARTES DECORATIVAS (NATIONAL MUSEUM OF DECORATIVE ARTS)

Calle Montalbán, 12

Hours: 10 A.M. to 1:30 P.M. Closed Mondays and the month of August.

MUSEO DEL PUEBLO ESPAÑOL

Plaza de la Marina Española, 9

Hours: 9 A.M. to 2 P.M.

Navarra
PAMPLONA

ETHNOLOGICAL MUSEUM OF THE PYRENEES

Calle de Santo Domingo

Toledo
TALAVERA DE LA REINA

MUSEO DE CERAMICA "RUIZ DE LUNA"

Plaza General Primo de Rivera, 5

Hours: 10:30 A.M. to 2 P.M.; 3:30 P.M. to 7 P.M.

See also **Crafts and Hobbies, Ceramics.**

Valencia
MANISES

CASANOVA DALFO-SANCHIS CAUSA MUNICIPAL MUSEUM

Calle Sagrario, 28

Hours: 4 P.M. to 8 P.M.

VALENCIA

NATIONAL CERAMICS MUSEUM

Rinconada Garcia Sanchiz, s/n

Eighteenth-century fans, Valencian silks, and a historical collection of Spanish ceramics. Hours: 11 A.M. to 2 P.M.; 5 P.M. to 8 P.M. In summer the afternoon hours are 6 P.M. to 9 P.M.

See also **Crafts and Hobbies, Ceramics.**

MUSEUMS

The listings below constitute only a small fraction of the museums of Spain. They have been compiled to demonstrate the great variety of collections that are on display. The museums are arranged by province.

Ávila
MADRIGAL DE LAS ALTAS TORRES

CASA NATAL DE ISABEL LA CATÓLICA (BIRTHPLACE OF QUEEN ISABELLA OF SPAIN)

Painting, sculpture, and tapestries of the fifteenth through the seventeenth centuries.

Balearic Islands
Mallorca
MARRATXI

VERI COLLECTION

"Son Veri"

LA CABANETA

Mudéjar paintings and panels owned by the Cotoner family.

VALLDEMOSA

REAL CARTUJA

The cells in which George Sand and Chopin spent the winter of 1838, including memorabilia of their visit to the former Carthusian monastery.

Barcelona
BARCELONA

MUSEUM OF CATALAN ART

Montjuich

A most important collection of Catalan primitive paintings from the eleventh to the fifteenth centuries. Also splendid Romanesque frescoes. Hours: 10 A.M. to 2 P.M.

CASA MUSEO GAUDÍ

Parque Guell

Memorabilia of the Catalan architect Antonio Gaudí, including some of his furniture designs.

FEDERICO MARES MUSEUM

Calle Condes de Barcelona, 8

Notable collection of religious and secular art dating from the twelfth to the eighteenth century. Hours: 10 A.M. to 1:30 P.M.; 3 P.M. to 6 P.M.

MUSEUM OF MODERN ART

Parque de la Ciudadela

Painting and sculpture of the nineteenth and twentieth centuries. Hours: 10 A.M. to 2 P.M.

PICASSO MUSEUM

Calle Montcada, 15

Drawings, engravings, paintings, and ceramics of Picasso. Hours: 10 A.M. to 2 P.M.

Cuenca
CUENCA

CASAS COLGADAS

The only museum of Spanish abstract painting and sculpture in the country. Hours: 11 A.M. to 6 P.M. Monday through Friday; 4 P.M. to midnight Saturday; noon to 6 P.M. Sunday.

Granada
GRANADA

NATIONAL MUSEUM OF HISPANO-MAURESQUE ART

Casa Real de la Alhambra

Hours: 10 A.M. to 7 P.M. with slight seasonal variations.

PROVINCIAL MUSEUM OF FINE ARTS

Palace of Charles V, Alhambra

Sculpture, paintings, and enamels of the Granada school from the fifteenth century to the present. Hours: 10 A.M. to 1:30 P.M.; 4 P.M. to 6 P.M.

León
LEON

REAL COLEGIATA DE SAN ISIDORO

Plaza de San Isidoro, s/n

This royal pantheon is decorated with some of the most beautiful Romanesque frescoes in Spain.

Madrid
EL ESCORIAL

MONASTERY MUSEUM

Paintings, tapestry, furniture, and other decorative arts. Hours: 10 A.M. to 1 P.M.; 3 P.M. to 6 P.M.

MADRID

SPANISH MUSEUM OF CONTEMPORARY ART

Paseo de Calvo Sotelo, 20

Nineteenth- and twentieth-century paintings, sculpture, drawings, and engravings. Hours: 10:30 A.M. to 2 P.M.

NATIONAL ENGRAVING MUSEUM

Calle Alcalá, 13

Engraving proofs and plates of the eighteenth to the twentieth centuries. Hours: 10 A.M. to 2 P.M.; closed Sundays and holidays.

GOYA'S TOMB

San Antonio de la Florida
Paseo de la Florida, s/n

The cupola was frescoed handsomely by Goya. Hours: 11 A.M. to 1:30 P.M.; 3 P.M. to 6 P.M. in winter. 10 A.M. to 1 P.M.; 4 P.M. to 7 P.M. in summer.

EL PRADO

Paseo del Prado, s/n

A superb collection of paintings. The Velasquezes and Goyas are not to be missed. Hours: 10 A.M. to 3 P.M. in winter and early spring; 10 A.M. to 3:30 P.M. in late spring and early autumn; 10 A.M. to 6 P.M. in summer. Cafeteria in the museum.

MUSEO DE LA REAL ACADEMIA DE SAN FERNANDO (ROYAL ACADEMY OF FINE ARTS)

Calle Alcalá, 13

Noteworthy paintings, sculpture, and drawings.

ROYAL TAPESTRY WORKS

Calle Fuenterrabia, 2

Eighteenth-century tapestries and carpets and some of the drawings for them. Hours: 10 A.M. to 1 P.M.; 4 P.M. to 6 P.M.

Salamanca
SALAMANCA

PROVINCIAL MUSEUM OF FINE ARTS

Calle Fray Luis de León, 1

Paintings from the fifteenth to the nineteenth centuries. Hours: 10 A.M. to 3 P.M. in winter; 9 A.M. to 1 P.M.

and 4:30 P.M. to 10:30 P.M. in summer.

Segovia
LA GRANJA

Charming royal palace richly decorated with tapestries. Hours: 10 A.M. to 1 P.M. and 2 P.M. to 6 P.M.

SEGOVIA

PROVINCIAL MUSEUM OF FINE ARTS

Casa del Hidalgo

San Agustin, 8

Paintings, sculpture, ceramics, crystal from La Granja, and ironwork. Hours: 10:30 A.M. to 1:30 P.M.; 3:30 P.M. to 6 P.M.

CHURCH OF SAN JUAN DE LOS CABALLEROS

Paintings and ceramics by Ignacio Zuloaga (1870–1945). Hours: 9 A.M. to 2 P.M.; 4 P.M. to 7 P.M.

Seville
SEVILLE

PROVINCIAL MUSEUM OF FINE ARTS

Plaza del Museo, 8

Paintings from the fifteenth century to the present. Also sculpture, drawings, ceramics, furniture, and weapons. Hours: 10 A.M. to 2 P.M.

Tarragona
TARRAGONA

DIOCESAN MUSEUM

Cathedral Cloister

Paintings from the fourteenth to the eighteenth centuries; prehistoric artifacts from the province, sculpture, tapestries, coins, costumes. Hours: 10:30 A.M. to 12:30 P.M.; 3:30 P.M. to 5 P.M.

Toledo
TOLEDO

EL GRECO HOUSE AND MUSEUM

Travesía del Tránsito, s/n

Paintings by El Greco and furniture

of his time. *Hours: 10 A.M. to 1:30 P.M.; 3:30 P.M. to 6 P.M.*

SEPHARDIC MUSEUM

Synagogue of Samuel-Ha-Levi
Travesía del Tránsito, s/n

Hebrew art and historical artifacts. Hours: 10 A.M. to 1 P.M.; 3 P.M. to 6 P.M.

Valencia
VALENCIA

PROVINCIAL MUSEUM OF FINE ARTS

Calle San Pio V, 9

Interesting Spanish primitives as well as Ribaltas and Riberas. Hours: 10 A.M. to 2 P.M.

Valladolid
VALLADOLID

IGLESIA DE LA PASIÓN

Calle de la Pasión

Paintings of the fourteenth to eighteenth centuries. Hours: 10 A.M. to 1:30 P.M.; 4 P.M. to 10 P.M.

NATIONAL MUSEUM OF POLYCHROME SCULPTURE

Calle Cadenas de San Gregorio, 1

The most important collection in Spain of carved wooden polychromed sculptures from the thirteenth to the eighteenth centuries. Hours: 10 A.M. to 1:30 P.M.; 4:30 P.M. to 6 P.M., except in summer, when the museum is open until 7 P.M. Sundays and holidays: 10 A.M. to 2 P.M.

Vizcaya
BILBAO

MUSEUM OF FINE ARTS

Parque de Da. Casilda Iturriza, 3

Paintings of the thirteenth to the nineteenth centuries. Hours: 10:30 A.M. to 1:30 P.M.; 4 P.M. to 6 P.M.

MUSEUM OF MODERN ART

Parque de Da. Casilda Iturriza, 3

Nineteenth- and twentieth-century

paintings. Hours: 10:30 A.M. to 1:30 P.M.; 4 P.M. to 6 P.M.

Zaragoza
FUENDETODOS

GOYA'S BIRTHPLACE

Plaza de Goya-Zuloaga, s/n

Memorabilia of Goya. To visit the house, ask at the town hall.

Crafts and Hobbies

The listings under each heading are arranged by province.

BOOKBINDING

This is a traditional Spanish craft and there are many binders active. Among the best are:

Barcelona
BARCELONA

BRUGALLA, ENCUADERNACIÓN DE ARTE

Aribau, 7

Madrid
MADRID

LOPEZ VALENCIA

Barbara de Braganza, 8

CERAMICS

Madrid
MADRID

INSTITUTO DE VALENCIA DE DON JUAN

Calle Fortuny, 43

This is a superb collection of early Spanish ceramics and tiles, as well as fabrics, jewels, and 10,000 coins.

See also **Folk Art, Toledo** and **Valencia.**

COINS

Barcelona
BARCELONA

NUMISMATIC CABINET OF CATALUÑA

Ciudadela Park

Nine rooms full of coins and medals. Hours: 10 A.M. to 2 P.M.

ACUÑACIONES ESPAÑOLAS S.A.

Calle Valencia, 193

Official commemorative issues on display and for sale.

NUMISMATICA IBÉRICA S.A.

Balmes, 195

Official commemorative issues on display and for sale.

Madrid
MADRID

MUSEUM OF THE FABRICA NACIONAL DE TIMBRE Y MONEDA

Calle Jorge Juan, 106

Collection of Spanish coins on display.

JUAN R. CAYON

Fuencarral, 41

Coins for sale.

FERNANDO P. SEGARRA

Clavel, 7 and Plaza Mayor, 26

Coins for sale.

See also **Crafts and Hobbies, Ceramics.**

LEATHERWORK

Barcelona
IGUALADA

LEATHER MUSEUM

Carretera de Manresa

Museum of the history of tanning and leatherwork.

MUSICAL INSTRUMENTS

Asturias
GIJON

INTERNATIONAL BAGPIPE MUSEUM

Antiguo Instituto de Jovellanos
Plaza del Generalisimo, 8

Barcelona
BARCELONA

MUNICIPAL MUSEUM OF MUSIC

Calle Bruch, 110

PAPER

Barcelona
CAPELLADES

PAPER MUSEUM AND MILL

Moli de la Villa
Calle Inmaculada Concepción, s/n

An extensive collection of artifacts used for making paper before the advent of machines. The mill can still turn out paper as it was made in the sixteenth century.

PHARMACOLOGY

Gerona
LLIVIA

PHARMACY MUSEUM

Ayuntamiento (Town Hall)
Plaza Mayor

With apothecary jars from the fifteenth to the nineteenth century, and

Sunday is *the* day for philatelists.

*other historical items relating to the
history of pharmacology, this is considered to be the most ancient museum of its kind in Europe.*

RAILROADS

Madrid
MADRID

RAILWAY MUSEUM

Calle de San Cosme y Damian, 1

STAMPS

Barcelona
BARCELONA

POSTAGE MUSEUM

Palacio de la Virreina
Rambla de las Flores, 99

> *Displays relating to the history of the
> postal service and examples of stamps
> from 1840 to 1940.*

Madrid
MADRID

PLAZA MAYOR

> *Every Sunday morning collectors
> gather to exchange stamps and the
> latest news about stamp collecting.*

SCIENTIFIC INSTRUMENTS

Madrid
MADRID

COLLECTION OF THE NATIONAL
ASTRONOMIC OBSERVATORY

Calle Alfonso XII, 3

TEXTILES AND COSTUMES

Barcelona
BARCELONA

TEXTILE MUSEUM

Calle Hospital, 56

TARRASA

BIOSCA TEXTILE MUSEUM

Calle General Sanjurjo, s/n

Textiles from Hispano-Mauresque times to the eighteenth century.

MUSEUM OF THE HISTORY OF COSTUME

Palacio del Marqués de Llio
Calle Montcada, 12

Displays of clothing from the sixteenth century to the present.

Education

Nearly sixty United States universities hold programs in Spain, although enrollment in the United States well in advance is necessary. For information about these universities and their Spanish programs contact:

INSTITUTO DE CULTURA HISPANICA
SECCIÓN DE NORTEAMÉRICA

Avenida de los Reyes Cátolicos, s/n
Ciudad Universitaria
Madrid 3

COURSES FOR FOREIGNERS

The majority of these courses require some knowledge of Spanish from participating students. Their locations are listed below by province, along with the addresses from which further information can be obtained.

Alicante
ALICANTE

SECRETARIA DE LOS CURSOS DE VERANO

Calderón de la Barca, 17

Balearic Islands
PALMA DE MALLORCA

DR. MARIANO BASSOLS DE CLIMENT
DIRECTOR DE LOS CURSOS DE VERANO
UNIVERSIDAD DE BARCELONA

Barcelona 7

Barcelona
BARCELONA

SECRETARIO DEL CURSO DE
ESTUDIOS HISPÁNICOS
FACULTAD DE FILOSOFÍA Y LETRAS
UNIVERSIDAD DE BARCELONA

Cádiz
CADIZ

SECRETARIO DEL CURSO DE VERANO
UNIVERSIDAD DE SEVILLA EN CÁDIZ

Apartado 151

Canary Islands
Gran Canaria

LAS PALMAS

UNIVERSIDAD INTERNACIONAL DE
CANARIAS

Bravo Murillo, 21

Tenerife
SANTA CRUZ

INSTITUTO DE ESTUDIOS HISPÁNICOS
UNIVERSIDAD DE LA LAGUNA

Puerto de la Cruz

Castellón
PENISCOLA

DIRECTOR DEL INSTITUTO DE ESTUDIOS
CASTILLO DE PEÑÍSCOLA
DIPUTACIÓN PROVINCIAL DE
CASTELLÓN DE LA PLANA

Castellón de la Plana

La Coruña
SANTIAGO DE COMPOSTELA

SECRETARIO DEL CURSO DE VERANO
UNIVERSIDAD DE SANTIAGO DE
COMPOSTELA

Plaza de la Universidad, 4

MUSIC COURSE FOR PROFESSIONALS,
AMATEURS, AND AUDITORS

Dirección de Relaciones Culturales

Palacio de Santa Cruz
Madrid 12

Guipúzcoa
SAN SEBASTIAN

Secretario del Curso de Verano
para Extranjeros

Calle Andía, 13
Apartado 205

Granada
GRANADA

Universidad de Granada
Facultad de Filosofía y Letras

Calle de Puentezuelas

Huesca
JACA

Secretaría de los Cursos de Verano
Ciudad Universitaria

Saragossa

León
LEON

Secretario General de los
Cursos de Verano

Avenida de Sanjurjo, 2

Madrid
MADRID

Facultad de Filosofía y Letras
Universidad de Madrid

Escuela Central de Idiomas

Avenida de Islas Filipinas

Escuela de Verano Española
Dirreción de Relaciones Culturales
Secretarió del Curso Español
para Extranjeros

Plaza de la Provincia, 1

International Summer Course
Centro Cultural Hispanico-Francés

Doctor Castelo, 32

Sección Norteamérica
Instituto de Cultura Hispánica

Ciudad Universitaria

Málaga

FUENGIROLA

Instituto de Idiomas
Universidad de Granada

Granada

MALAGA

Curso para Extranjeros

Alcazabilla, 2

Navarra
PAMPLONA

Universidad de Navarra
Dirección del Instituto de
Lengua y Cultura Españolas

Edificio Central de la Universidad de
Navarra

Oviedo
GIJON

Secretario de los Cursos de Verano

Plaza del Generalísimo, 8

OVIEDO

Director del Curso para
Extranjeros
Universidad de Oviedo

Salamanca
SALAMANCA

Secretario del Curso de
Filología Hispánica
Universidad de Salamanca

Apartado 19

Santander
SANTANDER

Universidad Internacional
Menéndez Pelayo
Pabellón del Gobierno
Ciudad Universitaria

Madrid 3

Segovia
SEGOVIA

Secretario de Cursos para
Extranjeros

Apartado 42

Sevilla

316

Secretario de los Cursos para
  Extranjeros
Facultad de Filosofía y Letras
Universidad de Sevilla

Saragossa
SARAGOSSA

Secretaría de la Facultad de
  Filosofía y Letras
Universidad de Zaragoza

Valencia
VALENCIA

Secretario de Cursos de Verano
  para Extranjeros
Cátedra Mediterráneo
Universidad de Valencia

Valladolid
VALLADOLID

Secretario de Estudios para
  Extranjeros
Universidad de Valladolid

Vizcaya
BILBAO

Carmelo Saenz de Santa Maria, S.J.
Universidad de Deusto

Apartado 1

Fashion

CLOTHES

Madrid rather than Barcelona is rapidly becoming the fashion center of Spain. Shows for store buyers are generally held in January and July; shows for individual shoppers in late February or early March and late September or early October. Those wishing to attend a showing should telephone in advance for an invitation. The chief couturiers are listed below.

ASUNCION BASTIDA

Paseo de Gracia, 96
Barcelona 8
Telephone: 2-27-84-95

Hermosilla, 18
Madrid 1
Telephone: 2-25-67-70

> *Best known for beaded evening wear. Moderate prices: from $150 to $300 for dresses, suits, coats.*

CARMEN MIR

Provenza, 245
Barcelona 8
Telephone: 2-15-13-46

> *Sporty daywear that tends to be classical. Moderate prices.*

ELIO

Ayala, 124
Madrid 6
Telephone: 2-76-43-24

> *Ultramodern, very elegant. Does some men's jackets. Accessories: boots, hats, perfumes. Prices: from $200 to $400 for suits, dresses, coats.*

LINO

Plaza de Santa Barbara, 3
Madrid 4
Telephone: 2-24-49-52

> *Well-tailored classical clothes, priced from $125 and $150 to $300 for dresses, suits, and coats.*

MARBEL JR.

Avenida de Nazareth, 1
Madrid 7
Telephone: 2-73-23-37

> *Flashy evening clothes, some men's jackets for evening.*

PEDRO RODRIGUEZ

Paseo de Gracia, 8
Barcelona 7
Telephone: 2-21-36-05

Alcalá, 54

Madrid 14
Telephone: 2-21-94-40

Also in San Sebastián

*Beaded evening clothes, classical day-
wear. Moderate prices.*

PEDRO ROVIRA

Rambla del Prat, 7
Barcelona 12
Telephone: 2-27-15-33

*Sporty daywear, pantsuits, moderate
prices.*

PERTEGAZ

Avenida del Generalisimo, 401
Barcelona 8
Telephone: 2-27-47-20

Montero, 8
Madrid 6
Telephone: 2-61-33-44

*Highly elegant, a perfectionist in
tailoring. Accessories: shoes, bags,
perfumes. Prices: $200 to $400 for
dresses, suits, coats.*

ROSSER

Pasaje Concepción, 10
Barcelona 8
Telephone: 2-15-09-33

*Extremely good tailoring. Accesso-
ries: shoes. Prices: moderate.*

SANTA EULALIA

Paseo de Gracia, 60
Barcelona 7
Telephone: 2-15-42-16

*Sporty, classical day and evening.
Moderate prices.*

VARGAS OCHAGAVIA

Avenida de Calvo Sotelo, 16
Madrid 1
Telephone: 275-05-12

Classical style, moderate prices.

FUR

ARTURO

Calle Fortuny, 12

Madrid
Telephone: 224-77-73

JOSE LUIS

Genova, 19
Madrid
Telephone: 419-38-80

VILLAGROY

Jorge Juan, 35
Madrid
Telephone: 276-91-09

LOBEL

Velazquez, 15

SUEDE

LOEWE

Avenida de José Antonio, 8 and Serrano,
25

The finest shop for suede in Spain.

MITZOU

Serrano, 27
Madrid
Telephone: 275-28-10

*Exclusive suede designs, very ex-
pensive.*

HERRERO Y RODERO

Avenida de José Antonio, 37
Telephone: 231-50-39

*Well-tailored suede fashion at mod-
erate prices.*

Festivals

Below are listed some of the
more unusual among the 1,500
festivals celebrated annually in
Spain.

January 5

*In most of the large towns there is a
parade of the Three Wise Men during
which presents are given to the chil-*

dren. It is the Spanish equivalent of Santa Claus. The most important parades are held at Madrid, Barcelona, Palma de Mallorca, Santillana del Mar, Lerida, and Villafranca del Panadés (Barcelona Province).

January 16
LA PUEBLA

26 miles from Palma de Mallorca

The Festival of St. Anton, the patron saint of animals, includes a parade of marchers dressed as animals.

January 19 and 20
SAN SEBASTIÁN

The traditional Basque festival of La Tamborrada.

February 1–3
ALMONACID DEL MARQUESADO

Province of Cuenca, 71 miles from Madrid

Picturesque festival of La Endiablada.

February 7
ULLDECONA

67 miles from Tarragona

On this date and succeeding Sundays the villagers perform a sixteenth-century Passion play.

February 28
VALCARLOS

Province of Navarra, 39 miles from Pamplona

The Fiesta de' Bolantes is a typical example of Navarrese folkloric tradition and costume.

March 12–19
During the weeklong festival of St. Joseph there are parades of the satirical wood and papier mâché figures known as las fallas. At the end of the festival most of these figures are burned.

April–Holy Week

The April fair in Seville

...rtant of the renowned ...ake place in Seville, Má- ...nada, Lorca (Province of ...i), Murcia, Cartagena, Hijar ...ovince of Teruel), Esparraguera (Province of Barcelona), Ulldecona (Province of Tarragona), Verges (Province of Gerona), Cuenca, Zamora.

April–April Fair

Held in Seville about a week after Easter Sunday, it is the best known of Spanish folkloric celebrations. There is flamenco singing, bullfights, and endless gaiety.

April 11–18
MURCIA

Spring festival.

April 13
POLA DE SIERO

Province of Oviedo, 8 miles from Oviedo

During the Festival of the Painted Eggs, thousands of painted Easter Eggs are sold, a costume parade is held, and there is dancing in the streets.

April 22
BARCELONA

The St. George's Festival dates from 1459. Roses of different colors are on sale, the color indicating the degree of a lover's passion when he buys one for his lady.

May 1–25
CÓRDOBA

Fairs and festivals.

May 2–9
JEREZ DE LA FRONTERA

Province of Cádiz, 15 miles from Cádiz

This is the most picturesque and important horse fair in the country.

May 30
ATIENZA

52 miles from Guadalajara

The fiesta called La Caballada has been held since 1162.

May–June

Corpus Christi is celebrated with particular solemnity in Toledo and Granada. In Sitges (about 23 miles from Barcelona) and in Puenteareas (about 28 miles from Pontevedra) the streets over which the procession passes are richly carpeted with flowers.

June 6
CALELLA

31 miles from Barcelona

One of the most important folklore festivals of the Catalan region.

June 17
LA OROTAVA

On Tenerife in the Canary Islands

Flowers gathered from around Mt. Teide are fashioned into carpets that are laid down in various parts of the city.

June 21–30
ALICANTE

Wood and papier mâché tableaux are exhibited around the city and then burned on St. John's Eve (June 23).

June 23–25
SAN PEDRO MANRIQUE

30 miles from Soria

The picturesque festival of the móndidas represents the ancient priestesses of the Celtiberians.

June 24–28
SORIA

141 miles from Madrid

The venerable, colorful, and varied festival of St. John.

June 29
IRUN

17 miles from San Sebastián

The Festival of San Marcial celebrates the battle of that name, in which Spain finally defeated Napoleon's troops.

July 6–20
PAMPLONA

The Festival of San Fermin has been held since 1519. During the famous Running of the Bulls, the bulls for that afternoon's fight are allowed to run through the streets to the arena, closely pursuing crowds of brave men and boys.

July 24–26
LLORET DE MAR

25 miles from Gerona

The Festival of Santa Christina features ancient dances and costumes.

August 1
RIBADEO

66 miles from Lugo

Bagpipe day is a festival of Galician music.

August 7
ARRIONDA-RIBADESELLA

21 miles from Oviedo

International kayak race down the river Sella.

August 15
LA ALBERCA

48 miles from Salamanca

The Festival of the Assumption is particularly rich in local color. A mystery play is given.

SADA

10 miles from La Coruña

Visitors to the Sardiñada are given free sardines grilled fisherman-style. Folklore troops perform in true Galician style.

August 29
VILLAFRANCA DEL PANADES

29 miles from Barcelona

The festival in honor of San Felix is the classic Catalonian festival. There are performances of the Xiquets de Valls or Castellers (human towers).

August 31
REQUENA

47 miles from Valencia

Grape harvest festival.

September 6
ALAJAR

69 miles from Huelva

An Andalusian folk festival of ancient date.

September 19
LOGROÑO

Festival celebrating the harvest of the grapes that will be used to make the renowned Rioja wines.

September 24
BARCELONA

The festival of Our Lady of Mercy, which includes an international music festival, is the most important of the festivities held in Barcelona.

October 10–18
Among the many events of the Festival of El Pilar are most interesting contests for the best dancers of the jota. Like the dance itself, these take place in Aragon, particularly around Saragossa.

October 17–20
MONDOÑEDO

Province of Lugo

This festival has been held since medieval times. Most interesting hand-crafted objects are on sale.

December 24
LABASTIDA

Province of Alava

Ancient songs and dances are performed in a midnight mass that dates from the early middle ages.

Industry

AVIATION

AVIACO (AVIACION Y COMERCIO, S.A.)

Madrid offices: Calle Aduana, 33

Air transport.

IBERIA LINEAS AEREAS DE ESPAÑA

Madrid offices (administration): Calle Velazquez, 130

Air transport.

SPANTAX, S.A.

Avenida del Generalisimo, 89
Madrid

Air transport.

CONSTRUCCIONES AERONAUTICAS, S.A. (CASA)

Madrid offices: Calle Rey Francisco, 4

Construction and repair of planes.

CHEMICALS AND PETROCHEMICALS

ALCUDIA

Madrid offices: Alberto Alcocer, 7
Plant: Puertollano (Province of Ciudad Real)

Product: low-density polyethylene.

AMONIACO ESPAÑOL, S.A.

Madrid offices: Felix Boix, 8
Plant: Málaga

Product: ammonia fertilizer.

CALATRAVA, S.A. INDUSTRIA PETROQUIMICA

Madrid offices: Generalisimo, 20
Plants: Puertollano (Province of Ciudad Real); Santander

Products: polyethylene (Puertollano), butadiene, and carbon black (Santander).

CALVO SOTELO

Madrid offices: Plaza de Salamanca, 8
Plant: Puertollano (Province of Ciudad Real)

Products: ethylene and polypropylene.

The Calvo Sotelo chemical plant at Puertollano, Province of Ciudad Real

CEPSA

Madrid offices: Avenida de America, 32
Plant under construction: Algeciras
(Province of Cádiz)

Products: aromatic-base petrochemicals and carbon black.

CARBON BLACK ESPAÑOLA (CABOT, S.A.
PRODUCTOS QUIMICOS)

Madrid offices: Sagasta, 15
Plant under construction: Bilbao

Product: carbon black.

CROS, S.A.

Barcelona offices: Paseo de Gracia, 56
Plants: Tarragona; Puertollano (Province of Ciudad Real)

Products: chloride (Tarragona) and ethylene oxide (Puertollano).

DOW-UNQUINESA

Madrid offices: Lopez de Hoyos, 6
Plants: Bilbao; Tarragona

Products: sulfuric acid and titanium oxide (Bilbao); low-density polyethylene (Tarragona).

FERTIBERIA

Madrid offices: Velazquez, 22
Plants: Castellón de la Plana; Huelva; La Coruña

Products: ammonia fertilizers (Castellón); ammonia and urea (Huelva); ammonia (La Coruña).

FIBRAS ESSO

Madrid offices: Felix Boix, 8
Plant under construction: Saragossa

Product: nylon fiber.

INDUSTRIAS QUIMICAS ASOCIADAS (IQA)

Madrid offices: Marqués de Villamagna, 4
Plant: Tarragona

Products: petrochemicals, oxygenated hydrocarbons, and vinyl chloride.

PRODUCTOS QUIMICOS ESSO

Madrid offices: Felix Boix, 8
Plant: Castellón de la Plana

Product: caprolactam (raw material for nylon fiber).

REPOSA

Madrid offices: Apolonio Morales, 13 and 15
Plant: Miranda de Ebro (Province of Burgos)

Products: plasticizers and polyester resins.

SOLVAY, S.A.

Madrid offices: Velazquez, 35
Plant: Torrelavega (Province of Santander)

Product: inorganic chemicals.

UNION EXPLOSIVOS RIO TINTO
Madrid offices: Castellana, 20
Plant: Huelva

Products: sulfuric acid, phosphoric acid, and chemical fertilizers.

ELECTRONICS

GENERAL ELECTRICA ESPAÑOLA

Madrid offices: Genova, 26
Plants: Bilbao; Algete (Province of Madrid)

Products: electrical generating equipment and household appliances.

MARCONI ESPAÑOLA, S.A. (ITT
SPANISH AFFILIATE)

Madrid offices: Calle de Alcala, 45
Plant: Villaverde (Province of Madrid)

Products: communications equipment of all kinds and television sets.

PHILIPS IBERICA

Madrid offices: Avenida de America, s/n
Plant: Barcelona

Products: television sets, radios, and household appliances.

STANDARD ELECTRICA (ITT SPANISH
AFFILIATE)

Madrid offices: Ramirez de Prado, 55
Plants: Villaverde (Province of Madrid); Maliaño (Province of Santander); Toledo

Products: communications equipment of all kinds.

WESTINGHOUSE IBERICA, S.A.

Madrid offices: Avenida de José Antonio, 10
Plants: Reinosa (Province of Santander); Erandio (Province of Vizcaya); Córdoba

Products: household appliances, brakes, and signaling equipment.

ENGINEERING ASSOCIATIONS

ASSOCIATION OF AGRICULTURAL ENGINEERS

Santa Cruz de Narcenado, 5
Madrid

ASSOCIATION OF ARMAMENT ENGINEERS

Conde de Xiquena, 13
Madrid

ASSOCIATION OF CIVIL ENGINEERS

Montalbán, 3 and 10
Madrid

ASSOCIATION OF CONSTRUCTION ENGINEERS

Victoria, 2
Madrid

ASSOCIATION OF INDUSTRIAL ENGINEERS

Carrera de San Jeronimo, 5
Madrid

ASSOCIATION OF COMMUNICATIONS ENGINEERS

General Goded, 38
Madrid

MOTOR VEHICLES

AUTHI (AUTOMOVILES DE TURISMO HISPANO INGLESES) BRITISH LEYLAND

Madrid offices: Plaza de la Independencia, 5
Plant: Pamplona

Product: passenger cars.

BARREIROS DIESEL (CHRYSLER)

Offices and plant: Villaverde (Province of Madrid)

Product: passenger, commercial, and industrial vehicles.

CITROEN HISPANIA, S.A.

Madrid offices: Doctor Esquerdo, 62
Plant: Vigo (Province of Pontevedra)

Products: passenger and commercial vehicles.

ENASA (EMPRESA NACIONAL DE AUTOMOVILES, S.A.)

Madrid offices: Calle General Sanjurjo, 2
Plants: Madrid; Valladolid; Mataró; Barcelona

Products: industrial vehicles of all kinds.

FASA RENAULT

Madrid offices: Carretera de Burgos, Km 5'5
Plants: Valladolid; Seville

Products: passenger and commercial vehicles.

SEAT (SOCIEDAD ESPAÑOLA DE AUTOMOVILES DE TURISMO, S.A.) (FIAT)

Madrid offices: Avenida del Generalisimo, 146
Plant: Paseo de Zona Franca, Barcelona

Product: passenger cars.

NUCLEAR POWER PLANTS

NUCLENOR, S.A.

Madrid offices: Juan de Mena, 6
Plant: Santa Maria de la Garoña (Province of Burgos)

UNION ELECTRICA, S.A.

Madrid offices: Madrid, 157
Plant: Zorita de los Canes (Province of Guadalajara)

OIL REFINERIES

CALVO SOTELO

Madrid offices: Plaza de Salamanca, 8
Plant: Puertollano (Province of Ciudad
Real)

Production: 3 million tons a year.

CEPSA (COMPAÑIA ESPAÑOLA DE
PETROLEOS), S.A.

Madrid offices: Avenida de America, 32
Plants: Tenerife (Canary Islands); Algeciras (Province of Cádiz)

Production: 4 million tons a year.

ESSO PETROLEOS

Madrid offices: Felix Boix, 8
Plant: Castellón de la Plana

Production: 3½ million tons a year.

GULF OIL (PETRONOR AND RIO GULF
DE PETROLEOS)

Madrid offices: Avenida del Generalisimo, 67
Plants: Bilbao; Huelva (Rio Gulf de
Petroleos)

Production: 4 million tons a year.

PETROLIBER (COMPAÑIA IBERICA DE
PETROLEOS, S.A.)

Madrid offices: Plaza Vazquez de Mella,
12
Plant: La Coruña

Production: 4 million tons a year.

REPESA (REFINERIA DE PETROLEOS DE
ESCOMBRERÁS, S.A.)

Madrid offices: Paseo del Prado, 28
Plant: Escombreras (Province of
Cartagena)

Production: 4 million tons a year.

RUBBER PRODUCTS

FIRESTONE HISPANIA, S.A.

Madrid offices: Prolongación R. Crellano, 4
Plants: Burgos; Bilbao

Product: tires.

MICHELIN, S.A.

Madrid offices: Dr. Esquerdo, 203
Plants: San Sebastian; Vitoria; Aranda
de Duero (Province of Burgos)

Product: tires.

PIRELLI, S.A.

Madrid offices: Genova, 15
Plant: Manresa (Province of Barcelona)

*Products: tires, electrical cables, and
other products utilizing rubber.*

GENERAL TIRE (NEUMATICOS GENERAL,
S.A.E.)

Madrid offices: Avenida del Generalisimo, 71-A
Plant: Torrelavega (Province of
Santander)

*Products: tires, adhesive products,
and industrial belts.*

SHIPBUILDING

ASTILLEROS DE CÁDIZ, S.A.

Madrid offices: Zurbano, 70
Shipyard: Cádiz

ASTILLEROS Y TALLERES DEL NOROESTE,
S.A. (ASTANO)

Madrid offices: Avenida del Generalisimo, 30
Shipyard: La Coruña

EMPRESA NACIONAL BAZÁN

Madrid offices: Paseo de la Castellana,
65
Shipyard: El Ferrol del Caudillo

STEEL

EMPRESA NACIONAL SIDERURGICA, S.A.
(ENSIDESA)

Madrid offices: Velazquez, 134
Mill: Avilés (Province of Oviedo)

ALTOS HORNOS DE VIZCAYA, S.A.

Madrid offices: Serrano, 3
Mill: Bilbao

UNION DE SIDERURGICAS ASTURIANAS,
S.A. (UNINSA)

Madrid offices: Prim, 12

Mill: Veriña (Province of Oviedo)

SOCIEDAD METALURGICA DURO-
FELGUERA, S.A.

Madrid offices: San Bernardo, 114
Mill: La Felguera (Province of Oviedo)

TEXTILES

CYANENKA, S.A.

Barcelona offices: Mayor, 49 (Prat de Llobregat)
Plant: Prat de Llobregat (Province of Barcelona)

FIBRAS ESSO, S.A.

Madrid offices: Felix Boix, 8
Plant: Saragossa

Product: synthetic fiber.

FABRICACION ESPAÑOLA DE FIBRAS
TEXTILES ARTIFICIALES, S.A.
(FEFASA)

Madrid offices: Nuñez de Balboa, 108
Plant: Miranda de Ebro (Province of Burgos)

Product: synthetic fibers.

LA SEDA DE BARCELONA, S.A.

Barcelona offices: Avenida de José Antonio, 654
Plant: Prat de Llobregat (Province of Barcelona)

Products: rayon and polyester.

National Parks

Visiting hours are from sunrise to sundown. Listings are by province.

Asturias
PARQUE NACIONAL DE LA MONTAÑA DE
COVADONGA OR DE PEÑA SANTA

50 miles from Oviedo

Covering 41,804 acres, the park ranges from a high of 6,412 to a low of 420 feet above sea level. Trees include beech, oak, birch, and ash, while among the animals are roebuck, wildcat, wild boar, wolf, bear, fox, and ibex.

Canary Islands
PARQUE NACIONAL DE LA CALDERA DE
TABURIENTE

At El Paso, on the island of Palma

This 8,645-acre park features wild goats and rare trees of the laurel and laburnum families.

PARQUE NACIONAL DEL TEIDE

33 miles from the capital of Tenerife

This 27,170-acre park is noted for its rare flora.

Huesca
PARQUE NACIONAL DEL VALLE DE
ORDESA O DEL RIO ARA

In the Pyrenees, 1 mile from the French border, 3 miles from the village of Torla

This 5,372-acre park is an average of 3,900 feet above sea level, while the highest point is Mount Perdido, at 10,065 feet. There are several waterfalls. The trees include black pine, beech, cedar, and linden, while among the wildlife are eagles, vultures, pheasant, falcons, wild boar, and trout.

Sports

AUTO RACING

The Circuito del Jarama race track, 28 miles from Madrid on the road to Burgos, holds auto races from mid-February to the end of November, usually on Sundays. Detailed information about racing schedules is obtainable from the track's Madrid office:

OFICINAS DEL CIRCUITO DEL JARAMA
Narvaez, 7

AUTO RALLIES

More than 100 are held in Spain each year. Backed by ten regional federations, the central body organizing the rallies is:

FEDERACIÓN ESPAÑOLA DE
    AUTOMOVILISMO

General Sanjurjo, 10
Madrid

BULLFIGHTING

The national sport is held at rings all over Spain from about the middle of April until the end of October. There is almost bound to be a ring in any town with more than 5,000 inhabitants.

A fight in which the animals are young cows and are not killed is called a *capea;* a fight in which the bulls are from two to three years old is called a *novillada;* a fight in which the bulls are from three to five years old is called a *corrida.*

Collection
Álava Province

VITORIA

ART AND HISTORY OF BULLFIGHTING

El Portalón
Calle Correria, 151

This is a private collection, entrance

free to serious visitors.

See also **Folk Art, Córdoba.**

FISHING

Trout
The season extends from the first Sunday in March through August 15 except in the high mountains, where stream fishing is permitted from May 16 to September 30. All fish less than 8 inches long must be thrown back. The limit is 25 trout per fisherman.

Salmon
The season extends from the first Sunday in March to July 18. Fish less than 18 inches long must be thrown back. The limit is 3 salmon per fisherman.

Licenses are required by all fishermen using public waters. For licenses to fish waters not under the control of the Spanish Fish and Game Service, tourists should apply to:

JEFATURA DE LA 4A. REGION DE PESCA
CONTINENTAL Y CAZA

Luchana, 17
Madrid

For the same license foreigners resident in Spain should apply to:

JEFATURA DEL SERVICIO NACIONAL DE
    PESCA FLUVIAL Y CAZA

Goya, 25 (5th floor)
Madrid

Special permits to fish in waters controlled by the Spanish Fish and Game Service are obtainable from:

4A. COMISARIA DEL SERVICIO DE
    PESCA CONTINENTAL

Trout fishing in the Province of Lérida

CAZA Y PARQUES NACIONALES

Calle de Jorge Juan, 39, 2o
Madrid

GOLF

The courses listed below are all 18-hole courses unless otherwise noted, and most of them offer temporary memberships for a maximum of two weeks. They are listed by province.

Barcelona
REAL CLUB DE GOLF EL PRAT

10 miles from Barcelona

27 holes

CLUB DE GOLF DE SAN CUGAT

San Cugat del Vallés
12½ miles from Barcelona

Cádiz
CLUB DE GOLF SOTOGRANDE

Guadiaro
18 miles from Gibraltar and Algeciras

Canary Islands
GRAN CANARIA

CLUB DE GOLF DE LAS PALMAS

Bandana
8½ miles from Las Palmas

TENERIFE

CLUB DE GOLF DE TENERIFE EL PEÑON

10 miles from Santa Cruz de Tenerife

Gerona

CLUB DE GOLF COSTA BRAVA

Santa Cristina de Aro

REAL CLUB DE GOLF DE CERDAÑA-
PUIGCERDÁ

Near Puigcerdá by the French border

Madrid
NUEVO CLUB DE GOLF DE MADRID

17 miles northwest of the capital

CLUB DE GOLF EL ESCORIAL
LA HERRERIA

San Lorenzo de El Escorial
31 miles from Madrid

REAL CLUB DE LA PUERTA DE HIERRO

2½ miles from Madrid

36 holes

REAL SOCIEDAD HIPICA ESPAÑOLA CLUB
DE CAMPO

2½ miles from Madrid

27 holes

Málaga
CLUB DE CAMPO DE MÁLAGA

Between Málaga and Torremolinos

GOLF ATALAYA PARK

Estepona-Marbella

GOLF RIO REAL

Los Monteros-Marbella

GOLF CLUB GUADALMINA

San Pedro de Alcantara-Marbella

Santander
REAL GOLF DE PEDREÑA

On a peninsula 15 miles from Santander

Valencia
GOLF EL SALER

At Dehesa de El Saler between La Al-
bufera and the sea

Vizcaya
REAL SOCIEDAD DE GOLF DE NEGURI
LA GALEA

Overlooking the sea 10 miles from
Bilbao

GREYHOUND RACING

Greyhounds (*galgos* in Spanish)
are native to Spain. They can be
seen in villages accompanying
small-game hunters, and in the
early morning along the Diag-
onal and on Castellana Avenue
in Madrid, where they are exercised in groups of four or six.
Greyhound racing is popular in
Spain. The main tracks, by
province, are:

Balearic Islands
Majorca

PALMA DE MAJORCA

CANÓDROMO BALEAR

Santacilia, 3

Barcelona
BARCELONA

CANÓDROMO AVENIDA

Avenida del Generalísimo Franco

CANÓDROMO MERIDIANA

Concepción Arenal, 164

CANÓDROMO PABELLÓN

Calle Llansá, 8

Canary Islands
Gran Canaria

LAS PALMAS

CANÓDROMO NUEVO CAMPO ESPAÑA

Madrid
MADRID

CANÓDROMO MADRILEÑO

Camino de las Ánimas, s/n

Málaga
MALAGA

CANÓDROMO AVENIDA

Campo Municipal de Deportes (Ciudad
Jardín)

Valencia
VALENCIA

CANÓDROMO AVENIDA

Avenida del Doncel Luis Felipe García Sanchóz, 127

HORSE RACING

By province the main tracks are:
Guipúzcoa
SAN SEBASTIAN

HIPODROMO DE LASARTE

Season: summer.

Madrid
MADRID

HIPODROMO DE LA ZARZUELA

Monte de El Pardo

Season: autumn.

Sevilla
SEVILLE

REAL CLUB PINEDA

Season: spring.

HORSE SHOWS

International horse shows are held each spring in Barcelona (at the Real Club de Polo) and in Madrid (at the Real Sociedad Hipica del Club de Campo). Each show lasts for about a week.

HUNTING

In addition to import permits for his guns, a nonresident foreigner will also need a hunting permit. The latter is valid for two months and costs about $30.

Information about hunting in Spain may be obtained from:

FEDERACIÓN NACIONAL DE CAZA

Plaza de Santo Domingo, 16
Madrid

or from the following division of the Ministry of Agriculture:

SERVICIO NACIONAL DE PESCA FLUVIAL Y CAZA

General Sanjurjo, 37
Madrid

Big game includes deer, mountain goat, boar, bear, wolf. Small game includes partridge, quail, pheasant, duck, a variety of doves, rabbits, and hares. The following organizations will obtain permits and organize hunting parties:

Big Game
EMPRESA NACIONAL DE TURISMO

Velazquez, 47
Madrid

CACERIAS AZOR

Nuñez de Balboa, 30
Madrid

Small game
ATESA

Ferraz, 87
Madrid

CACERIAS CAMPOS

Seis de Junio, 32
Valdepeñas
Ciudad Real

JOSÉ DELGADO DUVOS

Duque de Sesto, 41
Madrid

RODASVIEJAS

Generalisimo Franco, 23
Salamanca

ASOCIACIÓN DE CAZADORES

Travesia de Lirio, 6
Huesca

CACERIAS AZOR

Nuñez de Balboa, 30
Madrid

JAI ALAI

This Basque game, also called *frontón,* or *pelota vasca,* is also played in a number of cities outside the Basque country. The more important jai alai courts are, by province:

Álava
VITORIA

FRONTÓN VITORIANO

San Prudencio, 5

Barcelona
BARCELONA

FRONTÓN COLÓN

Rambla Santa Monica, 18

FRONTÓN PRINCIPAL PALACIO

Plaza del Teatro, 4

Guipúzcoa
SAN SEBASTIAN

FRONTÓN ANOETA

Barrio Anoeta

Madrid
MADRID

FRONTÓN MADRID

Dr. Cortezo, 10

FRONTÓN RECOLLETOS

Recoletos

Navarra
PAMPLONA

FRONTÓN EUZCAL-JAI

San Augustin, 7

FRONTÓN LABRIT

Calle Juan Labrit

Saragossa
SARAGOSSA

FRONTÓN JAI ALAI

Calle Requeté Aragonés, 12

Vizcaya
BILBAO

CLUB DEPORTIVO

Alameda de Recaldo, 28

MOUNTAIN CLIMBING

For information contact:

FEDERACIÓN ESPAÑOLA DE MONTAÑISMO

Alberto Aguilera, 2
Madrid

SKEET AND PIGEON SHOOTING

For information contact:

FEDERACIÓN NACIONAL DE TIRO AL PLATO (SKEET)

Espoz y Mina, 18
Madrid

FEDERACIÓN ESPAÑOLA DE TIRO DE PICHON (PIGEON)

Espoz y Mina, 18
Madrid

SKIING

There are ski resorts at Navacerrada, barely 30 miles from Madrid, and in the Pyrenees provinces of Huesca (at Candanchú) and Gerona (at La Molina). For further information contact:

FEDERACIÓN ESPAÑOLA DE ESQUI

Modesto Lafuente, 4
Madrid

SOCCER

Known as *fútbol,* the sport is the passion of almost every Spaniard. Millions participate vicariously through the football pools, called *quinielas.* Matches of the sixteen teams that compose the First Division take place every Sunday in major Spanish cities from autumn to early summer. Below are the main stadiums, by province.

Alicante
ELCHE

ELCHE CLUB DE FÚTBOL

Campo de Altabix

Capacity: 22,000.

Barcelona
BARCELONA

CLUB DE FÚTBOL DE BARCELONA

Estadio C. F. Barcelona

Capacity: 90,138.

REAL CLUB DEPORTIVO ESPAÑOL

Campo de Sarriá

Capacity: 38,300.

SABADELL

CLUB DEPORTIVO SABADELL

Campo de Cruz Alta

Capacity: 32,000.

Canary Islands
Gran Canaria
LAS PALMAS

UNION DEPORTIVO DE LAS PALMAS

Campo Insular

Mountain climbing at Potes, in the Province of Santander

Capacity: 30,000.

Córdoba
CORDOBA

CAMPO DE ARCÁNGEL

Capacity: 27,000.

La Coruña
REAL CLUB DEPORTIVO LA CORUÑA

Campo de Riazor

Capacity: 45,000.

Granada
GRANADA

GRANADA CLUB DE FÚTBOL

Campo de los Cármenes

Capacity: 22,000.

Guipúzcoa
SAN SEBASTIAN

REAL SOCIEDAD SAN SEBASTIAN

Campo de Atocha

Capacity: 32,000.

Madrid
MADRID

ATLETICO DE MADRID

Estadio Manzanares

Capacity: 57,000.

REAL MADRID

Estadio Bernabeu

Capacity: 90,123.

Málaga
MALAGA

CLUB DEPORTIVO DE MÁLAGA

Campo La Rosaleda

Capacity: 20,000.

Pontevedra
PONTEVEDRA

PONTEVEDRA CLUB DE FÚTBOL

Campo de Pasarón

Capacity: 21,000.

Saragossa
SARAGOSSA

REAL ZARAGOZA

Campo de la Romareda

Capacity: 33,766.

Valencia
VALENCIA

VALENCIA CLUB DE FÚTBOL

Campo de Mestalla

Capacity: 21,872.

Vizcaya
BILBAO

ATLETICO DE BILBAO

Campo de San Mamés

Capacity: 41,400.

Trade Fairs

For a complete schedule and exact dates of trade fairs in Spain in a given year contact:

COMISARIA DE FERIAS
MINISTERIO DE COMERCIO

Paseo de la Castellana, 16
Madrid 1

A list of the most important annual trade fairs follows.

January
NATIONAL FAIR OF LEATHER GOODS AND RELATED ACTIVITIES (IBERPIEL)

Avenida José Antonio, 32
Madrid

SPORTS AND CAMPING FAIR

Avenida Maria Cristina
Parque Montjuich
Barcelona

February

MONOGRAPHIC FAIR OF GOODS FOR
THE HOME
(TEXTILHOGAR)

Paseo del Mar, 2
Apartado 476
Valencia

FAIR OF READY-MADE WEAR
(AUTUMN AND WINTER WEAR)

Avenida Maria Christina
Parque Montjuich
Barcelona

Executive Committee: Avenida José
Antonio, 670, Barcelona.

TOYS AND CHILDREN'S GOODS FAIR

Paseo del Mar, 2
Apartado 476
Valencia

March
INTERNATIONAL NAUTICAL FAIR

Avenida Maria Christina
Parque Montjuich
Barcelona

INTERNATIONAL FAIR OF FOOTWEAR AND
RELATED INDUSTRIES
(AUTUMN AND WINTER WEAR)

Avenida Chapi. Fair Pavilion
Elda (Province of Alicante)

CERAMICS AND GLASSWARE FAIR

Paseo del Mar, 2
Apartado 476
Valencia

April
INTERNATIONAL FAIR OF AGRICULTURAL
IMPLEMENTS

Saragossa

"ART IN METAL" FAIR

Paseo del Mar, 2
Apartado 476
Valencia

INTERNATIONAL AUTOMOBILE FAIR

Avenida Maria Christina
Parque Montjuich
Barcelona

CONSTRUCTION AND PUBLIC WORKS FAIR

Avenida Portugal, s/n

Madrid

June
CRAFTS AND TOURISM FAIR

Town Hall
Palma de Mallorca
Balearic Islands

July
NATIONAL NAVAL INDUSTRIES FAIR

Frutos Saavedra, 158
El Ferrol del Caudillo
Province of La Coruña

September
INTERNATIONAL FAIR OF FOOTWEAR
AND RELATED INDUSTRIES
(SPRING AND SUMMER WEAR)

Avenida Chapi. Fair Pavilion
Elda (Province of Alicante)

SPANISH FAIR OF CHILDREN'S WEAR
AND FASHION

Paseo del Mar, 2
Apartado 476
Valencia

INTERNATIONAL ORANGE WEEK

Paseo del Mar, 2
Apartado 476
Valencia

October
FAIR OF READY-MADE WEAR
(SPRING AND SUMMER WEAR)

Avenida Maria Christina
Parque Montjuich
Barcelona

SPANISH FURNITURE AND WOODWORKING
MACHINERY FAIR

Paseo del Mar, 2
Apartado 476
Valencia

INTERNATIONAL CANNING AND
FOOD FAIR

Avenida José Antonio, 11
Murcia

Trade Unions

Sindicato Nacional de Construccion, Vidrio y Ceramica (Glass and Ceramics)

Paseo del Prado, 18–20
Madrid 14

Sindicato Nacional de Frutos y Productos Horticolas (Fruits and Vegetables)

Princesa, 24
Madrid 8

Sindicato Nacional de Ganaderia (Livestock)

Huertas, 26
Madrid 14

Sindicato Nacional de Industrias Quimicas (Chemical Industries)

San Bernardo, 62
Madrid 8

Sindicato Nacional de la Madera y el Corcho (Wood and Cork)

Flora, 1 and 3
Madrid 13

Sindicato Nacional del Metal (Metals)

Ferraz, 44
Madrid 8

Sindicato Nacional del Olivo (Olive)

Españoleto, 19
Madrid 4

Sindicato Nacional de la Piel (Fur and Skins)

Avenida José Antonio, 32
Madrid 13

Sindicato Nacional de la Vid, Cervezas y Bebidas (Wine, Beer, and Beverages)

Paseo del Prado, 18
Madrid 14

Index

Art, 2, 8, 40, 60–62, 84, 93; during political decline, 150, 154, 156. *See also* individual artists, museums
Artois, 151
Asia, 140
Astorga (Asturica Augusta), 130
Asturias, Province of, 11, 107, 111, 277; in Civil War, 193; coal mining in, 111; people of, 111; rebellion in, 172, 181, 193
Athens, 59
Attlee, Clement, 212
Augustus, emperor of Rome, 116, 129
Austria, 148, 153–54
Automobiles, 34–35, 52, *53*, 56–57, *78*, 219, *224*
Ávila, 15, 26, 67, *129*
Ayolas, Juan de, 146
Azaña, Manuel, 179, 180, 181, 182–83, 190, 198

Badajoz (Pax Augusta), *116–17*, 130, *229*, 266
Badajoz, Province of, 114
Bahamonde, Francisco Franco. *See* Franco, Francisco
Bajazet II, Sultan, 145
Bakunin, Mikhail A., 243
Balaguer y Albas, Josemaria Escrivá, 26, 272
Balboa, Vasco Núñez de, 145
Balearic Islands, 11, 66, 74, 79, 82, 124, 181. *See also* Ibiza; Majorca; Minorca
Balenciaga, Cristóbal, 80, 88
Balmoral, Madrid (bar), 44
Baracaldo, 108
Barcelona, 10, 11, 22, 32, 37, 40, 76, *77, 80, 82–83, 84, 85*–86, *87*–88, *89*, 94, 125, 127, *147*, 172, 178, 180, *199*, 228, 234, *239*, 248, 255, 262; cathedrals in, 85–86, *257, 261;* Civil War in, 86, 192, 193, 198; culture of, 79–80, 86, 88; hotels in, 86, 88; industry in, *78*, 79, 85, 219; language of, 81, 82; leftist revolt in, 181; religious clashes in, 256, 259, 260, 266, 268; restaurants in, 88, *90;* rising social standards in, 220; Sarría Monastery in, 259; University of, 81
Barcelona, Province of, 79, 81
Baroja, Pío, 108, 168
Basilica of the Valley of the Fallen, 26, 71, 189

Basque country, 11, 66, 104–11, 124, 165, 220, 225, *259*, 267–68; agriculture in, 104, 107; Basque Nationalist party, 105; Civil War in, 193, 194, 196; defiance of Franco in, 105, 107, 278, 284; fishing industry in, 108; industry in, 104, 107–8; invasions and conquests of, 68, 107; language of, 104, 105; mysticism in, 11, 108–9; people of, 104, 105, 107, *108–9, 110,* 111; separatism in, 104, 105, 107, 180, 194, 248, 277
Bassano, Jacopo, 60
Batista, Fulgencio, 222
Bay of Biscay, 107–8, 124
Beltrán, Luís, 93
Benidorm, 94
Benítez, Manuel. *See* El Cordobés
Berbers, 95, 97, 132
Berenguer de Aguilar Palace museum, Barcelona, 40
Bilbao, 11, 32, 37, 94, *104, 105, 106,* 107, 109, 193, 194, 198, 219, 220, 243, 267, 268
Bilbao, Marquis of, 226
Black Legend, 141, 248
Blasco-Ibáñez, Vicente, 240
Blood and Sand (Blasco-Ibáñez), 240
Bohemia, 148
Boix Luch, Joaquín, 256
Bonaparte, Joseph, 140, 159
Borgia, Alfonso. *See* Calixtus III, Pope
Borgia, Valenciano Rodrigo. *See* Alexander VI, Pope
Bosch, Hieronymous, 60
Botín, Madrid (restaurant), 42
Botticelli, Sandro, 60
Bourbon dynasty, 153, 156–59
Braga (Bracara Augusta), Portugal, 130
Brenan, Gerald, 100
Bullfighting, 27, *41*–42, 93, 220, 225, 255, 260; and sexual relations between men and women, 240
Burgos, 67, 107, 192, 284
Burial of Count Orgaz (El Greco), 150

Cabrera range, 122, 125
Cáceres, Province of, 114
Cádiz, 94, 99, 124, 125, 126, *163;* Cortes, 162, 163
Cádiz, Province of, 94
Caesar, Julius, 129
Café Gijón, Madrid, 55–56
Calabacillas, 156

Gil Robles, José María, 181, 183, 235, 277, 285
Giner de los Ríos, Francisco, 168
Goded Llopis, Gen. Manuel, 190, 192
Godoy, Manuel de, 158
Gómez de la Serna, Ramón, 40, 62–63
Gonzáles Ruíz, José María, 288
González Martín, Marcelo, 268
Government of Spain, bureaucracy in, 45–48, 49, 52, 206, 251; constitutions, 47, 163–64, 165, 168, 174, 179, 266, 276; Council of the Realm, 260; and economy, 223; liberalism vs. orthodoxy, 158, 162; liberals in, 164–65, 166, 167, 172; moderates in, 166, 284–86; National Defense Committee, 192; political police of, 46; and press censorship, 174, 279, 281; radicals in, 179, 180–81, 284, 286, 288–89; rightists in, 172, 178. *See also* Cortes; First Republic; Franco, Francisco; National Movement; Politics; Second Republic; individual kings, parties
Goya y Lucientes, Francisco de, 2, 3, 60, 75, 122, 141, 157, 158, 159, 165, 192
Grace, princess of Monaco, 223
Gracián, Baltasar, 246–47
Granada, 3, 11, 20, 24, 36–37, 94, 99, 150; Alhambra of, 96, 99, 135, 136, 173; Calahorra of, 231; Civil War in, 193; occupation of, 12, 91, 97, 132, 140
Granados, Enrique, 170
Graves, Robert, 91
Great Britain, 110, 140, 151, 153–54, 159, 198, 279; in World War II, 208, 209, 210, 211, 212
Greece, 219
Greeks, 134; conquest and occupation of Spain, 34, 88, 91, 125–26; ruins of, 91
Grimau García, Julián, 277
Guadalajara, Province of, 189, 194
Guadalquivir River, 11, 125, 134, 146
Guadiana River, 11
Guam, 168
Guardia Civil, 49, 84, 179, 212, 270, 277, 282, 287
Guernica, 196, 266
Guernica (Picasso), 196
Guerrilla warfare, 128, 132, 159, 167, 187, 189
Guevara, Ché, 288

Guipúzcoa, Province of, 105, 107
Guzmán el Bueno, 248
Gypsies, 54, 57, 116, 133

Hadrian, emperor of Rome, 93, 130
Hamilcar Barca, 79, 127
Hannibal Barca, 34, 91, 127–28
Hapsburg dynasty, 148, 150–53, 156
Hasdrubal, 127
Hemingway, Ernest, 3, 188–89, 240
Hendaye, France, 208, 209
Henry II, king of France, 150, 151
Herrera the Younger, Francisco de, 156
Hidalgo, Diego, 181
Historia de España y de la civilización española (Altamira y Crevea), 12
Hitler, Adolf, 9, 181, 186, 193, 195, 206, 207, 208, 209, 210, 211, 212
Hittites, 123
Hojeda, Alonso de, 141
Hospitalet, 82
Huelva, 99
Hungary, 148, 195

Ibarruri, Dolores, 241
Iberian Peninsula, 122–23
Iberians, 12, 91, 97, 104, 123, 124, 126, 128, 134. *See also* People, Spanish
Ibiza, 11, 74
Ifni, Morocco, 66
Industry, 9, 27, 78–79, 85, 104, 107–8, 112, 157, 219, 224–25
Inquisition, 22, 141, 143–44, 150–51, 164, 165; Jews and, 134, 141, 143, 144, 151, 211; Vatican and, 131, 143, 260
International Brigades in Civil War, 188, 195
Irving, Washington, 3, 99, 136
Isabella, queen consort of Charles V, 148, 240
Isabella I, queen of Spain, 12, 24, 74, 75, 86, 132, 141, 148, 240. *See also* Catholic Kings
Isabella II, queen of Spain, 60, 62, 166–67, 241
Itálica, 93
Italy, 123, 193, 194, 195, 196–97, 207, 212. *See also* Mussolini, Benito

Jaén, 20, 207
James I, king of Aragon, 76, 92
Jarama River, 189
Játiva, 93

Jerez de la Frontera, 100
Jews, 134, 144–45, 211; and
    Inquisition, 134, 141, 143, 144, 151,
    211; synagogues of, in Toledo, 71–
    72
Jiménez, Juan Ramón, 168
Jiménez de Cisneros, Francisco, 22,
    24, 26, 71, 102, 143
JOC, 261, 263
Jockey Club, Madrid (restaurant),
    42, 228
Jones, Robert Trent, 100
JONS, 182
Jordana, Count Goméz, 226
José Antonio. *See* Primo de Rivera,
    José Antonio
Juan, Prince, 248
Juan Carlos de Borbón, Prince, 76,
    162, 166, 223, 226, 227, 234, 235,
    260, 276, 278–79, 280, 284, 285,
    286

Kamen, Henry, 143
Kennedy, John F., 41, 86
Khrushchev, Nikita, 277

La Coruña, 11, 32, 112, 180, 231
La Coruña, Province of, 112
La Florida, 223
La Granja (palace), 8, *157,* 231
La Línea de la Concepción, 31, 210
La Mancha region, 66, 94, *102*–3, 188
La Moraleja, 223
Labor, clandestine organizations in,
    267; official trade unions, 46, 224,
    260; unrest among, 10, 255, 264,
    267, 277, 285, 286
Lacalle Zarraga, Lt. Gen. José, 288
Languages, 24, 66, 67, 76, 81–84, 93,
    97–98, 104, 105, 113, 145
Largo Caballero, Francisco, 178, 179,
    181, 182, 193–94, 198
Larra, Mariano José de, 163
Las Palmas, 191
Latin America, 112, 145–46, 216, 251,
    261
León (Urbs Septima Legionis), 67,
    75, 130
León, Kingdom of, 67, 75
León, Luis de, 150
Leoni, Pompeo, 62
Lepanto, battle of, 150
Lérida (Ilerda), 8, 93, 129
Lerroux, Alejandro, 179, 180–81
Levi, Samuel, 72
Linares, Paco, 42

Literature, 83–84, 113; during
    political decline, 150, 154
Llopis, Rodolfo, 285
Lojendio, Juan Pablo de, 226
López Bravo, Grégorio, 246, 269,
    273, 281
López de Legazpe, Miguel, 110
López Rodó, Laureano, 235, 269, 271,
    273, 281, 288
Lorca, 219
Lorca, Federico García, 187–88
Lorraine, 151
Los Caracoles, Barcelona (restaurant),
    88, *90*
Louis XIV, king of France, 152–53
Louis XV, king of France, 158
Louis XVI, king of France, 158
Louis XVIII, king of France, 165
Louisiana, 146, 158
Low Countries, 148
Loyalists, 8, 86, 141, 186, 187, 189,
    193, 194, 195, 196–97, 200, 248,
    266, 272–73. *See also* Republicans
Lozoya, Marquis of, 226
Luca de Tena, Marquis Juan Ignacio,
    226
Lucan, 131
Lugo (Lucas Augusti), 130
Lugo, Province of, 112
Lull, Ramón, 83
Lusitanians, 124

Machado, Antonio, 84, 168
Machiavelli, Niccolò, 147
Madariaga, Salvador de, 12, 75–76,
    97, 104, 123, 131, 140, 154, 174,
    178, 179, 243
Madrid, *2*–*3,* 10, 11, 20, 26, *28,* 35–
    37, 40–45, 52–*58,* 59–*63,* 67, 69, 74,
    80, 94, 97, *120*–*21,* 178, 180, *214*–
    15, 217, 223, 228, 231, 234, *241,*
    242, 251, 260, 262, 263, 266, 278,
    285; arts in, 40, 41, 60–61; buildings
    of, *47*–48, 49, 57, 59; bullfights in,
    41–42, 220; as capital of Spain, 12,
    15, 45–52, 66, 165; church of San
    Andrés in, 156; Ciudad Universi-
    taria of, 10, 200; Civil War in, 8,
    91, 187, 192, 193, 194, 198, 200;
    craftsmen of, *44*–45; Feria de San
    Isidro of, 41–42; Goyeneche Palace
    in, 156; housing in, *35,* 36, 59, 223;
    industry in, 27, 219; National
    Library of, 62; occupied by French,
    140; outdoor cafés in, *55*–56; Plaza
    Mayor of, 47, 54, *155;* Rastro of,